Rewriting Islamic Law

The Modern Muslim World

6

This series will provide a platform for scholarly research on Islamic and Muslim thought, emerging from any geographical area and dated to any period from the 17th century until the present day.

Rewriting Islamic Law

The Opinions of the 'Ulamā' Towards Codification of Personal Status Law in Egypt

Tarek Elgawhary

GORGIAS PRESS

2019

Gorgias Press LLC, 954 River Road, Piscataway, NJ, 08854, USA

www.gorgiaspress.com

2019 ,

ISBN 978-1-4632-3908-4

Library of Congress Cataloging-in-Publication Data

A Cataloging-in-Publication Record is available from the Library of Congress.

Printed in the United States of America

TABLE OF CONTENTS

ACKNOWLEDGMENTS

Any academic work requires the help of so many people. I am indebted to my colleagues at Egypt's National Fatwa Office (Dār al-Iftā' al-Miṣriyya) where I first encountered this topic. The access I was given to both the Grand Mufti and junior muftis during their fatwa sessions was a front-row education to the nuances of the Sharīʿa and personal status laws. I am grateful to my professors and colleagues at Princeton University for helping me form this raw material into a coherent academic argument. Their guidance, reviews, and suggestions were fundamental to my intellectual journey with this topic. My gratitude also to Adam Walker and Gorgias Press for helping this work see the light of day. Lastly, and certainly not least, this work would never have been were it not for the unwavering support of my family. Words can never repay them, and it is to them with humility I dedicate this work.

A Note on Transliteration, Spelling, and Other Conventions

In the interest of consistency, Arabic words and Muslim names follow the convention used for Arabic consonants by the *International Journal of Middle East Studies*. With the notable exception of the term 'ulamā' (singular *'ālim*), the plural forms of Arabic words are usually indicated by adding an "s" to the word in the singular, as in fatwas, not fatāwa, rather than transliterating their Arabic plural. Also, Arabic words are italicized at their first occurrence. I have mostly retained the definite article al- for names but have dispensed with it in certain circumstances for the ease of reading.

For Qur'anic references, while I have provided my own translation of the verses, I based my translation on: Muhammad Asad, *The Message of the Qur'an* (Bristol: The Book Foundation, 2003).

INTRODUCTION. ORIGINS OF CODIFICATION, CODIFICATION OF ISLAMIC LAW, AND THE RISE OF PERSONAL STATUS LAW

This introduction deals with two of the three main issues this study seeks to analyze: codification (as a theory and as applied to Islamic law) and personal status law. The third issue, the *'ulamā'*, will be dealt with in the subsequent chapters as I analyze their various opinions towards codification of personal status law. Not only was codification of law new for the Muslim world when the concept was introduced in the 19th century,[1] it was new to Europe and was a product of the Age of Enlightenment.[2] This chapter seeks to explain the theory behind codification and how European jurists have interpreted its effect on legal thought and jurisprudence, most prominently Jeremy Bentham (d. 1832)[3] who is considered the

[1] For an overview of the codification experience throughout the Muslim world see: Tarek Elgawhary, "Codification of Law" in *The [Oxford] Encyclopedia of Islam and Law. Oxford Studies Online*, http://www.oxfordislamicstudies.com/article/opr/t349/e0033 (accessed September 26, 2013).

[2] Nils Jansen, *The Making of Legal Authority* (Oxford: Oxford University Press, 2010), 16.

[3] A dual system of dating is used throughout this study (e.g., 911/1505). When both dates appear together, the first is the Hijrī date and the second is the Gregorian date. When a single date appears, unless otherwise specified, it will be the Gregorian date.

chief expositor of codification of law.[4] This chapter also provides an analysis of Ottoman codification, the first official codification of Islamic law throughout the Muslim world. In the process, I discuss the origins of the legal concept "personal status" and the importance and significance this has for Islamic law in the modern world. Lastly, the introduction turns to how scholars have interpreted the effects of codification on Islamic law and outlines both sides of the debate offering key tools to interpreting this issue.

GENEALOGY OF CODIFICATION

Codification, as it will be used throughout this study, is defined as the reduction of the whole of the law, whether statue law or common law, into a systematic form.[5] The whole of the law is a reference to all laws that encompass a given society's legal culture. In some cases, this may include laws that are written (statutory laws) or laws that have remained unwritten (common or custom law).[6] The process of codification is to bring these parts together and state them in clear, written form. This systematic form is made legitimate by direction from the state (or equivalent), but actually compiled and written by legal experts (jurists – sometimes privately and sometimes as part of the legislative branch of government) whose task it is to find the most appropriate laws to be included and therefore codified. This code of the law is to be complete and self-sufficient and not to be developed, supplemented, or modified except by legislative enactment.[7] Therefore, the salient features of a legal code are that it is to be simple (with respect to the law's prior, scattered state), written in clear form (whether its predecessor be

---

[4] I discuss Bentham as the father of codification in the sections that follow.

[5] Courtenay Ilbert, *The Mechanics of Law Making* (New York: Columbia University Press, 1914), 150.

[6] While common law is technically written, it remains unarticulated, and therefore from the point of view of codification, remains unclear until it is enacted and cited by a judge. See Henry Campbell Black, *Black's Law Dictionary*, 6th ed. (St. Paul, West Publishing, 1990), s.v., *common law*.

[7] Ilbert, *The Mechanics of Law Making*, 152.

statue law or common law), and should cause all previous laws to be forgotten and supplanted.[8]

Codification should not be confused with consolidation, another legal tool that will appear from time to time in this study. Legal consolidation is defined as the process of combining in a single measure enactments relating to a particular subject matter, but that exist scattered over different acts. Unlike codification, consolidation is aimed at improving the *form* of the law, without altering its actual *substance*.[9]

Codification in Europe was very much a product of enlightenment philosophy, particularly utilitarianism. As the feudal status quo of the European continent was being challenged, concerns for the future of law, a major tool used by kings to maintain this status quo, became a topic of much concern. In line with the general desire to usher in a new age that provided equal rights for citizens and protected special rights like the right to own property, legal reform not only was important, but shaped the new trajectory of Europe. Not only did legal reforms, and particularly codification, influence the development of these new nation states; they were also exported through various colonial experiments around the world. The need to provide "order" to colonized lands and to "reform" their legal systems, implying that these legal systems did not work and contained gross abuses, in order to make them "rational" and therefore "civilized" was a function of this spirit of codification and all it had to offer. Much of how we have come to understand and assess reform and the modernization of Islamic law in the colonial and post colonial period is largely, if not entirely, a function of using the standards of western notions of progress as envisioned in the post enlightenment age. The point here is not to analyze this, but rather to make the point that to understand the perspectives of the 'ulamā' towards codification of Islamic law, one must first understand what exactly codification is and the environment from which it came.

---

[8] Ibid.

[9] Ibid., 123. In this study a prime example of legal consolidation in Islamic law is the *al-Fatāwa al-Hindiyya* discussed in the next section.

Jeremy Bentham: "Legislator of the World"[10]

The theory of codification is seen as owing its genesis to the legal philosopher Jeremy Bentham (d. 1832). Bentham's theory of the need for codification stemmed from his view of utility. Since for Bentham man is either in a state of pain or pleasure and since pleasure is derived from that which is good or is itself considered the good, the study of the pursuit of pleasure, thus defined, is the basis for all things. Bentham argued that pain and pleasure are reducible to four broad categories: natural or physical, popular or public, political or legal, and religious. To understand and relate these to one another in a coherent manner is to approach them all through the theory of utility. The law for Bentham, therefore, is the process of finding the ultimate good for society, and the ultimate goal of the legislator is to increase pleasure and minimize pain for citizens.[11] Since all actions are either understood as pleasure or pain, good or evil, and since the task of legislation is to determine these, the process of determination itself (i.e. the process of legislation or in Bentham's case the process of codification) is a mere exercise in arithmetic.[12] The goal of this legal math is to maximize pleasures and minimize pains for people keeping in mind that government itself and the laws it produces are fundamentally an infringement on liberty and should therefore be kept to a minimum.[13] In other words, while the law is needed to maximize utility and pleasure for society, it is impossible to legislate everything.

As for the law itself, as actions for Bentham are reduced to pleasure and pain, so too are laws reduced to offences and obliga-

---

[10] This is a title given to Bentham by José Del Valle, a Guatemalan politician, in a letter written to Bentham in 1825. This appellation has also been adopted in one volume of the collected works of Bentham: Philip Schofield and Jonathan Harris eds., *The Collected works of Jeremy Bentham: Legislator of the World: Writings on Codification, Law and Education* (Oxford: Clarendon Press, 1988), 370.

[11] Jeremy Bentham, *Theory of Legislation* (Boston: Weeks, Jordan, & Company, 1840), 13, 45

[12] Ibid., 48.

[13] Ibid.

tions (and in some instances services).[14] Since each action could be interpreted as an obligation to do such and such or not do such and such, Bentham saw terms such as "law", "offence", "rights", "obligations", and "services" as being interchangeable.[15] The whole of law, therefore, being based on regulating actions that are essentially good or bad and being based on Bentham's general theory of utility, is reduced to securing four fundamental rights, or as Bentham would argue securing against infringements (i.e. offences) of four fundamental rights: security of person, honor, property, and condition.[16] The importance of this line of thinking is that it led Bentham to conclude that a legal system must contain three fundamental parts: The first part is entitled the *Civil Code*, which enumerates rights and obligations, the second part is entitled the *Penal Code*, which enumerates crimes and punishments, and the third part is the *Constitutional Code*, which enumerates laws related to the organization of society in a political entity.[17] An important point that I will come to later is that there is no section in Bentham's scheme of codification directly related to "personal status."

Bentham's conceptions of law generally and codification specifically were not just a deduction based on his theory of utility, he was also reacting to a legal system he saw as extremely dangerous. He offered his legal theory in juxtaposition to European feudal law; a law Bentham argued was arbitrary and uncertain. While these laws did emerge from the courts of kings to rule their subjects, they were not meant to maximize the utility of the people, but rather they were a function of the whim of monarchs to secure their own desires and needs. Furthermore, these inherited laws, Bentham argued, were laws that were not written in any concise manner but passed on as custom and tradition. One of Bentham's fundamental tenets for codification is that law must be written. Only a law that is written can be considered law, anything else is pure conjecture.[18]

---

[14] Jeremy Bentham, *The Collected Works of Jeremy Bentham*, 11 vols., (Edinburgh: William Tait, 1838–1843), 3:158.

[15] Ibid., 3:159.

[16] Ibid.

[17] Ibid., 3:162.

[18] Ibid., 206.

However, the need for law to be directed by the state and written by legal experts is not a means unto itself. Rather, the ultimate goal of the law for Bentham is clarity and certainty.[19] Bentham's critique of common, unwritten law is that it engenders a great deal of uncertainty and can oftentimes have various laws oppose one another. For Bentham this uncertainty oftentimes creates more harm than good. At one point in his writings, Bentham equated unwritten law to belief in false idols and gods![20]

Throughout his life, Bentham corresponded with nation states (including the United States of America) urging legislators to adopt his proposal for a codified system of law and to ask him formally to undertake this task on their behalf. This opportunity came when he was asked by the Portuguese Cortes in 1822 to work on a codification of law.[21] However, his legacy was not to be in this piece of legislation, but in his articulation of the need for and merits of codification in general. The Napoleonic codes of 1804 were the actual legislation that became an example to which European nation states turned in order to draw inspiration. Bentham wrote to President James Madison in 1811 that the French codes had been a success in creating a *Pannomion*, his own term for a complete, utilitarian code of law.[22] He also unblushingly observed to Madison that his works on codification were mentioned in the French Code of Criminal Instruction (1808) and the French penal code (1810).[23] The significance of the Napoleonic codes is not that it was the most complete or most revolutionary of legal codes. In fact, scholars argue that they were simply a reform of existing French laws.[24] Its significance is that it was associated with the French Revolution, and therefore with the idea of creating a new world order. Specifi-

---

[19] Ibid.

[20] Schofield, *The Collected works of Jeremy Bentham*, 124.

[21] This effort, which consumed the last years of Bentham's life, is preserved in the volume edited by Philip Schofield and Jonathan Harris.

[22] Schofield, *The Collected works of Jeremy Bentham*, 11.

[23] Ibid., 12.

[24] C. J. Friedrich, "The Ideological and Philosophical Background," in Bernard Schwartz, ed., *The Code Napoleon and the Common-Law World* (Westport, Connecticut: Greenwood Press, 1956), 2.

cally, for the purposes of analyzing perspectives of the 'ulamā' towards codification of personal status law in Egypt, the French codes became the premier example to be emulated. Starting with Khedive Ismā'īl (r. 1863–79) the Code of Napoleon was used as a model in the drafting of the code used by the Mixed courts[25] and the new Native courts.[26] The Napoleonic codes and subsequent French codes became synonymous with progress, order, and most importantly codification.

Napoleon (r. 1804–1815[27]), who considered the creation of the Napoleonic code to be his greatest achievement,[28] had a strong affinity with Rousseau's theory of a social contract and accordingly sought to instill this concept first amongst his troops, then amongst his fellow countrymen. Napoleon saw, like Rousseau, that law under the social contract is for the betterment of society and has the power to transform individuals.[29] This gave the legislator a god-like power, which certainly appealed to Napoleon's interest in political control. Similar to the goals of codification laid out by Bentham discussed above, the Napoleonic codes were drafted to first and foremost curb abuses of the ancient régime. It was a de-

---

[25] The Mixed Courts of Egypt were established in 1875 to litigate cases of foreigners inside Egypt. The code of law drafted by the court was an eclectic one adopting laws from many European nations. The Treaty of Montreux spelled out their demise and the doors of the Mixed courts closed finally in 1949. See: Jasper Yeats Brinton *The Mixed Courts of Egypt* (New Haven, CT: Yale University Press, 1968); Mark S.W. Hoyle, *Mixed Courts of Egypt* (London: Graham & Trotman, 1991).

[26] Established in 1884, the Native courts of Egypt and the newly drafted civil code were the government's response to the establishment of the Mixed courts. Over time, all legal jurisdictions would become subsumed in Egypt's Native courts. See: Egypt, *al-Kitāb al-Zahabī lil Maḥākim al-Ahliyya*, 2 vols., (Cairo: Maṭba'at Bulāq, 1937).

[27] Napoleon abdicated and was briefly exiled to the island of Elba from April 11, 1814–March 20, 1815.

[28] Friedrich, *The Code Napoleon*, 7–8.

[29] Ibid.

liberate process to demonstrate that man's freedom could only be limited by statue, not by the whim of other men.[30]

While Bentham proposed that a legal code first and foremost take into consideration obligations and offences regarding actions, the Napoleonic code, building on the social contract theory of Rousseau, arranged itself with regards to persons and their individual rights. The three main sections of the civil code were, therefore, persons (containing mainly issues related to marriage, divorce, paternity, and guardianship), property, and the acts of acquiring properties (which covers wills and marriage contracts).[31] These sections were regarded by other European nations, Italy for example, that were interested in adopting the French codes as essentially being Family Law. As we will see below, it is this focus on persons and therefore family issues that give rise to the use of and consideration of *personal status laws.*

Effects of Codification on Law

Since one of the essential functions of codification is that it makes law easier to access and understand, a question that should be asked at this point is what, then, is law? The legal traditions that form the backbone of any nation pre-date that nation by generations. Law, therefore, is an evolving body of knowledge that weds theory to practice; it is by nature discursive. In the European context, Roman law[32] and Canon law[33] were the largest influence on

---

[30] André Tunic, "The Grand Outlines of the Code," in Bernard Schwartz ed., *The Code Napoleon and the Common Law World*, (Westport, Connecticut: Greenwood Press, 1956), 22.

[31] France, *Code Napoleon or The French Civil Code*, (Baton Rouge: Claitor's Book Store, 1960 reprint of the original 1804 unnamed translation).

[32] This is a reference to the Justinian Codex *Corpus Iuris Civilis.* For details on the history and transmission of this text see: Charles Radding, *The Corpus Iuris Civilis in the Middle Ages: Manuscripts and Transmission from the Sixth Century to the Juristic Revival* (Leiden: Brill, 2007).

[33] This is a reference to the 12th century *Decretum Gratiani.* For details on this text and its origins see: A. Winroth, *The Making of Gratian's Decretum* (Cambridge: Cambridge University Press, 2000).

the development of modern laws and codes. As each nation-state gathered lawyers and legal scholars to engage in codification, it was previous juristic works, like those mentioned, that were turned to. In the French context, our main example in this study, the works of Jean Dumont (d. 1696) and Robert-Joseph Pothier (d. 1772), themselves discussions of earlier European legal theory, provided core guidance.[34] Bentham's own view of codification acknowledged that law itself is not stagnant, but a dynamic entity. Bentham mentions in several places the need to "update" laws and to incorporate customs and other social norms into the legal code periodically.[35] The process of codification, then, is to take existing law, law that has been developed for centuries, and to restate them in a succinct manner. It is not the process of inventing or creating laws, but of simply ordering existing law into a code. What, then, happens to the laws from which the code is taken, and how, then, do we come to understand the influences upon the code in the updating process Bentham mentioned as necessary? It should be clear from these questions that there are essentially two types of laws: official or public law and non-official or private law. Official or public law is defined as those laws that are composed under the direction of a political entity (in our case the modern state) and used in courts to adjudicate cases. Throughout this study, this is precisely what a code is. Non-official or private law is essentially everything else and defined as law that is carried out through the mechanism of juristic discussion and its various manifestations.[36] The legal traditions as

---

[34] For an account of this one should consult: Charles Donahue, "Historical Introduction: Comparative Law Before the Code Napoléon", in Mathias Reiman & Reinhard Zimmermann eds., *Oxford Handbook of Comparative Law* (Oxford: Oxford University Press, 2006): 3–32.

[35] Bentham, *The Works of Jeremy Bentham*, 3: 205, 210.

[36] My definition of private law is adapted largely from Charles Donahue and should not be confused with the distinction made by David Snyder of private law and privately made law which is not entirely relevant for our purposes here, but necessary to know. See: Charles Donahue Jr., "Law without the State and During its Formation", in *The American Journal of Comparative Law* 56(2008): 541–565; David V. Snyder, "Private Law Making", in *Ohio State Law Journal* 64(2003): 371–449.

found in the writings of Dumont and Pothier were the realm of private law. They discussed and summarized earlier existing legal works, especially Roman and Canon law, in addition to customs. Therefore, the authority that is presented in the Napoleonic code that emerged in the early 19th century comes not from the fact that it was a code and issued by the state, rather its authority comes from the legal sources the drafters of the code chose and picked form. As Nils Jansen argues, "the abstract authority of a text giving expression to a legal norm consists in the legal profession accepting it as an ultimate source of the law, without requiring further legal reasons to do so."[37] And for these sources to become authoritative and to be recognized as authoritative (admittedly an issue that while important falls outside the pale of this work) there must be a vibrant, continuous culture of juristic discussion surrounding these private law texts in which the concept and idea of legal-textual authority is accepted.

In attempting to understand the importance of private law, Charles Donahue shares a *mishna* from the Babylonian Talmud where Rabbis discuss the liability of a camel carrying flax that catches fire in a public space.[38] His point in so doing is to demonstrate that not only are such legal discussions identical to contemporary legal discussions of liability in public spaces, but that the juristic discussion that produced this mishna have been preserved over centuries by the mere fact that legal scholars of that tradition are, "involved in some way in the resolution of real cases."[39] The underlying theme, then, in any discursive legal tradition (Roman, Jewish, or Islamic), is that there is an eye to what practically will happen, or should happen, if such and such were to actually take place. This has led many modern legal authorities to define the law as simply a prediction or prophecy of what will happen in court as an outcome of a certain action.[40] The utility of this definition is that

[37] Jansen, *The Making of Legal Authority*, 43.

[38] Donahue, *Law without the State and During its Formation Law*, 541–542.

[39] Ibid., 545.

[40] Oliver Wendell Holmes, "The Path of the Law", in *Harvard Law Review*, 110(1997): 991.

it can apply to any system of law, any discursive tradition and most importantly includes both public and private law. Indeed, as Holmes himself says, "even if every decision required the sanction of an emperor with despotic power and a whimsical turn of mind, we should be interested nonetheless, still with a view of prediction, in discovering some order, some rational explanation, and some principle of growth for the rules which he laid down."[41]

Now, what is the relationship between the theory and practice of codification to the development of juristic discussions, i.e. private law? While codification was intended to make law easier and more accessible, in reality it did not. It is true that the Codes Napoleon were hailed as a triumph of enlightenment thought and that the rules of the code were concise, but that was precisely the problem, they were too concise. When one encounters a text such as, "if the husband is interdicted or absent, the judge, on cognizance of the cause, may authorize his wife either to plead in her own name or to contract"[42] many questions arise. How is "cognizance of the cause" defined, and can a wife, "plead in her own name" if she is a minor (article 145 allows government sanctioned dispensations to the marriage of minors)? Such questions and concerns appear for every single article of the entire code. If the point of law, and ultimately the code, is to help predict court outcomes, the code falls short. Another area where codification falls short of its definition is that it was not actually done by the state, but, and as demonstrated above, by legal scholars. The significance of both of these shortcomings is that private law and the juristic discussions that carried them referenced above were and are part and parcel of the codification process. This also means that, while law (particularly private law) cannot be a direct mirror of society,[43] it often times emerges

---

[41] Ibid., 997.

[42] France, *The French Civil Code*, Book 1: Chapter 6 article 222.

[43] Jansen, *The Making of Legal Authority*, 19–20. While this may be true in European and American forms of private legislation, the focus of Jansen's work, the private legislation machine of the ʿulamāʾ in Egypt regarding codification of personal status law was very responsive to social issues. In fact, one may argue that their response was too reactive and did

as a reaction and response to both political and social situations.[44] To address these shortcomings of codification and as a manifestation of this reality of the relationship between public and private law, an entire tradition of restatements and re-stating bodies (in our case we will see amongst many things the importance of explanatory notes to codes) have sprung up in Europe and North America. The process of explaining the law in a more full and robust manner has become a necessary part of the legal fabric of the Western world. As both Snyder and Jansen make clear, the industry of restatements and non-official legislation (Jansen's terminology) are often times larger and more influential than state legislation and the codes themselves.[45] In the American context for example, while the restatements were meant to clarify the law freely without concern for the restatement itself to play an authoritative role in legislation, they quickly became authoritative texts in themselves, often times more so than statue law itself.[46] The point I believe to take away from this discussion is that juristic discussions and non-legislative legal works continue to be authoritative and influence the process of codification after the formation of a code of law.[47] This necessitates, like in the story of the mishna cited above, that there is a continued juristic conversation about private law and it is this conversation that determines what is and what is not authoritative in the creation of a code. In addition, it is important to understand the socio-political milieu from which these discussions and ultimately codes emerge in order to have a proper, informed understanding of modern legislation. In our case, we will see the impact of the women's rights issue in chapter 2 on the thinking of 'ulamā' who supported the codification of personal status law and certain divorce reforms.

---

not allow for a measured "conceptual and discursive rationality" according to Jansen.

[44] Ibid., 82.

[45] Ibid., 85; Snyder, *Private Law Making*, 378, 384, 406, 419–20.

[46] Ibid., 54.

[47] Ibid., 18.

EXPERIMENTS IN CODIFICATION OF ISLAMIC LAW

From the time of the first generation of Muslims onwards, the fundamental intellectual goal of Islam has been to interpret the meaning of God's word (the Qur'an) and the teachings of the Prophet of Islam (his words, deeds, and actions collectively referred to as his sunna). Due to the inherent plurality of injunctions, contradictory statements, and plurality of interpretative possibilities imbedded in the Arabic language (the official language of Islamic thought and legislation), various approaches and schools of interpretations emerged.[48] Early textual discussions focused on ascertaining the veracity of the primary sources and in the process led to debates about law, one of the central focuses of Islamic intellectual discourse, as each group sought to spell out both orthopraxy and orthodoxy. Islamic law (what I refer to throughout this study as *Sharīʿa*) was the product of a discursive, dynamic process in which the various rulings (*al-aḥkām al-sharʿiyya*), the main object of Islamic law, were derived from the primary sources (Qur'ān and ḥadīth literature), the main subject of Islamic law, and catalogued in manuals of positive law (*furūʿ*). This process was initially regulated by the principles of Islamic legal methodology (*uṣūl al-fiqh*), a science created by the jurists and popularized by Imām Muḥammad ibn Idrīs al-Shāfiʿī (d. 204/820), and later by the particular rules and principles (*qawāʿid*) of the various schools of Islamic law (*al-madhāhib al-fiqhiyya*) as they began to form and become standardized around the 9th Islamic century. As this process progressed, the breadth of each legal school increased at a dramatic rate largely due to commentaries, meta-commentaries, and glosses on legal works.

[48] It is completely outside the scope of this work to trace the rise of the various interpretative schools as well as the schools of Islamic law. For a general overview one should consult the following works: Shāh Wali Allah Dahlawī, *Ḥujjat Allah al-Bāligha*, 2 vols., (Cairo: Dār al-Jīl, 2005); G.-H. Bousquet and Joseph Schacht eds., *Selected Works of C. Snouck Hurgronje* (Leiden: E.J. Brill, 1957); Wael Hallaq, *The Origins and Evolution of Islamic Law* (Cambridge: Cambridge University Press, 2005); Wael Hallaq, *Sharīʿa: Theory, Practice, Transformations* (Cambridge: Cambridge University Press, 2009), Parts I & II; Joseph Schacht, *An Introduction to Islamic Law* (Oxford: Clarendon Press, 1982).

A natural reaction to this great breadth in legal thought was the production of legal compendia (*mukhtaṣar*) for the different schools of law.[49] However, the process of composing these legal compendia necessitated that the ratio legis (*'illa*) of each ruling be dropped in order to provide a simple to use catalogue of Sharī'a rulings of a particular school for beginner and intermediate students to memorize by rote.[50] This streamlined process in legal thought was itself based on another more dire need: to determine what exactly *the* position or ruling was for a given issue of law according to a particular school of legal thought given the vast plurality of opinions that existed. Since the breadth and diversity within each school had increased so much, this often times proved challenging. In the world of Ḥanafī law, significant in this study for the role it played in developing legal thinking on personal status law in Egypt, various attempts were made to answer these challenges. One such approach was the *al-Fatāwā al-Bazzāziyya* compiled in 812 AH by Sheikh Ibn Bazzāz al-Kardawī (d. 827 AH) to be followed some 250 years later by the *al-Fatāwā al-Hindiyya*[51] which was complied under the patronage of the Mughal Emperor Aurangzeb Alamgir (r. 1658–1707) who assembled a committee of jurists to compile the most popular and agreed upon opinions of Ḥanafī law. Sheikh Niẓām, the leader of the committee Aurangzeb assembled, wrote in his introduction, after complaining of the difficulties of ascertaining sound positions in the Ḥanafī School, that the fatwa collection strives to clearly define the most agreed upon positions in the Ḥanafī school according to both their status vis-à-vis the legal school's legal methodology (for the Ḥanafī's this is termed *ẓāhir al-*

---

[49] Mohammad Fadel, "The Social Logic of *Taqlīd* and Rise of the *Mukhtaṣar*", in *Islamic Law and Society* 3,2 (1996): 193–223.

[50] The dropping of the 'illa from works of Islamic law generated a larger problem, particular in the late Ḥanafī school. See generally: Ya'akov Meron, "The Development of Legal Thought in Hanafi Texts", in *Studia Islamica* 30 (1969): 73–118.

[51] Shaykh Niẓām, *al-Fatāwā al-Hindiyya al-ma'rūf bi-al-Fatāwā 'Ālamkīriyya* 6 vols., (Beirut: Dār al-Kutub al-'Ilmiyya, 2000).

riwāya)[52] as well as opinions established by precedent (via collections of prior accepted fatwa collections such as the al-Bazzāziyya).[53]

A question that emerges is why could not there have been an easier, more direct way, similar to the codification process in western law, to make the development of Islamic law easier to access? Ibn al-Muqaffaʿ (d. 142/759) a Persian, ʿAbbāsid statesman observed this same problem as the plurality of Islamic law was reaching its creative climax and is perhaps the first to speak of codification of Islamic law.[54] Ibn al-Muqaffaʿ was very concerned with what he saw as a dangerous situation. In desperation he wrote a letter to the ʿAbbāsid Caliph Manṣūr (r. 136/754–158/775) to address several political concerns, and in the process highlighted the need for a state sponsored codification of Islamic law. Ibn al-Muqaffaʿ's concern was that there was a plurality of interpretations of the sunna that led, not necessarily to fruitful juristic conversations and debates, but unfortunately to bloodshed and civil strife.[55] Every group, he argued, used their interpretations as justification for killing others and in the process went outside the political order of the Caliph, a grave moral and political sin according to Islamic law. For Ibn al-Muqaffaʿ this led to his second major point that there has to be absolute obedience to the Imām (here understood as the legitimate political leader) and that this political leader is in turn required to adhere to God absolutely vis-à-vis the Sharīʿa for there can be no obedience to someone who is not obedient to God

---

[52] For basic terminology on the Ḥanafī School of law see: ʿAlī Jumuʿa, *Responding from the Tradition*, Tarek Elgawhary and Nuri Friedlander trans., (Louisville: Fons Vitae: 2011), 210–213; ʿAlī Jumuʿa, *al-Madkhal ilā Dirāsat al-Madhhāhib al-Fiqhiyya* (Cairo: Dār al-Salām, 2004), 73–138.

[53] Niẓām, *al-Fatāwā al-Hindiyya*, 1:3–4.

[54] Ibn al-Muqaffaʿ is usually cited as the first to advocate for a codification of Sharīʿa. See: Schacht, *An Introduction to Islamic Law*, 55–56. For a controversial account of this codification experiment and the development of Islamic imperial law see: Benjamin Jokisch, *Islamic Imperial Law* (Berlin: Walter de Gruyter, 2007).

[55] ʿAbd Allah Al-Muqaffaʿ, *Āthār Ibn al-Muqaffaʿ* (Beirut: Dār al-Kutub al-ʿIlmiyya, 1989), 312.

(*lā ṭā'a li makhlūq fī ma'ṣiyat al-khāliq*).[56] This discussion by Ibn al-Muqaffa' represents the hierarchy of political and religious authority that necessitates and allows for the Imām to codify Islamic law for his body politic. Only by so doing, Ibn al-Muqaffa' argued, can true obedience to God and His Prophet, via the Sharī'a, be established.

Ibn al-Muqaffa''s understanding of authority and obedience acknowledges that there are certain issues, central, agreed upon issues, that all must follow, including and most especially the Imām.[57] However, aside from these well-known matters (usually referred to in Islamic legal discourse as necessarily known facts (*al-ma'lūm min al-dīn bi'l ḍarūra*) the vast majority of legal matters are open to different interpretations and therefore within the purview of the Imām to choose and enact officially.[58] The process by which these controversial and conflicting matters should be settled, according to Ibn al-Muqaffa', is for each group to present their opinion alongside their *ratio legis*, in order to prove that these interpretations in fact have a basis and are valid, and for the Imām to choose one of these valid positions to enact. It is important to note that Ibn al-Muqaffa' specifically stated that the Imām should strive to arrive and enact "one *ḥukm*" (what I have likened above to the "object of Islamic law") and does not say that there needs to be "one Sharī'a" or one interpretation of the subject of Islamic law, what I have identified as the primary sources of Islamic law. In other words, Ibn al-Muqaffa' acknowledged that plurality of interpretation is part and parcel of Islamic law, but with regards to application by the state, there needs to be uniformity. This basic methodology, as we will come to see through the chapters that follow, remains the essential methodology of the 'ulamā' who both wrote codes and supported codification of personal status law.[59]

---

[56] Ibid.

[57] Ibid.

[58] Ibn al-Muqaffa' would perhaps argue, however, that such preferences and official enactments are the duty and responsibility of the Imām and not simply a good thing to do. See: al-Muqaffa', *Āthār*, 312.

[59] See chapters 1 and 2 below.

In his recommendation of codification, Ibn al-Muqaffaʿ argued, "that it is…the caliph's sole prerogative to enact and promulgate legal decisions and doctrines in the form of a uniform, binding code; and he alone must define what normative sunna should mean or consist of at any given time."[60] Now, while this is certainly a rational argument by Ibn al-Muqaffaʿ there seems to be no record that al-Manṣūr sought to develop a singular code of law based on the Sharīʿa according to Ibn al-Muqaffaʿ's recommendation. In fact, there is no record that he responded to the treatise addressed to him at all. Nonetheless, and to use the words of Goiten, Ibn al-Muqaffaʿ's recommendation represented a "cross-roads" for the development of Islamic law.[61] The state could have assumed the responsibility of controlling religion and law (the option that Ibn al-Muqaffaʿ was arguing for) or a "divorce" of the two and religion and law could grow independent and scholastic in nature (the option that both the state and the ʿulamāʾ chose).[62] The independent and theoretical direction that Islamic law took is what I have sought to describe briefly in the first paragraphs of this section as the discursive nature of Sharīʿa. My understanding is that Islamic law, like Jewish law before it and concurrent to it, developed in private juristic discussions, not through enactment by the state. Therefore, the activities and results of private legislation are part and parcel of the discussion of the development of Islamic law. One aspect of this I will return to in the pages that follow is that to ascertain what forms this private, juristic discussion one must look at the "intellectual footprint" of both individual jurists as well as the institutions they come from (in the case of ʿulamāʾ engaging in official state-sponsored codification) and the intellectual schools they belong to (legal schools such as-Shafiʿī, Mālikī etc, as well as interpretive schools-traditional, modernist, salafi, etc.).

While al-Manṣūr did not take Ibn al-Muqaffaʿ's codification process on, he did offer Imām Mālik ibn ʾAnas (d. 179/795) to

[60] Muhammad Qasim Zaman, *Religion and politics under the early ʿAbbāsids: the emergence of the proto-Sunnī elite* (Leiden: Brill, 1997), 83.

[61] S.D. Goiten, *Studies in Islamic History and Institutions* (Leiden: Brill, 2012), 164.

[62] Ibid.

codify and standardize his famous *al-Muwaṭṭa'*, consisting of approximately 1,800 reports: 527 ḥadīths of the Prophet of Islam, 613 rulings made by Companions (*ṣaḥāba*), 285 rulings of Successors (*tābi'ūn*), with the remainder being Mālik's own opinions.[63] According to the story, perhaps apocryphal, Imām Mālik refused the Caliph's offer citing the proliferation of Islamic legal thinking throughout the Muslim world and the impossibility of unifying this. As Zaman states, the moral of Mālik's refusal is that "no one, not even a prominent *'ālim*, has the authority to draw up a code which might be given the sanction of law. The story is not about the separation of religion and politics, as one might be tempted to suppose, but only about the way legal understanding (*fiqh*) properly evolves in an Islamic society."[64] While I agree with this point entirely, I believe there is more to Imām Mālik's refusal that sheds light on the ability to codify Islamic law. Mālik's refusal to standardize the Muwaṭṭa' is not due to a problem with codification as a legal concept vis-à-vis Islamic law, but rather indicates the impossibility of the Sharī'a, the interpretation of the subject of Sharī'a to be precise, to be uniform and singular, and therefore un-codifiable.[65] In other words, like Ibn al-Muqaffa''s references to the legitimate plurality of Sharī'a interpretations, to codify and standardize the Muwaṭṭa', a collection of Imām Mālik's own interpretation of sound primary sources, would be tantamount to unifying and singularizing interpretation of the Qur'an and sunna. All that could be codified, however, are rulings and positions as a function of state law, not the function of juristic discourse, conversation, discussion, and debate.

Development of *al-siyāsa al-shar'iyya*

Although for the rest of this introduction I focus on the codification attempts under the Ottomans as a segue into the larger topic of codification of personal status law in Egypt, it should be clear that the story of codification of Islamic law did not stop with Ibn Muqaffa' and Imām Mālik only to be resumed hundreds of years

[63] I am indebted to Professor Jonathan Brown for these statistics.

[64] Zaman, *Religion and Politics*, 85.

[65] I admit this is foreshadows one of my conclusions to which I will offer a fuller explanation at the end of this study.

later in Anatolia by the Ottomans. Since every Muslim body politic had to grapple with the rule of law and establishing their own legitimacy, the subject of *al-siyāsa al-shar'iyya* evolved over time to emerge as the body of writing and theory that governed the crossroads of politics and Islamic law.

As Frank Vogel says, siyāsa can be thought of as legal conceptions and institutions viewed from the perspective of the ruler.[66] It generally included rules governing the discretionary right of the ruler to enact laws when there was no clear text in the primary sources and no precedent in Islamic law. In exchange for this type of power, the 'ulamā' were the providers of legitimacy to rulers, ensuring that they were essential and thus allowing them to be the sole "protectors of the Islamic constitution."[67] This "circle of justice" as Wael Hallaq calls it, is its own topic with its own vast literature and genealogy.[68] What are the conditions for a legitimate ruler, who is allowed to pick the ruler (i.e. the *ahl al-ḥall wa'l 'aqd*), what are the boundaries of what he can or cannot do, how can one remove a ruler if needed, etc., all are questions that form the backbone of this genre of writing. Throughout this study, however, I will use al-siyāsa al-shar'iyya to refer specifically to the legitimacy, or lack thereof, of a political entity, including the highest-ranking official of that entity. In other words, in analyzing the perspectives of various 'ulamā' towards codification of personal status laws, and in discussing their opinions of al-siyāsa al-shar'iyya, I will focus on whether or not these 'ulamā' held their own political authorities as legitimate or non-Sharī'a compliant agents to carry out codification.

---

[66] Frank E. Vogel, *Islamic Law and Legal System* (Brill: Leiden, 2000), 171.

[67] Ibid., 195.

[68] "The Circle of Justice", as translated by Wael Hallaq, refers to the religious sanctioning of a ruler over his subjects. As Hallaq himself notes, "The sovereign himself was expected to observe not only his own code but, more importantly, the law of the Sharī'a....siyāsa, therefore, was in no way the unfettered power of political governance but in a fundamental way the exercise of wisdom, forbearance and prudence by a prince in rulings his subjects". See: Hallaq, *Sharī'a*, 208–216.

The role that the 'ulamā' played in keeping the political and social structure of Muslim societies led to a consolidation of the political structure and a strong integration of siyāsa by time of the Ottomans.[69] The Ottomans provided a vast government bureaucracy where the 'ulamā' played a vital role allowing siyāsa to take on a more formal role in Muslim politics. There were official state 'ulamā' (muftis, *qāḍīs*, and the position of *Shaykh al-Islām*) which provided a more structured role for the 'ulamā' in matters of state. Over time, the imperial laws and decrees that were issued were, in a sense, written and codified. They became known as *qānūn*s and provided a vast new body of legal literature that would impact the desire to codify Islamic law in the 19th century.

Part of the Ottomans legal efforts and bureaucracy was to standardize the sources of Islamic law used throughout its court proceedings. The Ḥanafī school, considered the most widely followed school of Sunnī Islam, gained great popularity in Transoxania and therefore received prominence under the Ottoman Empire, which enacted the Ḥanafī school as the official school of law throughout the Empire and its territory.[70] As I have mentioned above, the development of Islamic law after the formation of the legal schools represented a widening of the schools, but not necessarily a deepening of analysis of the primary sources. One way in which this was manifested was the plethora of opinions that formed within each school for almost every single point of law. While this characteristic is technically found in the four sunnī schools of law, for reasons that go beyond the scope of this current analysis, the Ḥanafī school in particular was not redacted in the same manner as some of the other schools and its rulings, therefore, have not been as uniform as the rulings and opinions of the other three sunnī schools. The explanatory note to the *Majalla* itself makes mention that the Ḥanafī school "was not redacted (*tanqīḥ*)

---

[69] Ibid., 205.

[70] See: Rudolph Peters, "What Does It Mean to Be an Official Madhhab? Hanafism and the Ottoman Empire," in Peri Berman ed., *The Islamic School of Law* (Cambridge: Harvard University Press, 2005).

like the Shafi'ī school."[71] Works such as the al-Fatāwā al-Bazzāziyya and al-Fatāwā al-Hindiyya (usually printed together) were meant to consolidate Ḥanafī law and provide legislators and judges with accurate and reliable rulings from the Ḥanafī school.

In the process of consolidation of the law, often times the ratio legis of rulings were discarded to make the law more accessible.[72] This phenomenon has led some authors to claim that jurists of the post classical period simply followed blindly and imitated (taqlīd) the various legal schools and made little effort to know why or how a particular ruling has emerged. Of particular relevance to the codification of personal status law in Egypt, stringent rulings of the Ḥanafī school relating to certain marriage and divorce practices, rulings that were expected to be enacted in Sharī'a courts upholding Ḥanafī law, became a rallying call for reform.[73] As I will discuss below, this type of narrative was even promoted by the 'ulamā' who supported the need for codification of personal status law.[74] However, even if the 'illa of rulings became lost or sidestepped for a more theoretical argument as to the reason for the particulars of law, the deep analysis of classical and post-classical Ḥanafī texts demonstrates that recourse was given to following other sunnī schools in these difficult matters.[75] The point to be made here is that jurists of the Ḥanafī school recognized these problems of late Ḥanfism and a pattern of cross-madhhab cooperation was both theoretically and operationally intact (Shafi'ī judges would sit alongside Ḥanafī ones to pass rulings in these situations) and, in a sense, the positions of other schools became Ḥanafī rulings since they were accessed through Ḥanafī judges in courts upholding, exclusively, Ḥanafī law.

---

[71] 'Alī Ḥaydar, *Durar al-Ḥukkām Sharḥ Majallat al-Aḥkām*, 4 vols., (Beirut: Maktabat al-Nahda, 1970), 1:9.

[72] This applies more to legal compendia than collections of fatāwa. See Meron, *Hanafi Texts*, 94–97.

[73] As I mention in chapter 2 below, Aḥmad Shākir highlights this point.

[74] See chapter 2 for details.

[75] Meron, *Hanafi Texts*, 100.

Ottoman Codification and the Story of the Majalla

While Islamic law as a scholastic discipline grew independent of the state, there was always a point of overlap where Muslim jurists served in government positions such as judges, muftis, and legal advisors to the ruling elite. There was also usually a form of al-siyāsa al-shar'iyya at play and Islamic law, if not directly used by the state, always found a way to inform state legislation. In the late modern period, this legal structure was most pronounced in the Ottoman Empire and reflected in the vast regions it controlled, including Egypt. There was a dominance of the Ḥanafī school in courts and official legal positions were more administrative than scholarly.[76] By the early 1800s the Ottomans began to feel tensions, particularly in commercial ventures, between European nations and the Sublime Porte. The capitulation arrangements that grew from the earliest days of the Ottoman Empire had slowly created a gap in commercial and criminal legislation pushing the Sharī'a to the side and even challenging its applicability. This same tension in Egypt, an inheritor of Ottoman capitulations, led to the creation of the Mixed courts in 1876 by Khedive Ismā'īl (r. 1863–1879).[77] While the Egyptian Mixed courts developed an eclectic legal code, largely influenced by French codes, the Ottomans sought a different route regarding commercial law.

The Ottoman Majalla was the first attempt in the modern Muslim world to carry out a full and official codification of Islamic law. Like the episode of Ibn al-Muqaffa' during the 'Abbāsid era, the production of the Majalla represented a new cross roads for Islamic law and the state that would permanently, and drastically alter the relationship between the two, an effect felt even today. Understanding the story of the Majalla and the methodology used

---

[76] As nominally part of the Ottoman Empire, Egypt strictly followed Ḥanafī law throughout its Sharī'a court system. Even though there was some oversight from the Ottoman appointed Chief Qadī (a Ḥanafī to be sure), he was not considered a true scholar by the *'ulamā'* of Egypt. See: 'Abd al'Azīz al-Shināwī, *al-Azhar Jāmi'an wa Jamā'atan*, 2 vols., (Cairo: Anglo-Egyptian Bookshop, 1983), 1:198. Also see: Peters, "What Does It Mean to Be an Official Madhhab?", 147–158.

[77] For details on this episode see chapter 1 below.

by its 'ulamā' drafters is paramount to understanding codification of personal status law in Egypt.

The *Tanzimat* reforms of the Ottoman Empire began in 1839 with the *Hatt-i Hümāyun* (Imperial Decree) seeking to clarify the adjudication of cases between Muslims (and non-Muslim Ottoman subjects) and non-Muslims (i.e. European nationals). Falling out with its key allies after the Crimean War, the Empire was pressed to make its legal positions clear regarding commercial and criminal laws for non-Ottomans. By 1847 secular courts were recognized to deal with international, commercial relations and another Imperial Decree was issued in 1856 (a second Hatt-i Hümāyun) seeking to provide more clarity.[78] The situation deteriorated, however, and an 1866 uprising in Crete, then part of the Empire, demonstrated the Ottoman's failure at protecting Christian subjects per the Imperial Decree of 1839 and its supposed improvement in 1856. Writing to the Sultan about the need to provide legal clarity, the Grand Vizer Ali Paşa suggested that the Porte follow the same path as Egypt in adopting aspects of the Code Napoleon for legal reform.[79] Ali Paşa went one step further than simply recommend this, and sent for a copy of Ṭahṭāwī's (d. 1873) translation of the French Codes to the Porte and entrusted them with one of his aides, Said, who later became himself Grand Vizier (Küçük Said Paşa).[80] Ottoman officials had noticed that their counterparts in Egypt had taken aspects of the Napoleonic Code and enacted them as a means to deal with mixed interests in commercial cases, the same mixed interest problem they were facing in the Sublime Porte. Writing in 1867, Ali Paşa reiterated his conviction that such an accommodation could take place in Ottoman lands without violating Islamic law and the grasp it had on Ottoman jurisprudence.[81] This sentiment, that a solution was needed that would not harm the Sharī'a underscores

---

[78] Dora Glidwell Nadalski, "Ottoman and Secular Law", in *International Journal of Middle East Studies* 8(4) 1977, 522; Sherif Arif Mardin, "Some Explanatory Notes on the Origins of the 'Mecelle'" in *The Muslim World* 51(4) 1961: 275.

[79] Mardin, *Explanatory Notes*, 276.

[80] I discuss Ṭahṭāwī's translation in chapter 2.

[81] Ibid., 276.

the great challenge that lay before Ottoman reformers. How could the Sublime Porte make its legal positions modern and clear to its European interlocutors, yet at the same time remain firmly based on Islamic legal jurisprudence? Realizing that they needed help from amongst the 'ulamā', the Grand Vizer wrote to the Şeyhülislām in 1856 to provide him with an ʿālim of "great learning and a liberal bent" to help with these difficult legal reforms.[82] The ʿālim that was sent would grow to be one of the greatest supporters and authors of codification of Islamic law in the modern period.

Ahmed Cevdet Paşa

Ahmed Cevdet Paşa (d. 1895) had always found himself as the translator of two opposing worlds: modern, western leaning Ottoman society, and the world of the traditional 'ulamā'. As will be common throughout this study, such liberal minded and reform leaning 'ulamā' always found themselves at the center of legal reform and especially the process of codification. Ahmed Cevdet had a traditional Islamic education.[83] At the same time, however, Cevdet had an intense curiosity in non-traditional subjects and spent a great amount of time and exerted great efforts to learn mathematics, philosophy, and Persian (a much more advance level than was typical at the time). His skills in Persian allowed him to be more familiar with the writings of the 15th century Persian philosopher, Jalāl al-Dīn al-Dawānī (d. 1502), whose political philosophy of the four pillars (*erkān-i erbaa*) had a tremendous impact on the thinking of 19th century Ottoman thought.[84] Later in his life, Cevdet would again turn to the Avicennian philosopher to offer a defense of secular (more accurately labeled non-religious) courts in

---

[82] Ibid., 274.

[83] The broad strokes of his Islamic education are covered in: Richard L. Chambers, "The Education of a Nineteenth-Century Ottoman Alim, Ahmed Cevdet Pasa", in *International Journal of Middle East Studies* 4 (1973): 440–464.

[84] Sherif Mardin, "The Mind of the Turkish Reformer 1700–1900" in *Western Humanities Review*, 14 (1960): 420–23. For a biography on Dawānī, see: *The Encyclopedia of Islam*, 2nd ed. (Leiden: 1960–2002), s.v., "al-Dawānī (article by Ann Lambton).

the Ottoman Empire. In any case, Cevdet's erudition was well established by the time he had matured and graduated to an official *'ālim* and he gained many fans amongst the intellectual elite of Istanbul. This was at a time when the state of traditional Islamic learning was waning and largely considered ineffective. Cevdet himself commented on this state of affairs and offered a four-tier ranking of the 'ulamā' at his time that left most 'ulamā' off the list.[85] Even though authors make a point to mention that Cevdet formally left the 'ulamā' class in 1866, he always identified with his origins as an *'ālim* and considered himself to be a continuation of the Islamic intellectual tradition.[86]

While Cevdet was indeed known and respected as an intellectual, he did have his share of enemies, particularly Şeyhülislam Hasan Efendi who had Cevdet removed from the Majalla commission and the authority of the commission itself transferred to the office of the Şeyhülislam.[87] In 'Alī Haydar's introduction to his commentary on the Majalla, he also makes references that Cevdet's actions, particularly his work in the Majalla, often counted against him with his fellow 'ulamā'. While there is no denying the fact that the 'ulamā' were not a uniform, homogeneous class, indeed this entire study demonstrates this fact, Cevdet's position as an open minded and liberal 'ālim, in the words of the Grand Vizer, was not so much outside the norm for 19th century Ottoman 'ulamā'. Even though, as I will discuss below, he used Dawānī as an argument for a justification of non-religious courts, Dawānī, as an Avicennian, Persian philosopher was a known and studied intellectual in 20th century Ottoman circles. Cevdet's level of open mindedness, then, is something that can be considered relatively proportional to his colleagues and therefore not as radical as his counterparts amongst Azhar 'ulamā' such as Ḥasan al-'Aṭṭār (d. 1835) or Rifā'a al-Ṭahṭāwī, figures that are essentially proto-supporters of codifica-

[85] Chambers, *Education*, 448–51.

[86] Ibid., 460. I understand his break in 1866, therefore, to be an indication that in the Ottoman hierarchical society of 19th century Cevdet moved away from the professional track the *'ulamā'* occupied, but he did not stop being an *'ālim*.

[87] Ibid., 452.

tion of Islamic law in Egypt. This is not to diminish from the importance of Ahmed Cevdet as a major contributor to the project of codification of Islamic law, but rather demonstrates that codification of Islamic law in the Ottoman context did not have the same intellectual and social ramifications as it did in Egypt.[88]

Methodology of the Majalla's Codification[89]

While there were systemic solutions to difficult rulings within the Ḥanafī school, the problems that Cevdet and the Ottoman 'ulamā' faced in the mid-1800s were much more serious than problems faced in the past by the 'ulamā'. The challenge was two-fold: the need to articulate Ottoman commercial law for European nations conducting major transactions with the Sublime Porte, a law that was purportedly based on Islamic law, and at the same time there was a need to face the challenges Islamic law, particularly Ḥanafī law, confronted in the modern context as well as reconciling the process of codification of Islamic law and legal norms to satisfy the first issue.

Cevdet's immediate task was to argue against the adoption of French law in lieu of Islamic law.[90] Cevdet made the following remarks regarding the proposal to adopt French law:

> With the increase in the number of Europeans coming to Turkey, and with the increase of contacts with them because of the Crimean War, the scope of trade widened. The commercial courts became unable to deal with the commercial lawsuits

---

[88] An obvious question is how one should interpret the "objection" of *Şeyhülislam* Hasan Efendi to Cevdet. I believe this was born out of a personal problem between the two, rather than a formal rejection by the *Seyhülislam* towards codification. See Chambers, *Education*, 452.

[89] The main sources for the methodology of codification in the *Majalla* are Ahmed Cevdet's memoirs as well as the explanatory note Cevdet and his committee provided for the project: Ahmed Cevdet Paşa, *Teẓākir*, 3 vols., (Ankara: Türk Tarīh Kurumu Basimevī, 1953); Haydar, *Durar al-Ḥukām*, 1:8–12; Dora Glidewell Nadolski, "Ottoman and Secular Civil Law", in *International Journal of Middle East Studies* 8 (1977): 517–543.

[90] Nadolski, *Ottoman and Secular Civil Law*, 523.

> arising every day. The foreigners did not like to go to the *şeriat* courts. The unacceptability of the testimony of non-Muslims against Muslims and of the *musta'man* (non-Muslim foreigners) against *dhimmi* (non-Muslim Ottoman subjects) in the *şeriat* courts became very annoying to the Europeans and they objected to the trail of the Christians in the *şeriat* courts. Thus, certain persons took up the idea of translating French civil codes into Turkish for judgment in the *nizami* courts.[91] This idea was not acceptable because changing the basic laws of a nation would entail its destruction. The 'ulamā' believed that those who had gone astray to hold Frankish ideas were unbelievers. The Franks, on the other hand, used to say "bring forth your code; let us see it and make it known to our subjects."[92]

Despite the fact that the concept of codifying Islamic law was controversial to some more conservative Ottoman 'ulamā', Cevdet most likely saw this as the only way to preserve the Islamic legal heritage of the Ottomans, a theme that will be echoed in later years by pro-codification 'ulamā' in Egypt.

Cevdet's next task, and just as challenging, was to provide a justification for codification itself. He found this justification in one of the scholars he came to be familiar with through his Persian studies, Jalāl al-Dīn al-Dawānī. In his memoirs, Cevdet referenced a treatise by Dawānī on the *maẓālim* courts and cites Dawānī's justification of secular courts alongside Sharī'a courts and coexisting within an Islamic legal tradition. The basic argument is that the maẓālim courts allow the testimony of non-Muslims and these testimonies have full legal effect, therefore there is room for purely non-Islamic forms of legal effect within the Sharī'a.[93] Another way of saying this is that the Sharī'a itself includes secular, non-Islamic

---

[91] As I make clear above, this was accomplished via the Arabic translation of Ṭahṭāwī.

[92] Quoted in Nadolski, *Ottoman and Secular Civil Law*, 539.

[93] Niyzai Berkes, *The Development of Secularism in Turkey* (New York: Routledge, 1998), 168.

law. This argument adduced by Cevdet assumes, then, that a code of law is itself secular, even if its origins are from Islamic law.[94]

As I have demonstrated in the first section of this introduction, codes are usually in need of explanations and accompanying texts, either officially or unofficially. Cevdet and his committee provided a concise explanatory note to introduce the Majalla and placed it in an Islamic context, perhaps, as others would do later in Egypt, to ward off claims that he has engaged in something heterodox. The note draws a distinction between rulings that do not change and those that do change based on time and custom.[95] The example given in the explanatory note is that amongst earlier Ḥanafī jurists, sales of homes were permitted if the buyer simply saw similar homes to the one being purchased, and did not necessitate that the buyer see the exact house being purchased. Later Ḥanafī jurists, however, stipulated that the buyer actually see the exact house being purchased. The note explains this discrepancy in that the custom of housing changed and necessitated that the exact house be seen since variation in building structures did not exist at the time of the earlier jurists. These changes, the report states, are

---

[94] I admit that this is my perspective regarding the nature of codification. However, it is appropriate to mention here that the "secular" nature of Ottoman law is not something that emerged with Cevdet. Constitutional and fiscal matters were dealt with by *firmans*, not Sharīʿa courts. Many of the laws that Caliph Mahmud II (r. 1808–39) enacted were laws based on customs that he inherited and then sought to Islamicize. Even before this, hailing back to the 16th century down to the Tanzimat period there was a coexistence of Islamic and non-Islamic laws. For a discussion of this see: Yunus Koç, "Early Ottoman Customary Law: The Genesis and Development of Ottoman Codification" in Walter Dostal and Wolfgang Kraus eds., *Shattering Tradition: Custom, Law and the Individual in the Muslim Mediterranean* (London: I.B. Tauris, 2005), 75–121.

[95] Haydar, *Durar al-Ḥukām*, 1:9. Although the explanatory note and its example cite one or two casues for the change of a ruling, there are typically four aspects that are cited as the cause of change in a Sharīʿa ruling: time, place, circumstance, and people. See: ʿAbdullah Rabīʿa ʿAbdullah Muḥammad, *Madā Taghyīr al-Aḥkām bi Taghyīr al-Jihāt al-ʿArbaʿa* (Cairo: Ministry of Endowments, n.d.).

the cause for need of works like al-Fatāwa al-Hindiyya.[96] However, as helpful as these works are, they too fall short since they were written with a certain historical perspective, a perspective that is not entirely relevant in the contemporary context, particularly those areas that are subject to change due to time and custom. To make this point clearer, the report cites the second article of the Majalla, a restatement of the uṣūlī principle that matters are based on their goals and results *(al-'umūr bi maqāṣidiha)*. Therefore, the point is not to follow the letter of the law, but to understand what the principle or goal of each ruling is in order to implement the spirit of the law. In addition, these rulings, which are subject to change and therefore subject to ijtihād, are within the purview of the Imām to choose and enact at his will and subsequently the obligation of the people to obey.[97]

Cevdet and the committee saw this essential sketch of Islamic law as a continuation of the work of the Ḥanafī jurist Ibn Nujaym (969/1561). Since a principled approach to the Sharī'a is called for in order to avoid applying rulings that are no longer cogent, the first one hundred articles of the Majalla are restatements of the major principles of Islamic law (al-qawā'id al-fiqhiyya). These principles were to serve as guides for future legislation and were aimed at encouraging a more principled approach to law, rather than a pure codification of one single madhhab. However, in reality, these principles themselves are so broad that it is nearly impossible to find utility in them as stated in the code without commentary, explanations, and examples. This itself has caused much misunderstanding regarding the nature of the Majalla. For example, Brinkley Messick, sees the Majalla as limiting the practice of ijtihād and enshrining this in article 14 stating there is no ijtihād when there is a clear text (*naṣṣ*), i.e. Qur'an or ḥadīth.[98] This is one of his main themes in his critique of the impact of codification on Islamic law as I will discuss below. One could in fact interpret this article to limit the practice of ijtihād, however when one reads commentaries

---

[96] Ibid.

[97] Ibid.,12.

[98] Brinkley Messick, *The Calligraphic State* (Berkeley, University of California Press: 1993), 57.

on this article, it is clear that the article not only does not limit ijtihād, but rather is established to affirm the practice, as is the entire first section of the Majalla.[99] In fact, the need to follow other opinions based on ijtihād conflicting with the Ḥanafī school (a form of legal eclecticism – *talfīq*) is affirmed in the Majalla itself. Cevdet recognized that situations requiring non-Ḥanafī positions allowing sales with trade could be needed one day, a position held by Ibn Shubruma who was a contemporary *mujtahid* to Abū Ḥanifa and allowed sales based on conditions (something Ḥanafī jurists do not allow). Not only is this a position outside the confines of the Ḥanafī school, but also a non-Sunnī position as it relies on a singular opinion outside the four canonical schools.[100]

The Majalla, as is expected from a code, is an extremely dense document and itself in need of commentary assistance. While there were many attempts at explaining it, the extensive commentary of ʿAlī Haydar became its most popular and studied. Haydar had been teaching in law schools in Istanbul and served as Minister of Justice. His commentary displaced earlier ones made by Cevdet and others, and Haydar's commentary became part of the legal curriculum throughout the Empire.[101] Although short lived in the Ottoman Empire, the Majalla was considered a major legal document that continues to have lasting effect in certain parts of the Muslim world.[102]

Similar to the Majalla project several decades earlier, the codification of family law in the Ottoman Empire was based on the Ḥanafī school as well. While there was an extensive approach at arguing for a clear Islamic methodology and justification for the codification of the Majalla, there seems not to have been the same need in codifying family law. Most areas of Ottoman law by the

---

[99] See: Yūsuf Āṣāf, *Mir'a al-Majalla*, 2 vols., (Cairo; al-Maṭbaʿa al-Amiriyya, 1894), 1:13; Haydar, *Durar al-Ḥukām*, 1:29; Muḥammad al-Ḥussayn Āl Kāshif al-Ghiṭā', *Taḥrīr al-Majalla*, 2 vols., (Najaf: Iraq, 1359 AH), 1:21.

[100] Haydar, *Durar al-Ḥukām*, 11.

[101] Haydar, *Durar al-Ḥukām*, introduction to the Arabic translation.

[102] The *Majalla* continues to be used for commercial law in the Palestinian territories and Iraq.

turn of the 20th century had already been occupied by various European codes. Family law, however, was still based on Islamic law and administrated in Sharīʿa courts. Significant for this study is that the Ottoman Family Law of 1917 introduced courts as a procedural point in the divorce process.[103] Although not completely satisfactory for the women's agenda at the time, this procedural innovation was influenced by the women's movement, and was an answer, although unsatisfactory, to what was starting to be perceived as a problem with Islamic-Ḥanafī divorce laws.

Although the Swiss Code of Personal Status replaced the Ottoman Family Law in the year 1926, the Islamic practices of the Turkish people in relations to personal status matters continued. By the mid-1950s only a third of the Swiss Code was actually used and the Turkish state was eventually forced to recognize religious marriages and practices after having them disbanded and outlawed.[104] Like the Ottoman *Majalla*, the Ottoman Family Code of 1917 was short lived in Turkey, but continues as the basic law of personal status in the Levant (including Israel) and Iraq.

The Age of Personal Status Law

The time period of this study, roughly the middle of the 19th century until the early third of the 20th century, is rightfully called the age of personal status law. As Wael Hallaq has adequately shown, colonial interest in law and codification was a form of control and a more efficient option than forced subjugation.[105] From the end of the 18th century through the middle half of the 19th century, European colonial interests in law were related to the areas of commercial, land, criminal, and international laws (often times Ottoman capitulations). In other words, these areas directly impacted the bottom line of the colonial enterprise as a whole and affected the "business-friendliness" of a particular region. There was virtually no concern for the day-to-day lives of Muslim populations, their family matters, marriage, divorce, inheritance, charitable endow-

---

[103] Judith Tucker, "Revisiting Reform: Women and the Ottoman Law of Family Rights, 1917", in *Arab Studies Journal* 4 (1996), 11.

[104] Nadolski, *Ottoman and Secular Civil Law*, 529–30.

[105] Hallaq, *Sharīʿa*, 359.

ments, etc., were left untouched. These areas, not all united in one jurisdiction, were exclusively governed and regulated by Sharīʿa courts and by default the Sharīʿa itself.

Both the French Napoleonic code and the subsequent Italian code introduced the concept of "statut personnel", a reference to laws relating to one's person vis-à-vis the law.[106] This was based on a distinction these codes made between laws of the state or laws pertaining to the state and laws dealing with persons. Therefore, French law would qualify *état* with *personnel* or *des personnes* and likewise with the Italian *stato*.[107] The emergence of statut personnel or personal status laws was common with jurists writing in international private law, more so than areas where common law was known and practiced. Its introduction to the Muslim world, and Egypt specifically, came from the influence that continental international jurisprudence (specifically French and Italian codes) had rather than common law traditions.

When Egyptian jurists began significant legal reforms in 1875, they formally adopted the term "laws of personal status" according to their understanding of its definition in the Italian code. This definition was first used by Qadrī Pasha, whom I discuss in the next chapter, and subsequently by all of the ʿulamāʾ who are discussed throughout this study. Except in extremely rare circumstances, the appellation "personal status laws" is an exclusive reference to Islamic law and the codification of personal status law in Muslim countries, then, is essentially a synonym for codification of Islamic law. While the process of codification certainly did impact all areas of the law in both the Ottoman Empire and in Egypt, most jurisdictions except personal status laws had already been subjected to extensive changes and alterations that the Islamic influence and nature of them had already been diluted by the late 1800s.[108]

---

[106] G. Tedeschi, "'Personal Status' and 'Statut Personnel'", in *McGill Law Journal* 459 (1969): 453–4.

[107] Tedeschi, *Personal Status*, 453.

[108] A notable exception to this would be land laws in Egypt. See: Richard Debs, *Islamic Law and Civil Code* (New York: Columbia University Press, 2010).

Therefore, I will treat personal status laws as synonymous with Islamic law, and in light of this it is essential to examine the juristic discussion or what I have termed the "intellectual footprint" of those 'ulamā' dealing with codification. Part of this unofficial juristic discussion is found in understanding the impact of the early women's movement in Egypt as well as understanding the changing trends of Islamic laws and how various 'ulamā' were reacting to these changes.

INTERPRETING THE EFFECTS OF CODIFICATION ON ISLAMIC LAW AND THE 'ULAMĀ'

In the final section of this introduction I turn to the discussions found in the secondary literature concerning codification of Islamic law and the impact this codification had on the Sharī'a. While much has been written about the effects of codification on the nature of law in general, something I discuss above, there has been no singular exhaustive discussion of the effects of codification on Islamic law specifically. This makes an analysis of the secondary literature's discussion of such a topic difficult. There has been a great deal written about Islamic law in the modern period and the impact of modernity on Islam and its legal tradition. It is in these works that one finds dispersed discussions and allusions to the impact of codification on Islamic law. Rather than discuss these one-by-one, it will be more useful to present a thematic discussion and discuss the assumptions that have formed them. Following this discussion, I will offer an analysis of these opinions with some critical tools necessary to carry forth the greater discussion of the perspectives of the 'ulamā' towards codification of personal status laws in Egypt. Before proceeding, it should be noted that the following opinions are written from the perspective of the effects that codification had on Islamic law and the 'ulamā', and not based on a value judgment of the importance of codification in general to the modern Muslim world as a tool for legal reform and modernization. The latter is something that is usually implied in most of these discussions as a positive and necessary step towards progress.

It is perhaps not surprising that the overwhelming opinion throughout the secondary literature is that codification had an overall negative and destructive impact on both the Sharī'a and the 'ulamā'. This opinion can be thought of as containing three central arguments.

The first argument is that since the nature of a legal code is that it is fixed and unchangeable, the Sharī'a, when subjected to the process of codification, became sterile.[109] This argument makes an implicit reference to the ijtihādic nature of Islamic law in which there are endless commentaries, opinions, and juristic discussions that serve as an internal, self-check mechanism. The discursive nature of Islamic law allowed for it to be updated and modified as needed over time, and allowed the Sharī'a to be "open" as Messick observes. However, since a legal code is forced to take specific rulings on various topics and in so doing ignores and leaves behind the rich, plural expression of juristic opinion within the Sharī'a, the interpretive and ijitihādic nature of Sharī'a can no longer exist in a code. Codification of Islamic law, therefore, makes Islamic law rigid and static, not flexible and dynamic. As for legal interpretation, this argument holds that the state has usurped the function of ijtihād for itself.

This argument is essentially based on an assumption that once the process of codification ended, there was no life or further discussion of the law after that. Codification is thought of here as being a type of freezing of legal opinion. After all, Bentham did argue that the code would need to be updated once every hundred years or so and not more frequently.[110] There is an assumption here also that there is neither need nor room for further legal discussions, as they play no necessary role vis-à-vis codification since the precise point of codification is to make law simple. The frozen nature of law, which the code provides, is seen as the main reason for this phenomenon.

---

[109] Hallaq, *Sharī'a*, 15–16; Malcolm Kerr, *Islamic Reform: The Political and Legal Theories of Muḥammad 'Abduh and Rashīd Riḍā* (Los Angeles: University of California Press, 1966), 217; Messick, *Calligraphic State*, 56; Nadav Safran, *Egypt in Search of Political Community: An Analysis of the Intellectual and Political Evolution of Egypt, 1804–1952* (Cambridge: Harvard University Press, 1961), 115.

[110] Bentham, *Works of Bentham*, 3:206.

The second argument is that the process of codification ultimately usurped the power and the influence of the 'ulamā' to both interpret the Sharī'a and to influence the state in such interpretations.[111] It follows that since the state by definition claims ultimate sovereignty, the codes that it enacts are superior to any other form of law and the interpretations of these laws can only be carried out through the state.[112] While some 'ulamā' were used in the interim codification process, their role became diminished and eventually non-existent vis-à-vis the law since they were not part of the legislative structure of the modern Egyptian state.

This argument assumes that codification was a process that started at some point in time and then ended with the production of the code, therefore ending the potential need of the 'ulamā' to play a role in interpretation and legal development. Again, the code is seen as a freezing of legal opinion and that certain 'ulamā' were coopted to provide rationales for conclusions the state opted for.[113]

The third and final argument, and perhaps the most significant, is that the process of codification pitted the structure of Islamic society, with Islamic law at its core, against the modern, secular nation state.[114] Since both Islamic law and the modern nation state claim ultimate, temporal authority, and since codification is one of the main functions and tools of the modern nation state to achieve sovereignty, Islamic law ultimately lost this battle sounding the death knell of Sharī'a in the modern Muslim world.[115] There-

---

[111] Hallaq, *Sharī'a*, 368–370, 381, 401; Aharon Layish, "The Contribution of the Modernists to the Secularization of Islamic Law", in *Middle Eastern Studies* 14 (1978): 268; Messick, *Calligraphic State*, 56–57; Safran, *Egypt in Search*, 113–115.

[112] Hallaq, *Sharī'a*, 360; Messick, *Calligraphic State*, 68

[113] Layish, *Modernists*, 267–271.

[114] Hallaq describes this as, "the most pervasive problem in the legal history of the modern Muslim world." Hallaq, *Sharī'a*, 359. Also see a longer exposition of this in Wael Hallaq, *The Impossible State: Islam, politics, and modernity's moral predicament* (New York: Columbia University Press, 2013).

[115] Hallaq, *Sharī'a*, 360; Kerr, *Islamic Reform*, 219; Layish, *Modernists*, 267.

fore, simply by the fact that codification occurred, the Sharīʿa was pushed to the side and left for dead. While this issue has much to do with the nature of the modern nation state and raises questions of its compatibility or lack thereof with Islam, issues admittedly outside the scope of this study, its relevance and inclusion here is due to its central argument that legal codification was and continues to be the main weapon used in this battle.

The main assumption of this argument is that there was indeed an active struggle for sovereignty between the state and the ʿulamāʾ and that this struggle was clearly lost by one group and clearly won by another. In other words, this argument assumes that the involvement of the ʿulamāʾ throughout the entire process of codification ignited a massive conflict pitting the ʿulamāʾ against the state. Furthermore, this argument assumes that either there are no longer ʿulamāʾ who play a role in national legal matters or that while there may be some ʿulamāʾ, their role and influence is insignificant and unsubstantial with respect to secular legal authorities.

A second group of scholars have argued for another narrative and interpretation of the effects of codification on Islamic law. These opinions can be summarized in the following three arguments:

First, the process of codification, rather than kill the Sharīʿa was its re-birth.[116] This argument likens the process of codification to the formative period of Islamic law when there was a renewed commitment by ʿulamāʾ to re-visit the primary sources and use interpretive tools to derive new rulings from the primary sources, and reconsider the validity and utility of inherited ones. This argument is itself an extension of "the gates of ijtihād closing" narrative, which argues that around the 4th Islamic century (roughly the 9th century CE) there was a stagnation of legal thought marked by a rigid view of taqlīd, and an argument that ijtihād was no longer valid. By the late 18th and early 19th century, however, there was a revival of ijtihād, itself leading to the rise of modernist-ʾulamāʾ, often

[116] J.N.D. Anderson, *Islamic Law in the Modern World* (New York: New York University Press, 1959), 18–19; N.J. Coulson, *A History of Islamic Law* (Edinburgh: Edinburgh University Press, 1964), 218–219; Schacht, *Islamic Law*, 102.

the central figures in this argument's vision of codification. The encounter with western legal thought and the process of codification inspired debates only found in the formative period of Islam and energized these modernist 'ulamā' to undergo ijtihād to answer the difficult questions codification posed.

This argument assumes that there were indeed wide, intense juristic debates in which 'ulamā' were using interpretive tools to derive new rulings from the primary sources. In likening the codification experiment to the formative period, this argument also assumes that the ijtihād practiced from the middle of the 19th century onwards was something universally recognized and accepted amongst the 'ulamā'.

The second argument is that the codification of Islamic law resulted in a code that contained, at its heart, not only Sharī'a rulings, but Islamic legal maxims.[117] There was a concerted effort to ensure that the final code was compatible with and derived from Islamic legal sources. Furthermore, when various laws of various jurisdictions are analyzed, not just personal status laws, there are clear genealogies back to Sharī'a sources.

This argument assumes that the laws based on Sharī'a where chosen because they were in fact based on Sharī'a in a deliberate way. In other words, this argument assumes that there was a purposeful selection of these laws and not an accidental overlap between these Sharī'a opinions and the European codes being considered.

The third argument is that codification was a preservation method that the 'ulamā' willfully accepted in order to continue having Islamic law be the heart and soul of Egypt's legal system.[118] Since codification and legal reform were essentially attempts to graft European legal styles and norms onto the Egyptian legal system, the 'ulamā' used their role throughout the codification process

---

[117] Coulson, *History*, 185; Debs, *Islamic Law*, 72; Anderson, *Islamic Law*, 82–91. Also see generally Muḥammad 'Ammāra, *Islāmiyāt Sanhūrī Bāsha*, 2 vols., (Cairo: Dār al-Qafā', 2006); Guy Bechor, *The Sanhūrī Code, and the Emergence of Modern Arab Civil Law (1932–1949)* (Leiden: Brill, 2007).

[118] Anderson, *Islamic Law*, 24; Schacht, *Islamic Law*, 102.

to ensure that Islamic jurisprudence played as large a role as possible in influencing the codes that were ultimately drafted.

This argument assumes that the various codes that emerged in Egypt at the end of the 19th and early 20th century in fact represented a preservation of Sharīʿa thinking as opposed to the assumption that this process destroyed or killed Islamic law as mentioned above. In other words, by preserving Islamic law, rather than destroy it, this argument assumes that Sharīʿa thinking has advanced directly as a result of codification and continues to play this role throughout the judiciary.

Following this discussion, it is necessary to lay down some basic points by which we can understand and assess these various arguments. The first point is that it is essential to make a clear distinction between Sharīʿa as a legal system on the one hand and modern legal codes based on or influenced by Sharīʿa on the other. As discussed in the first section of this introduction, codification does not negate the need for private law and juristic discussions, but rather necessitates and encourages it. Therefore, whatever the conclusion we have of the impact of codification on Islamic law, one thing that clearly did happen is that the Sharīʿa remained the Sharīʿa. Codification of Sharīʿa does not actually codify the Sharīʿa (what could be thought of here as uṣūl), but rather produces a code of Sharīʿa rulings (furūʿ).[119] A codification of Sharīʿa proper would be a codification of the interpretation of source texts to the exclusion of others, the reason I offer Imām Mālik refused to have the Muwaṭṭa' codified. While there were always different types of 'ulamā' throughout Islamic history, private and state, it was usually the private 'ulamā' who advanced the theoretical boundaries of the Sharīʿa, not the state. Therefore, unless codification was done in a private manner, the dramatic impact that both sides claim it had would only be secondary, not a primary influence.

Related to this point, there needs to be a clear understanding that Islamic law was at the same time a personal, spiritual legal guide as well as an imperial legal system serving vast political empires. Therefore, the Sharīʿa is an extremely vast and sophisticated

---

[119] Anderson observes that the *'ulamā'* used codification as a method to preserve "pure" Sharīʿa. Anderson, *Islamic Law*, 92.

jurisprudence with porous boundaries between the private and the public; the private 'ulamā' of the madhāhib and the state 'ulamā' who served as jurist consults to the government (often times they were one and the same). This vastness and porousness often facilitate a romantic view of the Sharīʿa and a false notion that it had overarching control over various Islamic political entities. For example, as Malcolm Kerr observes regarding al-Māwardī's (d. 450/1058) *al-Aḥkām al-Sulṭāniyya*, the "treatise tells us not how the state was actually organized in his time, but that government is a moral enterprise confided by God to the leaders of the Community."[120] In other words, while the Sharīʿa claims all temporal sovereignty for itself with no ambiguity, in reality it always coexisted with other temporal, political, and legal forces with the acknowledgement of the 'ulamā', not despite them. As mentioned above already by the middle of the 18th century throughout the Muslim world criminal, commerce, trade, and land jurisdictions were dominated by colonial influences and infused with western laws. As Hallaq observes, this was a cheaper and easier way to control the natives than war.[121] Since personal status laws were of no immediate interest, the Sharīʿa continued to be the sole legal force in this jurisdiction until the codification experiment to which this study is dedicated to analyzing.

Another point to consider is that regardless of one's opinion of the impact of codification on Sharīʿa, one thing that both groups should agree on is that Sharīʿa itself is needed in order to understand how codification of personal status law evolved. In this regard, again, the Sharīʿa continues to dominate the discussion and plays an active, on-going role vis-à-vis codification. Likewise, the 'ulamā' who continue to be regarded as the experts of the Sharīʿa, by default play an active role in the story of codification. One major way this influence is manifested today, for example, is through various fiqh bodies. In Egypt both the Islamic Research Council (*Majmaʿ al-Buḥūth al-Islāmiyya*) and the Supreme Council on Islamic Affairs (*al-Majmaʿ al-ʿĀli li'l Shu'ūn al-Islāmiyya*) have the absolute final say on Sharīʿa interpretation. While this has been exercised

---

[120] Kerr, *Islamic Reform*, 220.

[121] Hallaq, *Sharīʿa*, 372.

scarcely, a third institution, the office of the Grand Mufti of Egypt (*Dār al-Iftā' al-Miṣriyya*), plays a daily role in the interpretation of Islamic law for both individual citizens and the state. These three main legal bodies themselves constitute dozens of 'ulamā' and their collective scholarly writings and output is far greater than the opinions issued by the institutions they are affiliated with. This "intellectual footprint", in my opinion, is precisely the juristic discussion and private law making that is referenced in the first section of this introcution. Therefore, to truly understand the impact of codification on personal status law and the perspectives of the 'ulamā' of this, it is fundamental to not simply look at the codes and immediate commentary and debates on their drafting, but to also look at the "intellectual footprint" that has impacted, influenced, and sought to guide the entire process of not just codification, but legal reform in Egypt.

Lastly, it should be kept in mind that codification, although likened by Bentham to a mathematical equation,[122] was hardly straightforward. Even the most cherished of western codifications, the Code Napoleon, was not strictly in line with the theory laid out by Bentham.[123] Each codification effort is nuanced and different, and each code is therefore unique. While the fundamental goal of codification, to articulate law in a rational manner, is indeed a shared goal across various codification processes, what this exactly means and how it is implemented is not. Therefore, we have to understand exactly the unique process of codification of personal status law in Egypt in order to assess its impact on Sharī'a and more importantly the perspectives of the 'ulamā' towards this process.

---

[122] Bentham, *Theory of Legislation*, 48.

[123] It is true that Bentham's works are referenced in the first drafts of the Code Napoleon (Schofield, *The Collected works of Jeremy Bentham: Legislator of the World*, 11–12). However, Rousseau's thinking had much more of an impact on the development of French law. See: Friedrich, *The Ideological and Philosophical Background*, 7–9.

CHAPTER 1.
'ULAMĀ' OF THE CODE

This chapter discusses what I term 'ulamā' of the code, which describes 'ulamā' who not only supported the theory behind codification (a group discussed in chapter 2), but in fact composed different treatises of codified personal status law that were used either in the serious study and process of codification (as is the case with the works of al-Minyāwī and Qadrī) or legislatively (as in the case of law 25 of 1929). The emphasis in this chapter is on the fact that these works dealt with actual codes, rather than the general concept of the need for codification or problems with codification vis-à-vis Islamic law as discussed in chapters 2 and 3 respectively.

Before embarking, however, it is important to define the term 'ulamā'/'ālim (plural and singular respectively), which is rendered throughout this study as a scholar of the Islamic sciences, as well as the term Sharī'a, which is rendered here as both Islamic jurisprudence and Islamic law. While it is true that historically al-Azhar University was a main training ground for Islamic scholars inside Egypt, it was not, however, the only institute of learning. We know that, for example, the school established by the famous Sufi 'Abd al-Wahhāb al-Sha'rānī (d. 973/1565) rivaled the influence of al-Azhar and there was also the popular school at which the polymath Jalāl al-Dīn al-Suyuṭī (d. 911/1505) taught.[1] Not only were these

[1] The history of al-Azhar as a school and university is difficult to trace. It was established by the Fatimids in the year 359/971 and was used for educational purposes until the Ayyubid invasion in 1171. Under the rule of Salāḥ al-Dīn al-Ayyūbī (d. 1193), however, it was not used as a gathering for Friday prayer to avoid the prohibition of multiple Friday prayers in one city according to the Shāfi'īs. While it was certainly used as

popular centers of learning led by noted 'ulamā', but they also produced scholars who themselves emerged to be very much a part of the 'ulamā' class. The profession of being an 'ālim was and is akin to any profession in the modern period; it is bound by a methodology of instruction (there are typically certain texts that one must study and master), the rules of practice (in the case of the 'ulamā' this would be the interpretative methodology used to approach the primary sources of Islamic legislation), and a general code of ethics which binds similar professionals together. For my purposes, I will understand the 'ulamā' to refer to those Sunnī Muslim scholars who received a traditional[2] Sharī'a education of varying degrees.

---

a teaching facility from its establishment through the Ayyubid period, it was not until the turn of the 17th century that it gained widespread popularity, matched by the rise of the prominent position of Sheikh al-Azhar. Throughout the 15th, 16th, and 17th centuries, there were many other schools with large endowments that gained fame and prestige such as the Shaykhū school, the Sulṭān Ḥasan School, and Sha'rānī's school. For information about Suyūṭī's school see: E.M. Sartain, *Jalāl al-Dīn al-Suyūṭī Biography and Background*, 2vols., (Cambridge: Cambridge University Press: 1975), 1:37–46; Jalāl al-Dīn al-Suyūṭī, *Ḥusn al-Muḥādara fī Akhbār Miṣr wa'l Qāhira*, 2 vols., (Cairo: al-Maṭba'a al-Mawsū'āt, n.d.), 2:145–164. A more accessible edition is Jalāl al-Dīn al-Suyūṭī, *Ḥusn al-Muḥādara fī Akhbār Miṣr wa'l Qāhira*, 2 vols., (Beirut: Dār al-Kutub al-'Ilmiyya, 1997), 2:221–235. For information on Sha'rānī's school see: Idrīs 'Azūzī, *al-Shaykh Aḥmad Zarrūq wa Arā'uhu al-'Iṣlāḥiyya* (Morocco: Maṭba'at Fāḍila, 1998), 98–99; Jawda Muḥammad Abū al-Yazīdī al-Mahdī ed., *Manāqib al-Qutb al-Rabānī Sayidī 'Abd al-Wahhāb al-Sha'rānī* (Cairo: al-Dār al-Jūdiyya, 2005), 168–173.

2 Traditional Islam is meant to be a descriptive term referring to the classical period of Islam sometimes referred to as the Late Sunnī Tradition. This refers to a tripartite classification of the Islamic sciences: law and associated fields, theology and associated fields, and Sufism involving both academic and social practices. As far as law is concerned, this time period saw domination of the four sunnī schools of law (Ḥanafī, Mālikī, Shāfi'ī, and Ḥanbalī). In the context of al-Azhar, the Mālikī and Shāfi'ī schools were the strongest as demonstrated by the fact that from 1679–1870 the position of Sheikh al-Azhar was chosen from amongst these two schools exclusively. Theologically, al-Azhar was a leading Ash'arite institution and as for Sufism, it was part and parcel of the life of the *'ulamā'*. See:

This education allowed them to be heirs to and participants of the discursive process (uṣūl al-fiqh) that produced Islamic law (fiqh), both referred to as Sharīʿa throughout this study.[3]

The 'ulamā' themselves, however, are a large meta-group. Like any group there are various subgroups amongst them. The authors of the three works discussed in this chapter are a good example of one such subgroup amongst the 'ulamā'. The 'ulamā' of the code are what one could also refer to as state 'ulamā'. This is not meant to be a pejorative term, as is sometimes assumed in contemporary discussions, but rather a descriptive term to indicate that these were 'ulamā' who served in official roles: judges, ministers, professors of law, etc., and were in some way heirs to the concept, process, and complexities of al-siyāsa al-sharʿiyya. They would have been more attuned to actual problems amongst litigants, the challenges in dealing with the Islamic law in a rapidly changing Egypt, etc. They would have been highly proficient with the law, as they would have had extensive interactions with plaintiffs and the inner workings of the Sharīʿa court system in Egypt. However, this does not necessarily mean that they would have been famous or prolific, perhaps a reason why they are often discounted or not studied at all.[4]

Jonathan Berkey, *The Formation of Islam* (Cambridge: Cambridge University Press, 2003), Part IV; Jonathan Berkey, *The Transmission of Knowledge in Medieval Cairo* (Princeton: Princeton University Press, 1992); Richard McGregor, *Sanctity and Mysticism in Medieval Egypt* (New York: State University of New York Press, 2004).

[3] Talal Asad defines the discursive nature of Islam as being "a tradition of Muslim discourse that addresses itself to conceptions of the Islamic past and future, with reference to a particular practice in the present." See: Talal Asad, "The Idea of an Anthropology of Islam," *Occasional Papers Series, Center for Contemporary Arab Studies* (Washington D.C: Georgetown University Press, 1986), 14. I liken this definition to the science and discipline of uṣūl al-fiqh since the main task of the jurist is to arrive at new rulings using an understanding of the texts and maxims of law, an understanding of the modern context, and being able to wed these two compatibly into a new ruling.

[4] Even the most famous of Egyptian codifiers, 'Abd al-Razzāq al-Sanhūrī, who is credited with writing Egypt's civil code, has only recently

Throughout this chapter I analyze the codes that these 'ulamā' wrote and focus on *why* these works were authored. There is a common conception that codification of Islamic law, not just personal status law, developed as a function exclusively of the state. As some of the works studied below will indicate, such is not necessarily the case. There seems to be an inherent interest amongst the early state 'ulamā' to engage in comparative legal studies and to look primarily at French law as a source to benefit from and not necessarily to compete with Islamic law. However, I am also interested in *how* these works were compiled, i.e. what was the methodology used to codify the Sharī'a. The three works I analyze below will form my understanding of the how and why personal status law was codified in Egypt and by extension elsewhere in the Muslim world.

Aside from the how and why of codification, I will also pay special attention in this chapter and subsequent ones to the treatment of laws pertaining to divorce, specifically the issue of a thrice-pronounced divorce counting as one.[5] There were many controversial decisions made throughout the codification of personal status law (such as polygamy, the marriage age, the dowry, and divorce), none, however, were as contentious and more publicly debated amongst the 'ulamā' as the issue of a thrice-pronounced divorce counting as one.

---

been the subject of academic research. See: 'Amāra, *Islāmiyāt al-Sanhūrī* Bāshā; Bechor, *The Sanhuri Code.*

[5] This refers to the practice when a man says to his wife, "I divorce you threefold" (*antī ṭāliq thalāthan*). According to the four sunnī schools of law this type of divorce is considered an irrevocable, final divorce in which the husband and wife would be forced to separate and could only be re-married if the wife herself marries a second man, consummates the marriage, and is finally divorced from him allowing her the opportunity to return to her first husband.

MAKHLŪF AL-MINYĀWĪ AND HIS *MUQĀRANĀT AL-TASHRĪ'IYYA*

Makhlūf ibn Muḥammad al-Badawī al-Minyāwī was born in the year 1235/1819 and died in the year 1295/1878.[6] Very little is known of his life other than the fact that he studied at al-Azhar and served as a judge in the Minya district. He authored four works that we know of: a work on rhetoric,[7] a treatise on the *basmala*,[8] a treatise on celebrating *'āshurā'*,[9] and the comparative work on French and Mālikī law which is the focus of this section. Although little is known of al-Minyāwī's life, as has been mentioned in the introduction, we do know what someone of his stature was like and what kind of position he would have had in society. From his portfolio of written works, it is clear that he was not simply a judge who was consumed with adjudicating cases and tending to his own estates, but had an academic and scholarly interest in various subjects. His writing style indicates that he was trained primarily as a jurist and 'uṣūlī[10] and since he was tasked by the Khedive with undergoing this unique comparative legal study, it is safe to assume he was well grounded and known for his legal expertise. His position as a judge means that he most likely had exposure to litigants and the general problems of society as manifested through the Sharī'a courts. He also would have been well placed to see the advantages and disadvantages of the legal system he was operating in.

---

[6] Makhlūf al-Minyāwī, *al-Muqāranāt al-Tashrī'iyya*, 2 vols., (Cairo: Dār al-Salām, 1999), 5.

[7] Makhlūf al-Minyāwī, *Ḥāshiyat al-Minyāwī 'ala Sharḥ Ḥulyat al-Lub al-Maṣūn* (Cairo: al-Bābī al-Ḥalabī, 1357 AH).

[8] Makhlūf Al-Minyāwī, *Commentary on the Basmallah*, King Sa'ūd University collection, Manuscript 3617, 20 fols. It seems that the final few pages of this manuscript are not part of al-Minyāwī's original work, but rather an extensive quote from *Jam' al-Jawāmi'*.

[9] This work is mentioned in the introduction to the Dār al-Salām edition, but I have been unable to locate it. Dr. 'Alī Jumu'a, the former Grand Mufti of Egypt, mentioned to me that he has a copy of this manuscript in his personal collection.

[10] This is displayed mostly in his *Muqāranāt* and the many legal nuances he picks up which are discussed in the next section.

The Age of Ismāʿīl

The time in which al-Minyāwī lived is often referred to as the age of Ismāʿīl.[11] Khedive Ismāʿīl ruled Egypt from 1863–1879, which was a time of great change for Egypt and great pressure as well. Ismāʿīl was keen on reforming and modernizing Egypt to keep up with an advancing Europe. One of the many areas he devoted much time and resource to reforming was Egypt's legal system. At the heart of these legal reforms was the reorientation of Egypt's political and fiscal allegiance from the Ottomans towards European powers, particularly the English. His trust, often times interpreted as mistrust, of the English allowed them to gain a stronger foothold in Egypt, particularly with regards to financial matters. This, in addition to the power the newly formed Mixed courts had over the Khedive, ultimately became Ismāʿīl's downfall as he fell into massive debt and was eventually forced into exile in 1879.

In the early part of Ismāʿīl's reign he sought to reform and modernize the Sharīʿa courts as part of a larger legal makeover for the country. As it will be made clear by examining Muḥammad ʿAbduh's survey of the Sharīʿa courts at this time in Chapter 2, they were largely in disrepair and suffered many abuses.[12] Thus, both the structure of the courts and the mechanism used to adjudicate cases were in dire need of not just modernization, but general repair. Ismāʿīl saw the main problem of the Sharīʿa courts, aside from the obvious structural issues, being the law that was administered, i.e. the Sharīʿa itself. He saw that Islamic law, particularly the Ḥanafī school and its interpretation of Islamic personal status law, was in need of major reform and organization (read codification).

---

[11] For sources discussing this time period see: Evelyn Baring, *Modern Egypt*, 2 vols., (London: Adamant Media Corporation-Eliborn Classics Replica Edition, 2005), 1:9–146; Robert F. Hunter, *Egypt Under the Khedives 1805–1879* (Cairo: American University in Cairo Press, 1999), 70–79; Ḥusayn Kafāfī, *al-Khadīwī Ismāʿīl wa Maʿshūqatuhu Miṣr* (Cairo: al-Hay'a al-Miṣriyya al-ʿĀmma lil Kitāb, 1997); ʿAbd al-Raḥmān al-Rāfiʿī, *ʿAsr Ismāʿīl*, 2 vols., (Cairo: Dār al-Maʿārif, 1987).

[12] ʿAbduh's study and report can be found in: Muḥammad ʿAmāra, *al-ʿAmāl al-Kāmila li'l Imām Muḥammad ʿAbduh*, 5 vols., (Cairo: Dār al-Shurūq, 1993), 2:209–294.

Ismāʿīl turned to the 'ulamā' of al-Azhar for assistance with this. Rashīd Riḍā, whose position regarding codification of Sharīʿa is examined in chapter 3, speaks briefly of the tense interaction between Ismāʿīl and the 'ulamā' of the Azhar, and Ismāʿīl's request of the 'ulamā' to produce a simplified manual of Islamic law.[13] However, Riḍā also narrates a story he heard from the son of Rifāʿa Ṭahṭāwī, 'Alī Pāshā, that his father was asked directly by the Khedive to persuade the various 'ulamā' of al-Azhar to comply with his request to produce a simple to follow European modeled code of personal status law or else these laws would face being replaced by French law. Ṭahṭāwī politely declined this request citing his old age and dislike to be dragged into a messy controversy.[14] He never, however, disagreed with what the Khedive said or treated the approach of codification as strange. It is unclear why Ṭahṭāwī was reluctant given that he was very well-known for his comparative studies in law and translations of existing French law prior.[15] Although Riḍā drops the story here and goes on to lament how the 'ulamā's stubborn position was the direct cause of the Sharīʿa courts being lost, we know now that there is more to the story as Ismāʿīl finally found his man.

Ismāʿīl's interest in legal reform also extended to the capitulations system that was inherited from the Ottomans. Capitulations was a system that allowed foreigners conducting business throughout the Ottoman Empire and its territories to be tried in special tribunals and courts set up with the consent of the European nations that signed capitulations agreements with the Ottoman Empire.[16] Employing his Armenian Prime Minister Nubār Pasha,

---

[13] Rashīd Riḍa, *Tārīkh al-Ustadh al-Imām al-Shaykh Muḥammad 'Abduh*, 3 vols., (Cairo: Dār al-Fāḍila, 2006), 1.2:620.

[14] Ibid.

[15] I discuss Ṭahtāwī's translations in the section on Qadrī Pasha below.

[16] For a brief history of the legal impact of capitulations see: 'Umar Muṣtafa, *Uṣūl Tārīkh al-Qānūn* (Cairo: Mu'assasa al-Maṭbūʿāt al-Ḥadītha, 1960), 415, 418, 451–454; Nasim Susa, *The Capitulatory Regime of Turkey: Its History, Origin, and Nature* (Baltimore: The Johns Hopkins Press, 1933);

Ismāʿīl was able to negotiate an entire new legal system and legal code to govern and regulate what was seen and interpreted as an abusive and unfair system of favoring foreigners over natives. The Mixed courts and their newly drafted eclectic legal code were established on June 28, 1875. While a dramatic moment for Ismāʿīl and his efforts to move away from everything Ottoman, it was also an ironic historical moment as four years later it was the Mixed courts that litigated against him and forced him into exile.[17] The importance of the Mixed courts in Egypt vis-à-vis the topic of codification of personal status law is that the Mixed courts helped demonstrate the utility and strength of European legal codes for civil matters (understood here as business transactions, torts, and criminal areas of law). Since the Mixed courts were specifically for foreigners, there was a parallel need to develop Native courts.[18] Around the same time in the late 19th century a lengthy process began for developing a civil code and courts to administer this code in parallel to the codification of personal status law. Eventually these two were united into one code and the Mixed courts were abolished, giving rise to a singular legal system that emerged as the backbone of the modern Egyptian State.

The work

We have no indication that al-Minyāwī knew French. In fact, since he is not listed in any of the trip manifests of scholars taken to France,[19] it is unlikely that he had knowledge of European lan-

---

Maurits H. van den Boogert, *The Capitulations and the Ottoman Legal System* (Leiden: Brill, 2005).

[17] This episode in Ismāʿīl's life is chronicled in al-Rāfiʿī, *ʿAsr Ismāʿīl*, 2:29–83. Also see: Hunter, *Egypt Under the Khedives*, 70–79 and 179–180.

[18] The development of the Native courts, while important, falls outside the scope of this study. Two sources that outline the development of law in Egypt in the 19th century, including the Native courts are: Byron Cannon, *Politics of Law and the Courts in Nineteenth Century Egypt* (Salt Lake City: University of Utah Press, 1988); Egypt, *al-Kitāb al Dhahabī lil Maḥākim al-Ahliyya*.

[19] The definitive source on these trips including full travel logs is: HRH Prince Ṭūsūn ʿUmar, *al-Biʿthāt al-ʿIlmiyya fī ʿAhd Muḥammad ʿAlī*

guages or legal systems first hand.[20] Since Ṭahṭāwī's translation of the French Civil Code was published in 1866 and again in 1868 (which is cited throughout al-Minyāwī's work as his source for French law), this places the study and writing of al-Minyāwī's work sometime between 1866 and his death in 1878. There is no way of telling if Ṭahṭāwī recommended al-Minyāwī to the Khedive after he declined to take on the task of codification himself, or if the Khedive was finally able to find a jurist who agreed to take on the controversial task of comparing European law and Islamic law. One can assume, however, that al-Minyāwī was unique in his willingness to engage in the task.

General Methodology of the Work

In his own introduction to the work, al-Minyāwī states that the purpose of his writing is to draw comparisons (*muwāfaqāt*) or appropriate links (*munāsabāt*) between Mālikī positive law and the codes of France.[21] In this regards the work is not a comparison per se as there is hardly any discussion of what is not compatible and what is not an appropriate link. Rather, the work is one where similarities are sought and argued for based on core legal principles and methodologies. Although he states that he is drawing from the positive law of the Mālikī school, al-Minyāwī often presents and writes as a scholar of juristic methodology (uṣūl al-fiqh), often using the technique of *takhrīj*. Accordingly, he often abstracts a point of law

thumma fī 'Ahdi 'Abbās al-'Awwal wa Sa'īd (Alexandria: Maṭba'at Ṣalāḥ al-Dīn, 1934).

[20] There were no institutes in Egypt at this time that gave instruction in French. This was to come later with the School of Languages (*Madrasat al-Alsun*) discussed in the next section. There is a possibility, however, that he was self-taught. Susan Gunasti has demonstrated that late Ottoman *'ulamā'* were able to learn French on their own. I believe that this is unlikely in the case of al-Minyāwī, however. See Susan Gunasti, "Approaches to Islam in the Thought of Elmalili Muhammed Hamdi Yazir (1878–1942)" (PhD diss., Princeton University, 2011).

[21] Although he uses the word Europe (*Uruba*), he is discussing the French code of civil law, as it is the Arabic translation of these codes he uses throughout the work.

to its core legal principle and therefore finds compatibility in the principle, even if various points of law appear different. This type of thinking and writing is typical of *al-ashbāh wa'l nadhā'ir* writing in Islamic law, more so than strict discussions found in manuals of law of a particular school.[22] For example, the French code states that the laws of the code are for French citizens and describes how citizenship can be lost through adopting a foreign nationality, unlawful employment in a foreign government, and permanent residence in a foreign country without intent on return. However, there is no direct corresponding legal concept in Mālikī fiqh. To find the overlapping legal principle, al-Minyāwī discusses Mālikī sources that describe a man who swears an oath not to marry an Egyptian woman, and how this oath would also apply to a woman whose father was Egyptian, thus establishing a type of citizenship and belonging to a particular geographical location.[23] Likewise, a man who swears an oath not to marry a bedouin, but a particular bedouin women moves to a city has therefore lost her bedouin appellation and is therefore marriageable. For al-Minyāwī, the concept of citizenship has some similarities in Islamic law since one belongs to one region or another and this belonging (i.e. citizenship) can change as is stated in the French code.[24]

Al-Minyāwī also uses the technique of takhrīj to find where the Sharī'a inclines (*mayl* or *mutashawwif*) towards a particular principle or concept, such as in discussing article 197 where it is mentioned that it is not permissible to denounce or criticize the lineage of children who have grown up in the care of a married couple from infancy even if a marriage contract cannot be produced. Al-Minyāwī accepts this saying, "because the Law Giver inclines and desires to establish lineage."[25] He also uses this technique to find where Islamic law is silent and does not oppose (*la ya'bāhu al-Shar'*) certain principles, such as his discussion of article 41 that discusses

---

[22] For a discussion of this genre of writing see: Ahmad Atif Ahmad, *Structural Interrelations of Theory and Practice in Islamic Law: a study of six works of medieval Islamic jurisprudence* (Leiden: Brill, 2006).

[23] Al-Minyāwī, *al-Muqāranāt*, 1:54–55.

[24] Ibid.

[25] Ibid., 1.80.

the need to have proper pagination on legal documents and files. Since there is no direct corresponding principle in Mālikī law, he says, "the Law Giver does not reject this since there is more accuracy in it."[26]

Methodology and Understanding of Codification

Although his introduction is not lengthy, al-Minyāwī leaves us with a very concise and comprehensive discussion of his general opinion of codification of Islamic law. His opinion has three main parts:

The first is his understanding of siyāsā and the role of the ruler (*ḥākim*) in society. He begins this discussion acknowledging that man by nature is a social being that requires a polis to live in. Since there are natural disputes between humans over worldly objects, there is a need for laws to produce a just society and these laws are in need of being championed and defended by a just ruler.[27] The existence of this political leader, then, becomes a necessary part of life, as laid out by al-Minyāwī, and since the ruler is the vehicle to keep society just by upholding its laws, it becomes necessary to follow and obey this ruler. Concerning this point al-Minyāwī says "it is obligatory upon every Muslim to obey and follow [a political leader] whose leadership has been legally established, it is [also obligatory] to follow this leader in their independent legal reasoning (ijtihād) and their legal opinions in those areas in which there is no violation of the Sharī'a."[28] Al-Minyāwī goes on to provide evidence

---

[26] Ibid., 1.60.

[27] Ibid., 1.48.

[28] Ibid., 1:49 It is important to note that the Dār al-Salām edition quotes al-Minyāwī's source as being Muḥammad bin 'Alī al-Sanūsī (d. 1276 AH) and his commentary on the didactic poem *al-Jazā'iriyya.* This is in fact a mistake. The work that al-Minyāwī is citing here is the commentary of Abū 'Abduh Muḥammad bin Yūsuf al-Sanūsī (d. 899 AH) on *al-Jazā'iriyya.* The exact quote of al-Minyāwī quoted above can be found here: Abū 'Abduh Muḥammad bin Yūsuf al-Sanūsī, *al-Manhaj al-Sadīd fī Sharḥ Kifāyat al-Murīd,* ed. Muṣtafā Marzūq ('Ayn Malīla: Dār al-Huda, n.d.), 398–399.

from both the Qur'ān and ḥadīth literature to support this statement.[29]

Second, al-Minyāwī addresses the issue of taqlīd (following a specific school of law) and talfīq (legal eclecticism-choosing from different schools of law). He begins this discussion, and in fact the entire work, with a well-documented argument that, at least according to relied jurists of the Mālikī school, it is not agreed upon (*muttafaq 'alayhi*)[30] that a judge (qādī) must adhere to his own legal school's opinions in adjudicating cases. Only the Prophet of Islam is deserving of such obedience al-Minyāwī argues. His general principle in this regard, as he quotes the famous Mālikī jurists al-Qarāfī, is that, "it is permissible to follow and switch from one school of law to another (when a judge issues a verdict) in everything except those rulings that would violate the following: legal consensus (ijmā'), established legal principles (al-qawā'id), a clear text (naṣṣ – which refers to a text of the Qur'ān or the ḥadīth literature), or apparent analogy (*al-qiyās al-jalī*)."[31] Al-Minyāwī's understanding of legal consensus is that it is embodied in the agreed opinions of the four Sunnī schools of law. He negates the permissibility of applying rulings and opinions outside the four schools since no other legal schools, in his opinion, have gone through the proper redaction (tanqīḥ) that the four canonical sunnī ones have.[32]

---

[29] The position of al-Minyāwī regarding this point is one that is congruent with other sunnī writers on the topic of siyāsa. See for example: Imām al-Ḥaramayn al-Juwaynī, *al-Ghiyāthī: Ghiyāth al-'Umam fi'l Tiyāth al-Ẓulam*, ed., 'Abd al-'Aẓīm Maḥmūd al-Dīb (Beirut: Dār al-Minhāj, 2011), 241.

[30] Issues that are agreed upon (*mutafaq 'alayhi*) are interpreted as issues that have reached consensus (*ijmā'*) amongst mujtahid Imams and therefore legally binding and obligatory on Muslims to follow. Aside from this sort of consensus, there is room for dissenting opinions theoretically leaving most aspects of religion open for debate.

[31] Al-Minyāwī, *al-Muqāranāt*, 1:44.

[32] Following opinions found outside the four Sunnī schools becomes very important in the codification process as I discuss below in the divorce law of 1929.

Third, al-Minyāwī tackles the issue of independent legal reasoning (ijtihād) as it relates to newly occurring matters, i.e. matters that either were not found at the time of the Prophet of Islam or at the time of the writings of the various legal manuals that have been transmitted through the generations.[33] Al-Minyāwī cites major sources of the Mālikī school to prove his point. He cites al-Nafrāwī as saying:

> It is permissible for a mujtahid to initiate new rulings [regarding issues] not found at the time of the Prophet nor at the time of the Companions in proportion to what people invent in matters outside the Sharī'a…and these newly initiated rulings, initiated as a result of new conditions, are not considered foreign to the Sharī'a, rather they are from the Sharī'a itself since the principles of law have proven that these occurrences have no precedent during the time of the Prophet of Islam and his Companions due to a lack of their causes. And the delay of a ruling (ḥukm) due to a delay of its cause (*sabab*) does not necessitate that it is outside the Sharī'a.[34]

The permissibility of independent legal reasoning (ijtihād), according to al-Minyāwī's citation above, is one that is a natural progression of time and circumstance, which he does not see as something foreign to Islamic law. However, while it almost seems to be a natural necessity, he does equate this with a slightly negative outlook of history. He supports his claim by citing a famous statement of 'Umar ibn 'Abd al-'Azīz (d. 101/720), "[new] situations have emerged for people as a result of what they have engaged in that is unlawful and crooked."[35] Therefore, according to al-Minyāwī, the mujtahid's efforts at arriving at new rulings for these new occurrences become an essential tool for a ruler who, as discussed above, is essential to create a just society. Al-Minyāwī sees this as perfectly

[33] This refers to what is considered "the madhhab", i.e. opinions that have been accepted, catalogued, redacted, and transmitted from generation to generation as the core basis for a particular legal school's body of opinions.

[34] Al-Minyāwī, *al-Muqāranāt*, 1:45.

[35] Ibid., 1.44.

acceptable since jurists have said, "when a matter is restricted, it becomes expansive."[36]

Al-Minyāwī does not limit his discussion to simply creating new rulings by way of ijtihād for new occurrences, but also acknowledges the need and permissibility to extrapolate current rulings. To this effect, he sites al-Ḥaṭṭāb's discussion of the permissibility of using markings and signs in court cases as definitive proof based on an interpretation of certain verses found in the story of Joseph in the Qur'ān.[37] Al-Qarāfī comments on this issue by saying:

> Expanding rulings in governance…is not against the Sharī'a, rather there is much proof for it, [the most important] being that wrong doing has become common and there is a need for new rulings so that [society] does not go outside the Sharī'a completely due to the saying of the Prophet, "there is no harm and no reciprocating harm" and leaving common law and state law (qānūn) would lead to harm.[38]

In this regard, al-Minyāwī cites instances from the time of the Prophet of Islam and his Companions when they took independent actions dictated by the different and unusual circumstances they encountered. That is to say, that in concluding his discussion of the permissibility and need of ijtihād, he reverts to the original time of Islamic legislation to tie his argument together.

Before analyzing al-Minyāwī's theory and understanding of codification it is important to answer the following question: why does he provide such an argument to begin with? We know from the second paragraph of his introduction that his attempt is not to codify Islamic law per se, but rather to provide Mālikī rulings and equivalencies to the French legal code, article by article. In other words, the work is more typical of soliciting a fatwa (*istiftā'*) and issuing a fatwa (*iftā'*) issue by issue rather than a work of codifica-

---

[36] This statement refers to situations of dire circumstances, often termed *ḍarūra* in Islamic law. The common legal maxim is that *al-ḍarūrāt tubīḥ al-maḥdhūrāt*, dire circumstances make the impermissible, permissible.

[37] Al-Minyāwī, *al-Muqāranāt*, 1:46.

[38] Ibid.

tion. He does not quote from other schools of law and when an article in the French code does not correspond to Mālikī law, as I will show in more detail below, he is comfortable stating so in definitive terms.[39] Since we know from the same introductory remarks that he was asked by Khedive Ismā'īl to undertake this comparative study, it is possible that al-Minyāwī, like al-Ṭahṭāwī before him, feared that such a study would be seen as controversial and unorthodox by his colleagues, and would lead to the eventual replacement of current laws in Egypt that up until then were understood to be based on Sharī'a and therefore considered sound by the 'ulamā' establishment. It is also important to note that al-Minyāwī was a Mālikī jurist, not a Ḥanafī one. While it is true that Ḥanafī jurisprudence emerged at this time period as the official basis for personal status law and used throughout the life of the Sharī'a courts, this had more to do with the influence of the Ottomans in Egypt than it did with the makeup of Egyptian Muslim jurists at the time.[40] Turning to a Mālikī jurist could have been the Khedive's attempt to find an Egyptian-Islamic legal solution to breaking away from the Ottoman Empire, similar to Cevedt Paşha's efforts, which I discuss in the introduction above. As I will demonstrate in chapter 2, there was a lot a criticism of Ḥanafī positions regarding personal status laws and practical solutions to certain divorce situations were offered from the Mālikī school.[41] There is a strong pos-

---

[39] See for example his discussion on article 282. Al-Minyāwī, *al-Muqāranāt*, 1:100.

[40] While all four schools of law were taught at al-Azhar, the majority of Egyptian jurists were Mālikī and Shāfi'ī. The increase of importance given to the Ḥanafī School was a direct result of the Ottoman presences and the position of *qāḍī al-quḍā'* they instituted to the great disappointment of the Azhar *'ulamā'*. Accordingly, mostly Egyptian Mālikī's and some Shāfi'īs held the position of Sheikh al-Azhar from its inception sometime in the year 1690 until the first Ḥanafī was appointed to this position, ironically, by Khedive Ismā'īl in 1870. For a detailed discussion of this tension see: al-Shināwī, *al-Azhar Jāmi'an*, 1:187–208.

[41] This is found in my discussion of Muḥammad 'Abduh and Aḥmad Shākir in chapters 2 and 3 respectively.

sibility that al-Minyāwī was also writing to address these problems that he as a judge was certain to have faced.

Al-Minyāwī lays out a system for codification of Islamic law that he grounds in heavy references from central figures of the Mālikī school as well as references to the foundational period of Islam. Al-Minyāwī's understanding of codification is that it involves three key variables: siyāsa, ijtihād/taqlīd, and talfīq. For al-Minyāwī, these variables are defined as follows: siyāsā means codification is meant for application as it relates to governance and not as it relates to the private, scholarly discipline of fiqh. Ijtihād means that when it comes to understanding the object of governance, society at large, one must recognize that many of the occurrences and situations that exist were not in existence at the time of the Prophet, his Companions, and the early jurists of Islam. Ijtihād also means that there is a necessity to expand, extrapolate, and even adopt nuances to current, established, and inherited fiqh (what is often times referred to as al-fiqh *al-mawrūth*). Talfīq means that the ruler and his judiciary are not to be bound by a singular school of Islamic law while a student or private scholar might be and might have to be.

Codification and Divorce Law

The writing of al-Minyāwī's comparative work preceded the great debates surrounding divorce reform in Egypt, including the issue of a thrice divorce counting as one. One will neither find mention of these reform issues in his writings nor a discussion of problems he would have faced in actual cases pertaining to marriage and divorce practices amongst mid-19th century Egyptians. His focus throughout the two volumes is to find comparisons of Mālikī law to French law, even if such a comparison leads the discussion to other areas of law. For example, his discussion of article 1402 of the French code, which states that all real estate belonging to one spouse, is assumed to belong to the couple unless proven otherwise. To find a corresponding ruling in the Mālikī School, al-Minyāwī quotes from Dusūqī's gloss discussing partnerships in the section of trade, not a corresponding discussion found in the rights of husbands and wives.[42] Also, as discussed above, his brief discussion of citizenship leads him to find compatibility in the sections of law dealing with oaths, as there is no discussion of citizenship in Mālikī fiqh per se.

In general, al-Minyāwī's discussion of divorce seeks to reduce divorce to its essential component as found in Islamic law. While the French code sees adultery to be the main reason for initiating divorce for both men and women, al-Minyāwī distinguishes, as is commonly found in Islamic law, between a man initiating a divorce and a woman initiating a divorce. A man initiating a divorce is not contingent on adultery, although that could lead to a public imprecation (*li'ān*),[43] but rather is a right he possess regardless of the circumstance and can be initiated without cause. For a woman to initiate a divorce, adultery is but one manifestation of the more central cause of harm (*ḍarar*). This type of harm could include: that her husband stops speaking to her, that he fails to engage in intercourse with her, that he favors another wife over her (assuming a man has multiple wives as is allowed by Islamic law), or he favors a mistress over his wife.[44] He goes on to expand on this list by saying harm towards a woman is also in the form of "striking her, engaging in anal intercourse, cursing her and her father such as saying 'you daughter of a dog, you daughter of a disbeliever, you daughter

---

[42] Al-Minyāwī, *al-Muqāranāt*, 2:391–392.

[43] A public imprecation (*li'ān*) is a legal tool used to deny paternity in cases of doubt. It consists of a husband stating publically in front of a judge that, "I testify to God that I am truthful in charging her (his wife) with adultery." This is repeated four times in a row. Then after being warned by a judge, the husband repeats the statement a fifth time adding the phrase, "and may the curse of God be upon me if I am lying." The wife is allowed to rebut this imprecation by her own public imprecation following the same sequence. The public imprecation of the husband invalidates the marriage and paternity while the wife's public imprecation prevents a punishment for adultery. See: Kuwaiti Ministry of Religious Endowments and Islamic Affairs, *al-Mawsū'āt al-Fiqhiyya*, 45 vols., (Kuwait: Maṭābi' Dār al-Ṣafwa, 1993), 29:7.

[44] Al-Minyāwī, *al-Muqāranāt*, 1:96.

of an accursed man' as is found amongst lowly people."[45] This last comment is a good foreshadow to the type of discussions that will occur in following decades.

In other sections al-Minyāwī highlights where French law is too limiting in its understanding. For example, article 268 of the French Code allows and encourages a woman before being divorced to leave her husband's home for a temporary home, paid for by the husband, until the divorce process is concluded. Al-Minyāwī rejects this as a standard divorce procedure and rather discusses when it might apply according to Mālikī jurists.[46] Likewise, in discussing article 295 which claims all divorces are final, al-Minyāwī reminds readers that there is a revocable divorce (*raj'ī*) and an irrevocable divorce (*bā'in*) according to Islamic law.[47] In article 63 the French code lays out elaborate procedures for registering a marriage contract. Al-Minyāwī says, "this article is too strict in [this matter]."[48] He argues, instead, that the Sharī'a would see these procedures as undo harm (*mashaqqa*) and that religion is meant to be easy, not difficult.[49]

It is unfortunate that there is no way of knowing exactly what Khedive Ismā'īl did with al-Minyāwī's work, or if his contemporaries studied his *al-Muqāranāt*. However, it is known that the genre of contemporary legal writing was to continue in Egypt and its impact on the codification process only increased with time.

MUḤAMMAD QADRĪ PASHA AND CODIFICATION

Muḥammad Qadrī Pasha (d. 1886) was a product of a new Egypt. He came from an ethnically mixed family, his father was Turkish, and his mother was Egyptian, and grew up to be bi-lingual in both Arabic and Turkish. He was amongst the first generation of young Egyptians to bypass the traditional grammar schools (*kuttāb*) and instead studied at a local government school in his hometown. Up-

---

[45] Ibid.

[46] Ibid., 1:99–100.

[47] Ibid.

[48] Ibid., 1:61.

[49] Ibid.

on completion of these studies he traveled to Cairo to attend the newly formed School of Languages (*Madrasat al-Alsun*) where he was trained under the tutelage of Ṭahṭāwī as one of Egypt's first modern lawyers. A typical path of study at this time would have been to attend a local kuttāb were a student typically memorized the Qur'an and was exposed to the basic tenets of Arabic grammar and syntax, then matriculate to al-Azhar University in Cairo and receive a classical Islamic education consisting of the basic Islamic sciences (advanced grammar, law, ḥadīth, theology). A student's time at al-Azhar usually, but not always, culminated in the prestigious *'ālimiyya* degree granting one the official title of 'ālim.[50] The changes that Muḥammad 'Alī Pasha brought to Egypt as well as the reforms brought by his heirs developed parallel and often competing educational and vocational structures to this traditional Islamic system of learning. Not only was al-Azhar not a necessary path any more by the middle of the 19th century, but there was a larger state bureaucracy and civil service class that was emerging giving the 'ulamā' as a class competition in prestige and land ownership. Although Qadrī was not a traditionally trained 'ālim like al-Minyāwī, we know that he did frequent lessons of Islamic jurisprudence at al-Azhar as well as received a comprehensive education in comparative law under Ṭahṭāwī.[51] From the great output of his writings and from what we know of his works as commented by others after him, as we will see in detail below, Qadrī excelled at his studies of

[50] This degree currently corresponds to the PhD level of study.

[51] The *'ulamā'* who taught Ḥanafi law at the Alsun School were: Muḥammad Manṣūr and Khalīl al-Rashīdī. The Alsun School also contained some of the most prestigious Azhar 'ulamā' at the time including: Muḥammad al-Damanhūrī, 'Alī al-Farghalī al-Anṣaarī, Ḥasanayn al-Ghamrāwī, Muḥammad Quṭṭa al-'Idwī, Aḥmad al-Ṭahṭāwī, 'Abd al-Mun'im al-Jijāwī, Naṣr al-Hūrīnī, Muḥammad al-Marṣafī, and Muḥammad Abu Su'ūd. See: J. Heyworth-Dunne, *An introduction to the History of Education in Modern Egypt* (London: Luzac & Co., 1938), 268; Muḥammad 'Izzat Karīm, *Tārīkh al-Ta'alīm fī 'asr Muḥammad 'Alī* (Cairo: Maktabat al-Nahda al-Miṣriyya, 1938), 337.

Islamic jurisprudence.[52] Regarding this point and the boundaries and definition of the term 'ulamā', it is important to note that while the majority of 'ulamā' at this time would most likely have attended al-Azhar university, and while al-Azhar was not only a major center of learning in Egypt, but also throughout the Sunnī world, it alone did not have a monopoly on the training of 'ulamā'.

Ṭahṭāwī, Qadrī, and al-Alsun School

Muḥammad 'Ali's concern with modernization, particularly creating a modern military power, led him to look to the advice and experience of western Europe. He employed many European advisors in his court and also sent many young students from Egypt to Europe to study.[53] Of these many trips, one in particular stands out as it relates to the impact of comparative legal studies: the Paris bound trip that departed Alexandria in 1826 and returned in 1831. Sheikh Hasan al-'Aṭṭār (d. 1835), known for his pro-reform stance vis-à-vis al-Azhar, close to Muḥammad 'Alī, and one-time Sheikh al-Azhar, recommended that one of his students, Rifā'a al-Ṭahṭāwī, be placed in charge of the trip. At the young age of twenty, Ṭahṭāwī em-

---

[52] His major Sharī'a legal writings are: *al-Aḥkām al-Shar'iyya fi'l-Aḥwāl al-Shakhṣiyya* (a compilation of Ḥanafī rulings related to personal status laws) published in 1298/1880 and commented on by Sheikh Muḥammad Zayd al-Ibayānī (d. 1936), *Murshid al-Ḥayrān ilā Ma'rifat Aḥwāl al-Insān* (a compilation of Ḥanafī rulings pertaining to trade) published in 1890, *Qānūn al-'Adl wa al-Inṣāf lil qadā' 'alā Mushkilāt al-Awqāf* (a work seeking to codify rulings of religious endowments) published in 1894, and *Taṭbīq mā wujida fi'l Qānūn al-Madanī Muwāfiqan li Madhhab Abī Ḥanīfa* (manuscript). This is a comparison of French law to Ḥanafī law, in much the same way as was done by Makhlūf al-Minyāwī prior. I have been unable to verify the date of this manuscript and the use of it by scholars after him. I have found, however, that Ziadeh makes mention of it as a well-known fact. See: Farahat Ziadeh, *Lawyers, the Rule of Law, and Liberalism in Modern Egypt* (Stanford: Hoover Institution on War, Revolution and Peace, 1968), 20.

[53] For details on these trips see Ṭūsūn, *al-Bi'athāt al-'Ilmiyya.* Pertinent information can also be found in the following two sources: Heyworth-Dunne, *An introduction to the History of Education in Modern Egypt* and Karīm, *Tārīkh al-Ta'alīm.*

barked on what was to become a very transformative journey.[54] He excelled at his studies and wasted no time in engaging in translations as he was learning and mastering French. While still in France he began to translate French enlightenment literature (particularly the works of Voltaire, Rousseau, Montesquieu, and Racine).[55] He also translated the French constitution and the Napoleonic codes.[56]

---

[54] Rifā'a Rāfi' Ṭahṭāwī's personal account of his years in Paris are an invaluable window into this period. See: Maḥmūd Fahmī Ḥijāzī ed., *Uṣūl al-Fikr al-'Arabī al-Ḥadīth 'ind al-Ṭahṭāwī ma'a'l-Naṣṣ al-Kāmil li-Kitāb "Takhlīṣ al-Ibrīz"* (Cairo: al-Hay'a al-Miṣriyya al-'Āmma lil Kitāb, 1974). A recent English translation of this work is: Daniel L. Newman, trans., *An Imam in Paris* (London: Saqi Press, 2004). The *Takhlīṣ* was translated into Turkish under the name *Siyāḥat Nāmeh* and published by the Bulāq press in 1840. Heyworth-Dunne mentions that it "had a wider circulation in Turkish than in Arabic, for Muḥammad 'Alī had it distributed to all his officials and had copies sent to Constantinople." See Heyworth-Dunne, *An introduction to the History of Education in Modern Egypt*, 266.

[55] A good discussion of these translations can be found in: Albert Hourani, *Arabic Thought in the Liberal Age* (Cambridge: Cambridge University Press, 2008), 69–84.

[56] Ṭahṭāwī left a large amount of writings, both original and translations. He is perhaps the first to have ever translated French legal and political works into Arabic. In his travel log of his trip to Paris he translated the French Constitutional Charters of June 4, 1814 and September 4, 1830 with commentaries on numerous articles. Much less known are the French legal codes that he translated and published: Arabic Translation of French Trade Law (published 1285/1868), Arabic Translation of French Civil Code (published 1283/1866), Translation of the Code of Napoleon alongside the Ottoman Constitution. (Published with Qadrī Pasha in 1866 and again in 1868.) This later work was translated at the behest of Khedive Ismā'īl in his efforts to reform the judiciary that began in 1863 alluded to above. On the translation of the French Constitution see: Newman, *An Imam in Paris*, 194–213; Ṭahṭāwī, *Takhlīṣ*, 229–243 and notes 66–159 for the original French. For the translations of various French codes see: Muḥammad 'Amāra, *Rifā'a al-Ṭahṭāwī Rā'd al-Tanwīr fī'l-'Asr al-Ḥadīth* (Cairo: Dār al-Sharq, 2007): 99–100, 126, 130. One should also consult these works as listed in: Joseph Ilān Sarkīs, *Mu'jam al-Maṭbū'āt al-'Arabiyya wa al-Mu'āraba*, 2 vols., (Cairo: Sarkīs Press, 1928), s.v., Rifā'a al-Ṭahṭāwī.

Ṭahṭāwī's education in France, however, was a supplement to his basic and original training as an Azharite ʿālim. Aside from being close to ʿAṭṭār, he also studied with many leading Azharite scholars including the famous Ibrahīm al-Bayjūrī (d. 1860) who became at one-point Sheikh al-Azhar.[57] When he returned to Egypt in 1831, he embodied a new hybrid of scholar that had until this time not existed in Egypt. In 1836 Ṭahṭāwī drafted a proposal to Muḥammad ʿAlī for a translation school which the Walī accepted immediately. The School of Languages (Madrasat al-Alsun) was formed in June 1836 and by January 1837 Ṭahṭāwī was running it.[58] In 1849, a school and faculty of law was added to the Alsun school and both remained in operation until they were temporarily closed during the reign of ʿAbbās II. They were reopened during Ismāʿīl's reign under the name *Madrasat al-Idāra*. By 1882 the law school was spun off to become an independent school as it has remained until this day.[59]

Under Ṭahṭāwī, the School of Languages provided an ambitious program of study. It was to offer Arabic, Turkish, French,

---

[57] Ibrāhīm al-Bayjūrī (d. 1277/1860) was an important figure throughout this time period. He is also one of the main sources for the conclusion drawn by early Orientalists that Islam fell into a state of intellectual stagnation with the "closing of the doors of *ijtihād*" after the Golden Era of Islam. C. Snouck Hurgronje uses al-Bayjūrī's famous legal gloss in Shafiʿī law to demonstrate that Muslim jurists of the late Sunnī period themselves claimed that *ijtihād* was no longer possible. See Bousquet, *Selected Works of C. Snouck Hurgronje*, 266 and 280. For Bayjūrī's original comments that are quoted by Hurgronje, see: Ibrahīm al-Bayjūrī, *Ḥashiyat al-Bayjūrū ʿala Sharḥ al-ʿĀllama Ibn Qāsim*, 2 vols., (Beirut: Dār al-Fikr, n.d.), 1:20. It is important to note that Bayjūrī's work is itself based on an older gloss on Ibn Qāsim by al-Baramāwī. Therefore, the opinion on *ijtihād* cited by Hurgonje is not necessarily one offered by Bayjūrī alone. In addition, the type of *ijtihād* that Bayjūrī claims is no longer valid is absolute *ijtihād* (al-*ijtihād al-muṭlaq*). He does offer as valid other forms of *ijtihād* that can occur iner-madhhab.

[58] Heyworth-Dunne, *An introduction to the History of Education in Modern Egypt*, 266.

[59] Ziadeh, *Lawyers*, 21.

math, and geography as core subjects. The five-year program was often extended to a sixth where a student underwent a translation project that took place in the Translation Bureau (*Qalam al-Tarjama*), one of which was dedicated to legal translation. The resulting translation was published under the direction of Ṭahṭāwī. In actuality, the languages taught were French and Arabic, the latter being taught by various 'ulamā' from al-Azhar giving the program an extremely rigorous course of linguistic study.[60] In addition, Ṭahṭāwī taught classes in comparative law (i.e. French law and Sharī'a). These classes on Islamic law were supplemented in 1847 by a full program that taught Ḥanafī law.[61]

It is not known exactly what year Qadrī Pasha entered the Alsun School, but it is clear that he was amongst the first students, and perhaps the most famous, to attend.[62] Qadrī became very close to Ṭahṭāwī and by the time he graduated, he was assigned a teaching and translation post at the school. This early relationship with Ṭahṭāwī and the Alsun School provided Qadrī with a solid education in the process, challenges, and nuances of codification, particularly between French law and Ḥanafī law. He was also able to apply this theoretical framework while at the Alsun through the many translation projects he engaged with alongside his teacher Ṭahṭāwī and his colleagues.

---

[60] Arabic studies at al-Azhar were and continue to be advanced. High school Azhar students study various sections of Ibn Mālik's *Alfiyya* and university students are taught the different commentaries and glosses of the work such as al-Mākudī, Ibn 'Aqīl, and al-'Ashmūnī. Advanced classes focus on works such as Ibn Mālik's *Awḍaḥ al-Masālik* and the works of Ibn al-Jinnī.

[61] See note 51 above for a list of these instructors.

[62] In his list of famous students to enter the school, Heyworth-Dunne lists Qadrī as entering, "shortly after 1837." Heyworth-Dunne, *An introduction to the History of Education in Modern Egypt*, 270.

Corpus and Reception

Despite having a vast career in government positions,[63] Qadrī's passion for translation and composition continued throughout his life. His corpus falls into three categories: linguistic works, historical works, and legal works.[64] His legal works, however, are the cause of his inclusion in this study, and most likely the reason why he gained popularity as a serious intellectual during his lifetime and beyond. His four legal works are:

1. *al-Aḥkām al-Shar'iyya fi'l-Aḥwāl al-Shakhṣiyya* (a compilation of Ḥanafī rulings related to personal status laws) published in 1298/1880 and later commented on by Shaykh Muḥammad Zayd al-Ibayānī (d. 1936).
2. *Murshid al-Ḥayrān ilā Ma'rifat Aḥwāl al-Insān* (a compilation of Ḥanafī rulings pertaining to trade law) published in 1890.
3. *Qānūn al-'Adl wa al-Inṣāf lil qaḍā' 'alā Mushkilāt al-Awqāf* (a work seeking to codify laws of religious endowments) published in 1894.
4. *Taṭbīq mā Wujida fi'l Qānūn al-Madanī Muwāfiqan li Madhhab Abī Ḥanīfa* (manuscript). This was a comparison of French law to Ḥanafī law, similar to the style of al-Minyāwī prior.[65]

Although most of these legal works were published after Qadrī's death, his expertise in comparative legal matters was a known fact due to his translation of French legal codes mentioned above. He was brought onto a committee to translate into Arabic the newly formed code of the Mixed courts in 1874 as well as tasked with heading a committee to re-write and edit the newly drafted Egyptian civil code in 1881.

---

[63] Upon graduation from the *Alsun* school Qadrī landed several positions as a translator for various government agencies. After a time, he was appointed a main tutor for the Crown Prince. He then advanced to being an advisor to the Mixed courts, and then became Minister of Justice. See Qadrī, *al-Aḥkām al-Shar'iyya*, 1:8.

[64] For a full list of his known works (published and manuscript) see: Qadrī, *al-Aḥkām al-Sahr'iyya*, 1:9–12.

[65] See note 52 above regarding this source.

Aside from teaching law and writing extensively concerning issues of codification, Qadrī's three main published works were used as core curricula in legal training for both secular lawyers and 'ulamā' seeking to serve in the Sharī'a courts. It must be remembered that just as Qadrī was a product of a new Egypt, there were dozens of young students who were following in his footsteps by forgoing traditional Islamic studies at al-Azhar and entering the newly formed school of law to be trained as modern lawyers. And in these new legal schools there was overlap from al-Azhar 'ulamā'. For example, Sheikh al-Ibayānī was the head of the Khedival school of legal studies while he undertook his lengthy commentary on Qadrī's work on personal status law.[66] He mentions in his introduction to his commentary that Qadrī's work was a textbook used in the core curriculum of the school.[67] In regards to Qadrī's other legal works, we know that posthumously, Qadrī's family, particularly his son Maḥmūd Afandī, worked with the Ministry of Justice to have his father's works published. Since these legal works were meant to be used in government schools as legal texts, they were in need of government and religious approval. In the early published version of both the Murshid al-Ḥayrān ilā Ma'rifat Aḥwāl al-Insān and the Qānūn al-'Adl wa al-Inṣāf lil qadā' 'alā Mushkilāt al-Awqāf[68] approval letters are provided. The Murshid's approval process required 'Alī Mubārak (Minister of Education d. 1893) to write to Shaykh Muḥammad al-'Abbāsī al-Mahdī who was a Ḥanafī mufti. Al-Mahdī reviewed the work in consultation with Sheikh Hassūna al-Nawāwī who at that time taught Islamic law at the newly formed Dār al-'Ulūm, which housed a law faculty, and later became Shaykh al-Azhar. Al-Mahdī seems to have made some adjustments to the Murshid, including supplying much needed corresponding Ḥanafī text citations to each of Qadrī's articles, in order

---

[66] Qadrī, *al-Aḥwāl al-Shar'iyya*, 1:20.

[67] Ibid.

[68] I relied on the second edition (1891) and fourth edition (1909) of both works respectively. See: Muḥammad Qadrī, *Murshid al-Ḥayrān ila Ma'rifat Aḥwāl al-Insān* (Cairo: al-Maṭba'a al-Kubra al-Amīriyya bi Bulāq, 1891); Muḥammad Qadrī, *Qānūn al-'Adl wa'l Inṣāf li'l Qadā' 'ala Mushkilāt al-Awqāf* (Cairo: al-Maṭba'a al-Amīriyya, 1909).

for the work to comply with the soundest opinions of the Ḥanafī school. Both al-Mahdī and al-Nawāwī endorsed the work for publication and use in law schools on the 15th of Muḥaram 1308 AH (August 31, 1890). The ten letters and statements back and forth leading to the approval of both the Ministries of Justice and Education as well as the Azhar establishment provides an important insight into how Qadrī, his work, and codification was received at this time. In ʻAli Mubārak's initial letter to the mufti, the Murshid is defined as "the main rulings of the Ḥanafī School ordered similar to the ordering of common law (qānūn)."[69] This description is acknowledged by al-Mahdī and used in his further correspondences to describe and subsequently approve the work. Furthermore, Mubārak states as a fact that, "as it is well-known, Islamic law is currently taught in schools [i.e. non-religious schools]." The same approval process was applied to Qadrī's work on endowments, but the main figure to reconcile the articles Qadrī chose with corresponding texts in the Ḥanafī school was Shaykh Muḥammad Zayd al-Ibayānī, then a professor of Islamic law at the Khedival law school, who later would go on to lead the law school and provide an extensive commentary on Qadrī's al-Aḥkām al-Sharʻiyya fi'l-Aḥwāl al-Shakhṣiyya.

Qadrī's works on law gained popularity for their utility in teaching the complications of Islamic law. These works were accepted as part of the core curriculum for secular legal education in Egypt at the turn of the 19th century and ensured that a basic level of proficiency with the Sharīʻa would be necessary not only to deal with personal status law, but other areas as well. Qadrī's legal works were also accepted by the orthodox Islamic establishment of al-Azhar and were treated as legal texts (nuṣūṣ) and commented on by other ʻulamā' in ways congruent with legal commentaries of the late classical period of Islamic law.[70] In this regard, Qadrī's works are at par with the Ottoman Majalla, which was subject to both Arabic and Ottoman commentaries and treated as a modern text of Ḥanafī law.

---

[69] Qadrī, *Murhsid*, 2.

[70] Ibayānī's commentary and the Dār al-Sālām's critical edition of this being prime examples.

Methodology of Codification

As is evident by the title of his work on religious endowments (awqāf) and its introduction, Qadrī's works were written to solve immediate legal problems and not theoretical concerns. This is a fundamental difference between his works and the comparative one of al-Minyāwī examined above. By the end of the 1800s, legal codification of Islamic law was no longer a theoretical discussion and debate, but an actual process in Egypt.

On one level, Qadriī's approach to codification of Sharī'a, including personal status law, is one that echoes previous attempts by certain Ḥanafī jurists to compile works of jurisprudence that contain *the* main and agreed upon rulings of every subject matter, a sort of legal consolidation. In particular, his approach is similar to the al-Fatāwā al-Hindiyya as well as earlier works. The exchange cited above between Shaykh al-Mahdī and Shaykh al-Nawāwī provides a clear understanding of what Ḥanafī texts Qadrī relied on to arrive at his rulings. He used many, too many to enumerate here, but relied mostly on the 19th century gloss *Ḥāshiyat ibn 'Ābidīn* as well as, and as expected, the al-Fatāwā al-Hindiyya. Since he provides only the appropriate rulings without their ratio legis ('illa), his work can be thought of as a modern mukhtaṣar.

However, Qadrī's process of codification is also different than his Ḥanafī predecessors. His focus is not to find the most agreed upon opinion in the Ḥanafī school for all legal issues dealt with in the maddhab. Rather, Qadrī's goal was to find what Ḥanafī jurists have to say about issues relating to personal status laws, a terminology he was introducing to Ḥanafī works. Therefore, he chose the areas that need to be codified, rather than codifying the entire madhhab. For example, a madhhab-based approach to the topic of marriage would usually begin with a discussion on the rulings concerning marriage itself, i.e is marriage obligatory or simply recommended, and does the ruling change for people in varying circumstances?[71] Qadrī, however, assumed that marriage is something that

---

[71] Muḥammad Amīn Ibn 'Ābidīn, *Radd al-Muḥtār 'ala al-Durr al-Mukhtār (Ḥāshiyāt Ibn 'Ābidīn)*, 12 vols., (Beirut: Dār al-Ma'rifa, 2000), 4:73–76.

should be pursued and began his code with a discussion of what type of women a man could marry.[72] Likewise, a section on divorce in Ḥanafī texts typically begins with the precise definition of divorce excluding other forms of spousal separation and continues to discuss the various kinds of divorce: divorce according to the practice of the Prophet of Islam and divorce that is considered a reprehensible innovation (*bid'a*).[73] Qadrī began article 217, however, describing who in the marital relationship can initiate a divorce.[74] The point to be made is that Qadrī's code assumed many things about the legal subject matters he seeks to codify. He assumed definitions, placement of a particular subject matter in its greater legal context, and most importantly the ratio legis, which he did not provide.

In addition, the Ḥanafī sources Qadrī used to draw out his code were themselves a series of commentaries and meta-commentaries on earlier fiqh works. Qadrī did not, however, copy this language into the code as this might have proved too difficult and would lead to a terse legal document. On the issue of a divorce pronouncement initiated by a drunkard, the 16th century Ḥanafī jurist al-Timirtāshī (d. 1004/1596) said in his *Tanwīr al-Abṣār*, "a divorce pronouncement from a husband has effect if he is of age, of rational faculty, whether he be a slave or coerced, whether he be jesting or dimwitted, or intoxicated."[75] Al-Ḥaṣakfī's commentary on this adds the following qualification to "intoxicated", "if (intoxicated) by wine, hashish, opium, or henbane plant."[76] Ibn 'Ābidīn's meta-commentary is even lengthier with a discussion on the precise definition of intoxication, the opinions of other schools of law on intoxication, and the difference between intoxication by choice and by coercion.[77] When Qadrī came to codify this portion of divorce law, he simply stated, "the divorce pronouncement of a drunkard has effect as long as he has become intoxicated with that which is

[72] Qadrī, *al-Aḥwāl al-Shakhṣiyya*, 1:25.

[73] Ibn 'Ābidīn, *Radd al-Muḥtār*, 4:412–427.

[74] Qadrī, *al-Aḥwāl al-Shakhṣiyya*, 2: 507.

[75] Ibn 'Ābidīn, *Radd al-Muḥtār*, 4:427–432.

[76] Ibid., 4:432–433.

[77] Ibid.

forbidden and on his own volition, not by coercion and out of need."[78] There is nothing necessarily wrong or incorrect with Qadrī's wording and it indeed captures the Ḥanafī opinion regarding the divorce pronouncement of a drunkard, but it is written in a concise way, what one would expect from a code of law, and is different than the original texts being analyzed.

Unlike al-Minyāwī before him, Qadrī did not provide us with a methodology of codification. This is deduced, rather, from his works and it is safe to assume he saw it as a necessity and a forgone conclusion in Egypt. As the letter of Alī al-Mubārak to Shaykh al-Mahdı stated, Sharī'a was already being taught to lawyers who needed to learn the material in an efficient manner.

Codification and Divorce Law

Qadrī stuck to the standard Ḥanafī opinion that a thrice pronounced divorce, either orally or by gesture, constitutes a final and irrevocable divorce (bā'in).[79] He did, however, mention that the number of divorces in the pronouncements needs to be stated explicitly, for if a man utters a divorce pronouncement to his wife and intends more than one, the divorce only counts as one and is therefore revocable (raj'ī).[80] Qadrī, as well as his commentator Ibayānī, made it clear that to issue a divorce in the first place requires exact language.[81] There is no mention in Qadrī's codes or its commentary to the behavior of people and the actual effects of these opinions and rulings on married and divorced men and women, as is discussed in the marriage and divorce law of 1929, nor to opinions found in other schools of Islamic law.

THE 1929 LAW OF MARRIAGE AND DIVORCE

The 1929 law of marriage and divorce, which sparked the debates that are analyzed throughout this study, and the process of formally codifying personal status law in Egypt is really a function of two

---

[78] Qadrī, *al-Aḥwāl al-Shakhṣiyya*, 2:514.

[79] Ibid., 2:585 article 239.

[80] Ibid., 2:558 article 228.

[81] Ibid., 2:536 article 225.

realities. The first reality is that by the turn of the 20th century the momentum for codification reached a climax. A memo written by the Justice Minister, Fakhrī Pasha, on December 7, 1882 (26 Muḥarram 1300) laid out the need for a new civil code, and at the same time foreshadowed the important work that 'Abd al-Razzāq al-Sanhūrī would accomplish some sixty five years later.[82] This led to a new codified civil law that was administered through a series of newly formed civil courts (*al-maḥākim al-ahliyya*). This only increased the importance of the newly recognized legal field and the many who flocked to these courts for positions. At the same time, the Mixed courts continued to function with its own eclectic legal code providing a nagging need for nationalists and reformers to address the never-ending problems of capitulations. It was logical at this point in time for legal reformers to turn to the Sharī'a courts to address the need for codification of personal status law.

The second reality to affect this type of codification was the rise of the women's movement in Egypt. The last half of the 19th century and early part of the 20th century witnessed a tremendous movement of women's rights throughout Egypt. Issues of the veil, polygamy, women working, and even voting rights, were publically debated and, as Ron Shaham has made clear, affected the trajectory of legal reform and particularly Sharī'a attitudes towards these traditionally conservative issues.[83] Both Muḥammad 'Abduh and Aḥmad Shākir, main actors in this drama, saw certain marriage and divorce practices and opinions as too stringent which in turn had detrimental effects on women and their families. For example, Aḥmad Shākir narrated a debate between his father and Muḥammad 'Abbāsī al-Mahdī in the introduction to his *Niẓām al-Ṭalāq fi'l Islām*. The debate involved the possibility of following an opinion from the Mālikī school granting a woman a divorce from her husband who has been given a lengthy jail sentence or who has been missing for an extended period of time. Al-Mahdī refused on grounds that only a Ḥanafī opinion would suffice. This story is significant as both 'Abduh and Riḍā narrate similar situations as rea-

---

[82] Egypt, *Al-Kitāb al-Zahabī fi'l Maḥākim al-Ahliyya*, 1:107–115.

[83] Ron Shaham, *Family and the Courts in Modern Egypt: A Study Based on Decisions by the Sharī'a Courts, 1900–1955* (Leiden: Brill, 1997), 7–18.

sons to follow other legal opinions. In addition to issues of marriage and debate, and perhaps the hallmark of this movement, was the issue of the veil.[84] Women leaders such as Hudā Sha'rāwī and their supporters such as Qāsim Amīn were strong forces that advocated for the liberation of women using the veil, or lack thereof, as the symbol for their movement while conservative scholars like Muṣṭafā Ṣabrī and Muḥammad Zāhid al-Kawtharī wrote works defending these practices as authentic and necessary.[85]

Part of Fakhrī's 1882 memorandum was the necessity of forming committees of personal status laws. While it is extremely difficult to identify who exactly served on these committees and what exactly they discussed, we do have some traces.[86] It is certain that these committees were a mix of secular and Azhar trained jurists. Part of their task was to investigate abuses of certain practices, recommend changes, and most importantly argue from a Sharī'a standpoint their rational behind these often times contentious recommendations.

While majority Ḥanafī positions were adopted throughout the codification of personal status law, along the same fashion of

---

[84] The issue of "veiling" is a reference to the Islamic practice of *niqāb*, which is a reference to women covering their face in addition to covering their hair and neck. I discuss this term in greater detail in the next chapter.

[85] For primary sources on these issues one should consult: Qāsim Amīn, *Taḥrīr al-Mar'a* (Cairo: Maktaba al Jāmi'a, 1928); Muṣṭafa Ṣabrī, *Qawlī fi'l Mar'a* (Beirut: Dār al-Qādirī, 1993); Hudā Sha'rāwī, *Muḥādarāt Dawr al-Mar'a fi'l Nahḍa al-Sharqiyya* (Cairo: al-Maṭba'a al-'Aṣriya, 1935). For secondary sources one should consult: Soha Abdel Kader, *Egyptian Women in a Changing Society, 1899–1987* (London: Boulder & London, 1987); Beth Baron, *The Women's Awakening in Egypt: Culture, Society, and the Press* (New Haven: Yale University Press, 1994); Majid Khaduri, "Marriage in Islamic Law: The Modernist Viewpoints," *The American Journal of Comparative Law* 26 (1978), 213–18; Judith Tucker, *Women in Nineteenth Century Egypt* (Cambridge: Cambridge University Press, 1985).

[86] An excellent source for these discussions is Muḥammad Aḥmad Faraj Sanhūrī, *al-Qawānīn al-Miṣriyya al-Mukhtāra min al-Fiqh al-Islāmi*, 2 vols., (Cairo: Maṭba'a Misr, 1949).

Qadrī's methodology, there were topics that proved highly contentious and incompatible with what had become customary amongst the majority Muslim population in Egypt. In this regard, many amendments to the personal status code were issued along with lengthy explanatory notes. Law 25 issued in 1929 is the focus of the following discussion.

The law itself is straightforward and simple in its language and conclusions, again consistent with what one would expect from a code of law. For example, the first article reads, "the divorce initiated by a drunkard does not count" and so on and so forth.[87] The amendments, and ultimately the code of personal status itself, are written in standard and simple legal language. However, while the language is simple, the process of arriving at these amendments and codes was not. Al-Minyāwī and Qadrī were both working within the confines of a particular school of law (Mālikī and Ḥanafī respectively), however the 'ulamā' of the committees of personal status laws were not. They concluded, as will be discussed below, that some standard Ḥanafī rulings were incompatible and often times the source of social ill. Accordingly, the real text that was produced and what is in need of analysis is the explanatory note that accompanies this law.

Anatomy of the Explanatory Note to Law 25 of 1929

The explanatory memorandum, issued with law 25 and signed by the minister of justice Aḥmad Muḥammad Khashaba, begins with a basic understanding of the Sharī'a concept of what exactly the meaning and purpose of divorce is. The authors begin this discus-

---

[87] Throughout this study, I will be using the following two sources containing both the text of law 1929 and its explanatory note: Muḥammad Ḥilmī 'Abd al-'Āṭī, *al-Mabādi' al-'Āmma fī Tashrī'āt al-Aḥwāl al-Shakhṣiyya* (Cairo: Maktabat al-Qāhira, 1962); Paul Geuthner and M.L. Massignon, eds., *Revue Des Études Islamiques* (Paris: Librairie Orientaliste, 1929), 137–153. Regarding this last source, it is important to note that it is not a French translation of the original Arabic law, but rather an original text of the 1929 law. All laws at this time in Egypt were issued in both Arabic and French simultaneously. This text, therefore, provides us with original language of the law and its explanatory note.

sion by mentioning that although divorce is legislated in Islam, it is something that is disliked (*makrūh*).[88] The proof adduced is the statement of the Prophet of Islam, "the most disliked of permissible acts for God is divorce."[89] The note then goes on to support this general notion by citing the Qur'an 2:229 in its discussion of sequential divorces. The writers of the explanatory note conclude that the original intent of the verse and the institution of divorce in general is that it takes place sequentially, one after another. However, it should be noted that this verse is traditionally adduced to prove the opposite, namely that coupled divorce pronouncements have effect. This leads to the explanation that divorce in Islam is something that the Lawgiver intends to be restricted. Concluding this argument is the fact that great harm, actual and potential, effect women through divorces practices that are abused.[90]

The explanatory note continues with the general methodology of both al-Minyāwī and Qadrī Pasha regarding codification of Islamic law. It invokes the concept of al-siyāsā al-shar'iyya to highlight the necessity of finding Sharī'a compliant solutions to social problems, which in this case apply specifically to divorce. It should be recalled that al-Minyāwī called the abuse of divorce the habits of "lowly people."[91] It is not a surprise, then, that the same sorts of abuses found in al-Minyāwī's time continued into the early part of the 20th century. The note also speaks of the "looming harm" traditional divorce (read Ḥanafī) created for women and their families.[92] Both the social harm, more of which I will say in the following

---

[88] This is both a descriptive and technical term. The sentence that, "divorce is disliked in Islam" refers to the fact that it is something that is permissible, yet not favorable. Technically disliked actions (*makrūh*) in Islamic law mean actions that lead to no bad deed if one were to engage in them, but would lead to a good deed were one to leave them.

[89] 'Abd al-'Āṭī, *Mabādi' al-'Āmma*, 122; Geuthner, *Revue des Études Islamiques*, 142. The ḥadīth can be found in the collection of al-Bayhaqī, ḥadīth 1208.

[90] Ibid., 123 and 143 respectively.

[91] Al-Minyāwī, *Muqāranāt al-Tashrī'iyya*, 1:96.

[92] 'Abd al-'Āṭī, *Mabādi' al-'Āmma*, 123; Geuthner, *Revue des Études Islamiques*, 143.

chapter, as well as the right of the sovereign to choose laws that are appropriate led the authors of the explanatory note to conclude that a legal solution must be sought out through ijtihād. However, this type of ijtihād was not a type of ijtihād in which jurists returned to the proof texts of certain rulings and specific legal maxims governing the various schools of law. Rather, the ijtihād employed by the explanatory note of the law was to re-think and re-apply the traditional and classical methodology of the Sharī'a itself. This approach led firstly the jurists to consider opinions found throughout Islamic legal history *outside* the four canonical suunī schools, and secondly to take an eclectic approach (talfīq) to which singular opinions will be adopted. In other words, these jurists were advocating and indeed working outside the classical madhhab construct.

As I mention in the introduction, I have a specific concern throughout this study to analyze the process of codification of a thrice-pronounced divorce (*al-ṭalāq al-mut'adid lafẓan*) counting as only one, revocable divorce. The general introduction to the explanatory note concluded that the solution to the social abuses of divorce in Egypt was to take the approach of restricting divorce and therefore making it more difficult for pronounced divorces to have effect. Therefore, while the four canonical schools of sunnī law (Ḥanafī, Mālikī, Shāfi'ī, and Ḥanbalī) form a consensus that any pronounced divorce associated with a number, has effect regarding that number, law 25 of 1929 concluded that such is not the case. Rather, the law's conclusion is that *any* numbered pronounced divorce counts only as one, revocable divorce. The ratio legis for this opinion, i.e. what the explanatory note adduced, was that this is the position found amongst some of the Companions and other mujtahid Imams of the past.[93]

---

[93] Article 3 of the memo states: "La repudiation par plus d'une fois, faite verbalement ou par geste, n'est qu'une repudiation unique. C'est l'opinion de Mohamed Ibn Ishak et c'est l'opinion attribueé á Aly, ā Ibn Massoud, á Abdel Rahman Ibn Of et á Zobeir. Elle est également attribueéaux Cheikhs de Cordoue, entre Mohamed Ibn Taki Ibn Mokhled et Mohamed Ibn Abdel Salam. D'aprés Ibn El Monzer, elle est celle disciples d'Ibn Abbas, tells que Ata, Taous et Amr Ibn Dinar. Des "Fetwas" dans

As was found in the introduction of al-Minyāwī and in the writings of Ṭahṭāwī, recourse to the formative period was usually paired with recourse to the primary texts. Although there is mention of some jurists from amongst the Mālikīs and Ḥanafīs, these are quoted by Ibn al-Qayyim (d. 751/1350) whom we know based his opinion largely on the argumentation of Ibn Taymiyya (d. 728/1328).[94]

ce sens ont été émises par Akrama et Daud. Selon Ibn El Kayyem, cette opinion est celle de la plupart des Compagnonsdu Prophéte, dequelques disciples de Malek, de quelques docteurs hanafites et de quelques disciples d'Ahmed [i.e. Ibn Ḥanbal]. Geuthner, *Revue des Études Islamiques*, 145.

[94] As I will demonstrate in the following chapter, Ibn Taymiyya has provided the most thorough argument for the strength of this position basing his opinion of the ḥadīth of the Companion Rukāna.

CHAPTER 2. DEFENDERS AND ADVOCATES OF CODIFICATION

This chapter turns to the 'ulamā' who defended and advocated for codification of personal status law in Egypt. The main distinction between these 'ulamā' and those of the previous chapter is that the 'ulamā' of this chapter did not compose codes of personal status law that were used legislatively, but rather provided arguments for the importance of and need for codifying Islamic law. It is true, as I will show below, that Muḥammad 'Abduh (d. 1905) and Aḥmad Shākir (d. 1958) both offered codes as suggestions for various aspects of marriage and divorce law. These were, however, just that, suggestions that were not taken as part of the official statutes drafted into law at the time, although they would come to influence the process of codification in later years. In addition, these suggested codes did not form the bulk of their thought concerning this subject matter and were relatively brief in nature. The fact that these codes were suggestions often times meant that these 'ulamā' were not directly part of the actual process of codification the way the 'ulamā' of the previous chapter were. Even though the 'ulamā' of this chapter played more of an observer role in the official process, they found the importance of codification of Islamic law something too important to ignore.

The 'ulamā' of this chapter fall under what is often termed Islamic reform thinkers. Some of the earlier narratives on this topic argue that Islamic reform thinkers are generally good for the future of Islam versus more traditionally oriented 'ulamā' who are backward and considered part of the problem. While this narrative has matured and there are newer discussions[1], its remnants still impact the dearth of written material around these thinkers, particularly Muḥammad 'Abduh and Rashīd Riḍa, which I feel is important to address briefly in order to understand their opinions concerning codification. This presents a challenge, however, to my discussion since my purpose is not to discuss the reform movement, but rather to discuss 'ulamā' who supported and defended the process of codification of Islamic law, regardless of their overall attitude towards reforming or not reforming Islam. Earlier authors writing of these reform thinkers tend to highlight their theological and philosophical discussions or their re-interpretation of traditionally controversial issues.[2] Rarely, however, is there a discussion of their treatment of the details and minutiae of Islamic law.[3] This is not to say that their views of reforming or re-interpreting Islam are irrelevant to their opinions of codification. In fact, there is oftentimes a direct relationship, particularly if we think of the three main com-

---

[1] One such approach is found in the writings of Riḍwān al-Sayyid. See for example his discussion of 'Abduh, Amīn, and Riḍā and their dealing with legal issues related to women: Riḍwān al-Sayyid, *Jawānib min al-Dirāsāt al-Islāmiyya al-Haḍītha* (Dār al-Fanak: Casablanca, 2000), 85–126.

[2] Some of these early works include: Charles C. Adams, *Islam and Modernism in Egypt* (London: Oxford University Press, 1933), 104–176; M. Horten, "Muhammed Abduh: Sein Leben und seine theologisch-philosophische Gedankenwelt-Eine Studie zu den Reformbestrebungen im modernen Ägypten (part I)," in *Beiträge zur Kenntnis des Orients* (Halle: Gebauer-Schwetschke Druckerei und Verlag, 1916), 83–114; M. Horten, "Muhammed Abduh: Sein Leben und seine theologisch-philosophische Gedankenwelt-Eine Studie zu den Reformbestrebungen im modernen Ägypten (part II)," in *Beiträge zur Kenntnis des Orients* (Halle: Gebauer-Schwetschke Druckerei und Verlag, 1917), 74–128; Hournai, *Arabic Thought*, 130–160; B. Michel and Moustapha Abdel Razik trans., *Rissalat al-Tawid du Cheikh Mohammed Abdou* (Paris: Librairie Orientaliste Paul Geuthner, 1925), ix–lxxxv.

[3] A notable example of an early discussion of 'Abduh's treatment of law is: Ignaz Goldziher, *Die Richtungen Der Islamischen Koranauslegung* (Leiden: E.J. Brill, 1952), 322–344.

ponents of codification in the previous chapter.[4] However, the topic of codification of Islamic law is not a function of reforming Islam or re-interpreting Islam entirely, but has more to do with negotiating the specific nodes of authority necessary to interpreting the Sharī'a (issues such as qiyās, ijmā', and ijtihād). Islamic reform thinkers were largely seeking to make Islam more palatable vis-à-vis contemporary realities and to go back to a better and more pristine Islam. It is true that one can argue this is exactly what codification of Islamic law is about. My contention with this notion, however, is that codification is specifically about three components: al-siyāsa al-shar'iyya, ijtihād, and talfīq, and the interaction between the three. It is not the reform agenda that unites the pro-codification camp ('Abduh and Riḍa fell on opposite sides), but rather the negotiation of these three components in a certain methodological manner.

This chapter also touches on the rise of the feminist movement in Egypt. By the turn of the 20th century there was a vibrant, and often times contentious, nationwide conversation on the role of women in society generally and the need to reform various aspects of marriage and divorce laws specifically. Since Islam was the dominant culture and legal system that governed these social issues at this time, it was natural that what Islamic law and Islamic thinkers had to say on these issues became part and parcel of these conversations. In this regard, we find that the earliest writings of the feminist movement, I discuss Qasim Amīn's works below, were filled with such references and discussions. The voices of the 'ulamā', therefore, became part of this movement and the manner in which Islam was discussed also became an important, central topic. There are too many areas of overlap and points of influence that the feminist movement had on the process and decisions taken throughout the codification of personal status law in Egypt that to not include a discussion of the relationship between the two is to ignore the great amount of social change in Egypt that grew along-

[4] These main components are: independent legal reasoning (*ijtihād*), legal eclecticism (*talfīq*), and the intersections of religion and politics (*al-siyāsa al-shar'iyya*). See note 68 in the introduction above.

side the story of codification of personal status law and what continues to make this topic important today.[5]

WOMEN AT THE TURN OF THE 20TH CENTURY IN EGYPT

While it is important to provide an outline of the feminist movement in Egypt and the impact this movement had on reinterpreting rulings of marriage and divorce and the overall process of codification of personal status law, it is equally important to state that this is not meant to be a thorough study of women's rights in early 20th century Egypt as much has been written about this.[6] My purpose, rather, is to demonstrate the importance that these social issues had on influencing the 'ulamā' who began to advocate for codification and who took certain positions that were historically considered weak or even heterodox. The 'ulamā' who wrote actual codes (previous chapter) and those who supported codification (this chapter) managed to weave the social issue of women into their writings, making it important to discuss.

---

[5] I have avoided insinuating that the rise of the feminism movement influenced reform Islam or vice-versa as this issue is one that is not settled throughout the secondary literature, and it is not my goal to do so here. Both the feminist movement and the Islamic reform movement were linked from their inception. Muslim urban elite women, not in opposition to Islam, but in order to promote a more accurate reading of Islamic moral and legal norms, began the feminist movement itself. Therefore, the early manifestations of the feminist movement in Egypt were not a transfer of western ideals to upper class women in order for these ideals to supplant Islamic norms. See: Abdel Kader, *Egyptian Women*, 3,5, and 50–52; Margot Badran, *Feminism in Islam* (Oxford: Oneworld Publications, 2009), 67–68.

[6] Some of the most prominent works in this field are: Soha Abdel Kader, *Egyptian Women*; Leila Ahmed, *Women and Gender in Islam: Historical Roots of a Modern Debate* (New Haven: Yale University Press, 1992); Margot Badran, *Feminism in Islam*; Margot Badran and Miriam Cooke eds., *Opening the Gates* (London: Virago Press, 1990); Beth Baron, *Egypt as a Woman* (Berkely: University of California Press, 2005); Huda Sha'rawi, *Harem Years* (New York: The Feminist Press, 1986); Tucker, *Women in nineteenth-century Egypt.*

It is difficult to put a start date to the rise of feminism in Egypt. Many authors have given the publication of Qasim Amīn's *Taḥrīr al-Mar'a* in 1899 as the catalyst for the movement.[7] While there is no doubt that Amīn's work was a monumental step in the direction of feminism in Egypt, he was certainly not the first to address the issue of women in society. As Margot Badran writes, women themselves had been publishing on various proto-feminist issues several decades before Amīn's work.[8] In addition to these writings by women, 'ulamā' like Tahṭāwī and 'Alī Mubarāk were drawing attention to the importance of educating women for the improvement of the nation even earlier. It is clear, however, that by the turn of the 20th century the feminist movement and the reforms it called for were very much a part of the national conversation in Egypt. And this conversation impacted the codification of personal status laws throughout the 1920s.

'Abduh commented in the introduction to his report on the Sharī'a courts that the courts and the personal status laws that governed them dealt with the most sensitive of areas: the family and, by extension, women.[9] Even though there was a wide range of cases adjudicated in the Sharī'a courts, the majority dealt with situations of marriage and divorce, which is why the codification of personal status law largely dealt with these two issues. In addition to this, and as 'Abduh made note of, these courts were very popular amongst different classes of people and were, for the most part, trusted.[10] This trust largely stemmed from the role of the qādī who served as a bridge between the world of the 'ulamā' and the world of social trends.[11] By analyzing data on the Sharī'a courts, particu-

---

[7] Huda Sha'rāwī herself claimed that Amīn was the first to address issues of concern for women: Huda Sha'rāwī, "Dawr al-Mar'a fī Ḥarakat al-Taṭawwur al-'Ālī" (A speech given at the American University in Cairo November 12, 1929), 18.

[8] Badran, *Feminism in Islam*, 55–57.

[9] 'Amāra, *al-'Amāl al-Kāmila lil Shaykh Muḥammad 'Abduh*, 3:213.

[10] 'Amāra, *al-'Amāl al-Kāmila-'Abduh*, 3:213; Tucker, *Women in nineteenth-century Egypt*, 13.

[11] Shaham, *Family and the Courts in Modern Egypt*, 15–18; Tucker, *Women in nineteenth-century Egypt*, 14.

larly in the late 19th, and early the 20th century, scholars have been able to provide us with a window into some of these dynamics. For example, we know that polygamy as a practice was in fact limited in incident, but that divorce was epidemic.[12] Furthermore, these situations of divorce often played out to the disadvantage of women, both socially and financially. For example, Tucker demonstrates that judges were unlikely to grant women *faskh*-divorces (allowing women to retain their dowry) and inclined more towards *khul'*-divorces (in which a women would have to return the dowry) which was often economically disadvantageous to women, particularly lower class women who could not afford such release payments or even the court fees involved in processing these cases.[13] There was also the problem of absent husbands and the inability of women to receive divorces (the Ḥanafī position) to enable them to move on to another marriage, an issue I address below. At the same time the Sharī'a courts were also a place in which women could exert significant power by negotiating and protecting their own financial assets.[14] Women were able to manage these affairs with a great deal of freedom and success and the sources tell many stories of the Sharī'a courts preventing relatives attempting to defraud women of their inheritance.[15] The Sharī'a courts, therefore, were an important meeting point of Islamic law and societal issues concerning women.

A third part of this nexus was the state.[16] However, it seems that the problem between the Sharī'a courts and the state was not too much intervention, but a lack of intervention, oversight, and care. Both 'Abduh and Shākir lamented the state of the Sharī'a courts; Shākir even claimed that they were beyond repair as they had been neglected for too long.[17] It is important, therefore, to read the laws and opinions of the court not as points of tension

---

[12] Tucker, *Women in nineteenth-century Egypt*, 52–54.

[13] Ibid., 54.

[14] Ibid.

[15] Ibid., 60.

[16] Ibid., 12–14.

[17] Aḥmad Shākir, *Taqrīr 'an Shu'ūn al-T'alīm wa'l Qaḍā'* (Cairo: Maktabat Imām al-Bukhārī, 2009), 57.

between Islamic law and the state, but rather the meeting point of Islamic law and society.[18]

The feminist movement in Egypt arose primarily as an urban movement involving upper class women.[19] These women were educated in European languages and subjects, and French played an important role as the main language of discourse. As Badran makes clear in her introduction to Sha'rāwī's memoirs, French was the social language of upper-class women in Egypt.[20] These were not women that frequented the Sharī'a courts personally, women could always send a *wakīl*, and their major social functions revolved around family, and if accessible, the Royal court. Aside from the Arabic discourse at the time that occurred amongst the 'ulamā',

---

[18] In her introduction, Judith Tucker uses as an example of the "tension" between the state and the Sharī'a courts a particular fatwa issued by Shaykh al-Mahdī opining on a forced divorce from a judge to indicate that the State had interfered and forced Mahdī to rule a certain way. However, this is a misreading of Mahdī's actual fatwa. The text of Mahdī's fatwa reads, "*ṭalāq al-mukrah wāqi'un 'indinā, wa Allahu ta'āla 'a'lam*" meaning that a coerced divorce is valid in the Ḥanafī school and has effect. The pronoun *naḥnu* refers to Mahdī's school of legal thought and not to "what is found common today" as Tucker translates it. In addition, the closing statement "God is most high and knows best" is how fatwas are traditionally concluded as a sign that one's position is based on probability not absolute certainty. Therefore, Mahdī's fatwa was not coerced by the state and this is not a phrase used by him to lament the current state of affairs. There is an issue, however, with Mahdī's fatwa. It demonstrates that he was a strict Ḥanafī and since this was the legal school being used to issue fatwas and adjudicate cases of personal status, the coerced act is valid. Tucker's point, as well as many other scholars, that Islam alone is not the singular force operating in these circumstances, and that there are a multitude of forces at play is very important to understand for women's issues, particularly divorce, were very much a part of how personal status law came to be codified. For the actual text of the fatwa see: al-'Abbāsī al-Mahdī, *al-Fatāwa al-Mahdiyya fi'l Waqā'i al-Miṣriyya*, 6 vols., (Cairo: al-Maṭba'a al-Azhariyya, 1301 AH), 1:154. For Tuker's discussion of this fatwa see: Tucker, *Women in nineteenth-century Egypt*, 13.

[19] Abdel Kader, *Egyptian Women in a Changing Society*, 50.

[20] Sha'rāwī, *Harem Years*, 1.

French served as a main language of intellectual exchange. It is no coincidence, then, that Amīn's first work was in French and the journal issued by Egyptian Feminist Union was also published in French. Even though Badran states that Sha'rāwī made an effort to turn to Arabic towards the end of her years, her memoirs were written in Arabic for example, the effects of her European education and social discourse lasted her whole life. Since it was not common for the 'ulamā' to have learned French, it remains to be determined the exact impact the early phase of the feminist movement had on the thinking of the 'ulamā'. We know that some 'ulamā' like 'Abduh knew French and were able to access works in French, but this most likely was the exception, not the rule. In this regard, the participation of the 'ulamā' in the feminist movement is largely based on what they *saw*, not what they read. Since, as Badran asserts, the feminist movement had to be translated into practice from theory, it was issues of veiling and women's general seclusion in society that became hotly contested areas and not necessarily issues of gender.[21]

QĀSIM AMĪN

Qāsim Amīn (d.1908) was born to a Turkish father and an Egyptian mother. From the time of his birth Amīn was part of the Turkish-Circassian elite community in Egypt. This meant that he attended elite schools in Alexandria where he received a primarily French education. In a similar fashion to Qadrī Pashā several decades earlier, Amīn completed his primary education and was bound

[21] Throughout discussions of feminism in Egypt, the word ḥijāb is often used and often misunderstood. The term *ḥijāb* as used by early feminist writers is a reference to the seclusion of women from society, and not a reference to the head covering today also commonly known as ḥijāb. The issue of "veiling" is a reference to the Islamic practice of *niqāb*, which is when a woman covers her face in addition to covering her hair and neck. The *sufūr* that writers refer to in this regard is the act of women uncovering their faces and only later became a reference to removing the head covering altogether. For some discussion on terminology see: Badran, *Feminism in Egypt*, 87; Baron, *Egypt as a Woman*, 35–36; Elgawhary, *Responding from the Tradition*, 317–319.

for the newly formed Khedival School of Law and Administration. He was amongst the first to graduate from the school in 1881 having received a degree in French law.[22] He left for France to continue his studies and received a law degree from the University of Montpellier in 1885. Amīn returned to Egypt to serve as a judge, first in the Mixed courts then in the Native courts, a position he retained for the duration of his life.[23]

In discussing his educational background and the various influences on him, Amīn's chief biographer Muḥammad 'Amāra claims that Amīn first met Jamāl al-Dīn al-Afghānī (d. 1897) in Cairo and joined his study circles. He further asserts that Amīn later reunited with both Afghānī and 'Abduh when the two were exiled in Paris.[24] 'Amārā also states that Amīn served as a translator for 'Abduh during this period providing 'Abduh with the needed language skills to translate certain French works in addition to helping in the production and publication of the journal *al-'Urwat al-Wuthqā*.[25] There are virtually no sources that discuss who exactly attended Afghānī's circles in Cairo and even less information about what exactly happened behind the scenes in the production of al-'Urwat al-Wuthqā.[26] However, there was a strong relationship and deep friendship between Amīn and 'Abduh that developed over time.[27] It is difficult to know, however, the extent of Amīn's involvement with Afghānī's study circles and what exactly he studied from the Islamic sciences, which would have had to be supplemental lessons he sought out outside his formal education. I assume that he did have a cursory knowledge of some of the funda-

---

[22] Muḥammad 'Amāra, *al-'Amāl al-Kāmila li Qāsim Amīn* (Cairo: Dār al-Shurūq, 1989), 21.

[23] Ibid., 25.

[24] Ibid., 21–22.

[25] Ibid.

[26] One source I have been able to locate, however, cites that Shaykh Bakhīt al-Muṭī'ī, whom I discuss in chapter 4, did in fact attend the lessons of Afghānī. See: Aḥmad ibn Siddiq al-Ghumārī, *al-Baḥr al-'Amīq fī Marwiyāt Ibn al-Siddīq*, 2 vols., (Cairo: Dār al-Kutbā, 2007), 1:208–209.

[27] See for example his eulogy of 'Abduh: 'Amāra, *al-'Amāl al-Kāmila li Qāsim Amīn*, 312–317.

mentals of Islamic law and he most likely had some classes on this at the law school, but his core training was in French law.

More than anyone, Qāsim Amīn is credited with being a catalyst for the feminist movement in Egypt.[28] Although, as alluded to above, there were women writing about similar topics before him, it was not until Amīn's famous work Taḥrīr al-Mar'a (published 1899) that the issues of the feminist movement came to public attention and in so doing caused a massive response.[29] His Arabic works on this subject (Taḥrīr al-Mar'a – 1899 and *al-Mar'a al-Missriyya al-Jadīda* – 1900) remain essential components to any discussion about Islam and feminism in Egypt not because they were necessarily or fundamentally feminist writings,[30] but because Amīn was able to provide a bridge between the French elite discourse of Egypt in the late 19th/early20th century Egypt and the discourse of the 'ulamā', particularly vis-à-vis Muḥammad 'Abduh, which was a discourse that had hitherto been isolated and contained amongst the 'ulamā'. Amīn's writings, therefore, were a first attempt to link aspects of the feminist movement to a corresponding dialogue and conversation within the world of Islamic thought and law.

Taḥrīr al-Mar'a and the Collaboration of Muḥammad 'Abduh

Amīn addressed issues related to women, and specifically marriage and divorce in his three books. [31] Since my study is focused on the

---

[28] Huda Sha'rāwī also held this view. See note 7 above. This notion, however, is currently being re-examined mostly by Leila Ahmed. See: Ahmed, *Women and Gender in Islam.*

[29] Badran mentions that over thirty works were written in response to *Taḥrīr al-Mar'a.* See her introduction in Sha'rāwī's Harem Years. Also consult Hourani, *Arabic Thought*, 164.

[30] This is one of the main points of Leila Ahmed's *Women and Gender in Islam.*

[31] Qasim Amīn, *Les Égyptiens* (Cairo: Jules Barbier, 1894). This work has been translated into Arabic: 'Amāra, *al-'Amāl al-Kāmila li Qāsim Amīn,* 219–307; Qāsim Amīn, *Taḥrīr al-Mar'a* (Cairo: Maktabat al-Taraqī, 1899); Qasim Amin, "*al-Mar'a al-Jadīda*", in *al-'Amāl al-Kāmila li Qāsim Amīn*, ed. Muḥammad 'Amāra, 419–517. Both these works have been translated into English: Peterson, Samiha Sidhom trans., *The Liberation of Women and The*

codification of personal status law generally, and the codification of divorce law specifically, it is Tahrīr al-Mar'a that will occupy the discussion below.[32]

The publication of Taḥrīr al-Mar'a itself produced over thirty books and pamphlets in response, some against and some in support. While his first work was addressed largely to a French audience and was done with the purpose of defending Egypt and Islam, both his later works were addressed to Egyptians first and foremost and took a more critical approach to Islamic practices. Taḥrīr al-Mar'a was written by Amīn to address two main points: social issues relating to women that became problematic (women's seclusion, lack of education, and other associated social mores), as well as the treatment of other issues in classical Islamic legal discourse (the face-veil, divorce practices, and polygamy) as opposed to how they have been manifested in a particular Islamic culture.

Amīn's opening lines in Taḥrīr al-Mar'a admit that the book is indeed an innovation (bid'a), not against Islam, but rather against social norms that have gone awry. Amīn argued for the equality of men and women and saw this as a fundamental right protected by the Sharī'a.[33] This is often times obfuscated, in Amīn's opinion, because of a conflating of cultural and religious matters regarding gender.

Stemming from his concept of women as equals, Amīn discussed the issue of women's education. He equated universal education for women as the key to their liberation from seclusion and isolation in society as well as the path towards winning them more

---

New Women (Cairo: The American University in Cairo Press, 1992). Regarding the French work, it is very unlikely that it had a wide readership in Egypt outside the French reading elite. Most of the sources consulted for this section exclusively cite the *Taḥrīr al-Mar'a.* One notable exception is: G.WJ. Drewes, "Qasim Amin, Egyptisch Feminist: (1865–1908)" *Bijdragen tot de Taal-,Land-en Volkenkunde, Deel 114, 1ste/2de Afl (1958)*, 55–71.

[32] Amīn's *Taḥrīr al-Mar'a* contains a very nuanced discussion of Islamic law's treatment of marriage and divorce. These discussions are largely absent from his first and last work.

[33] Amīn, *Taḥrīr*, 12.

respect from within their own family structures.[34] A woman cannot be respected by her spouse, or be capable of raising her children, if she is not educated. For Amīn, this education goes beyond what he viewed as the superficialities of what was termed women's education at the time.[35] He wanted to see girls attend schools alongside boys and to see women be part of the workforce as they were in Europe, his model for a just and equitable society.[36]

The discussions that are most relevant to our topic, however, are those that Amīn links directly to Islamic legal discourses. These sections take on the issues of women's face veil, marriage, polygamy, and divorce. However, Amīn never provided a detailed account of Islamic legal sources and their discussions of these topics. Not only are the legal discussions in Taḥrīr al-Mar'a very similar to what was being said by other 'ulamā' on similar topics, it is peculiar that such a detailed Sharī'a discussion should take place by an untrained, secular lawyer. In light of this, Muḥammad 'Amāra, who collected and published the complete works of both Amīn and 'Abduh, has posited that these sections were most likely written by 'Abduh himself, not Amīn.[37] 'Amāra's arguments can be distilled to three central themes:[38]

1. There are some references by contemporaries that demonstrate that the book Taḥrīr al-Mar'a was a joint project between both Amīn and 'Abduh.[39]
2. The writings in the sections under question resemble earlier writings by Muḥammad 'Abduh.[40]

---

[34] Amīn, *Taḥrīr*, 25–26.

[35] Amīn laments the fact that the entirety of French education had been reduced to women learning to say good morning and good evening in French. Amīn, *Taḥrīr*, 53.

[36] Amīn observed that the middle class in France was better and more moral than its counterpart in Egypt. Hourani, *Islamic Thought*, 169.

[37] This discussion can be found in: 'Amāra, *al-A'amāl al-Kāmila lil Shaykh Muḥammad 'Abduh*, 1:254–275. Margot Badran also holds this opinion: Badran, *Feminism in Islam*, 61.

[38] Amāra, *al-'Amāl al-Kāmila lil Shaykh Muḥammad 'Abduh*, 1:264–265.

[39] Ibid., 1:262–263.

[40] Ibid., 1:263–264.

3. The Sharīʿa discussions in the sections under question would have had to be written by a Muslim jurist, which Amīn was not.[41]

Of these themes, I find the first and the third to be the most significant. ʿAmāra quotes from the memoirs of Aḥmad Shafīq Pasha, the Khedive's personal secretary, that he was propositioned by Qasīm Amīn to help with Taḥrīr al-Mar'a and that in fact it what was ʿAbduh who offered assistance after he declined to help. This notion is seconded by Shafīq's daughter, Ḍurriyya, in her work co-authored with Ibrahīm ʿAbduh *Taṭawwur al-Nahḍa al-Nisā'iyya fī Miṣr*.[42] These are the two main historical documentations that ʿAmārā relies on to support his claim. The second theme, and perhaps the most convincing, is that Amīn, a secular trained lawyer with no formal Sharīʿa education, would most likely not have been able to write these sections at all. The language of these sections is the language of Islamic jurisprudence, with extensive quotes from legal sources within the different schools of law and providing preferences (*tarjiḥ*) on which ones are more appropriate in light of modern realities. This is essentially the process of ijtihād and is the style that someone like Muḥammad ʿAbduh would write in, as in fact he did later as Grand Mufti. The personal status law training that Amīn might have had in the Khedival school would have been in Ḥanafī law.[43] Since the legal discussion in Taḥrīr al-Mar'a gave preferences to Mālikī positions, and since ʿAbduh was originally trained in the Mālikī school and had an interest in printing earlier Mālikī works like the *Mudawanna*, this gives further reason to assume that ʿAbduh had a large role in writings these sections.[44] Lastly, the codes that are offered at the end of Taḥrīr al-Mar'a would have had to include the input of not just a Muslim jurist, but a

---

[41] Ibid.

[42] Aḥmad Shafīq, *ʿAmālī bʿad Mudhakkirātī* (Cairo: Maṭbaʿat Miṣr, 1941), 352; Ḍurriya Shafīq, *Taṭawwur al-Nahḍah al-Nisā'īyah fī Miṣr min ʿahd Muḥammad ʿAlī ilā ʿahd al-Fārūq* (Cairo: Maktabat al-Ādāb, 1945), 252, 274–275.

[43] See note 51 in chapter 1.

[44] Riḍa, *Tārīkh al-Ustādh al-Imām*, 1:940–941.

Sharīʿa court judge, which ʿAbduh was at the time of the works composition and publication. While I cannot definitively say, as ʿAmāra has, that ʿAbduh is indeed the author of these sections, my position is that they were at least influenced by Muḥammad ʿAbduh and his perspectives on Islamic law and the codification of personal status law.

The discussion of divorce begins with language similar to that found in law 25 of 1929 discussed in the previous chapter. Divorce is something that is frowned upon in Islam and something that the Sharīʿa intends to be restricted, not widespread.[45] The nature of the human condition and the nature of marriage have made divorce a necessity and therefore it is to be approached with great care.[46] The discussion turns to cite the standard Ḥanafī position that a divorce pronouncement associated with a number has effect equal to the amount of that number. For example, if a man were to tell his wife, "you are divorced two times" this would count as two divorces, not one. The Ḥanafī position also holds that the divorce of a coerced man (*mukrah*) has effect, as does the divorce initiated by an intoxicated person. Acknowledging that this is not just the Ḥanafī position, but the dominant position amongst the jurists, the discussion equally acknowledges that this is not the only opinion on this subject that has existed throughout Islamic jurisprudence and there are others that have taken into consideration the general welfare of society (*al-maṣlaḥa al-ʿāmma*) over the explicit readings of the source texts.[47] These dissenting positions are referenced as belonging to Ibn al-Qayyim, al-Shawkāni (d.1250/1834), and jurists of the

---

[45] Amīn, *Taḥrīr*, 165–166.

[46] Ibid.

[47] The difference being that the ratio legis for the Ḥanafī school is following the source texts as they are graded soundly, while other schools look to different issues. However, this argument is not entirely accurate since the position that a thrice-pronounced divorce only counts as one is not due to social welfare, but because those jurists find the ḥadīth of Ibn ʿAbbās (discussed below) involving divorce to be sounder than the ḥadīth of ʿUmar. It is the choosing of one opinion over the other (*ikhtiyār*) that takes into consideration social welfare, not the ratio legis of the position itself.

Imāmī school. The main ratio legis given for this dissenting opinion in this discussion, and something that will be discussed in greater detail in the section on Aḥmad Shākir below, is the ḥadīth narrated by Ibn ʻAbbās concerning the Companion Rukāna's thrice pronounced divorce and the Prophet informing him that this divorce only counted as one, and to take back his wife.[48] This section on divorce is concluded with offering five recommended codes that:

1. Introduces a magistrate into the divorce proceeding and obligates the husband intending to issue a divorce to do so in front of this magistrate.
2. If the husband still intends on divorce after being warned of its effects by the magistrate, a representative from both the husband's family the wife's family are required to intervene to attempt a reconciliation (*ṣulḥ*).
3. If this does not work a divorce is granted.[49]

The proposed codes conclude that only this type of divorce be recognized, and no other divorce be given legal weight.[50]

From the brief discussion of divorce in Taḥrīr al-Mar'a, it is clear that it follows a very similar pattern to the ʻulamā' of the pervious chapter who wrote actual codes of personal status law. The argument includes the key elements of: the need to look for other opinions (this being a form of ijtihād), the importance of following opinions outside one's main school when the situation calls for it (talfīq), and the introduction of the courts to help regulate and mitigate the divorce process (the courts being a function of the state – al-siyāsa al-shar'iyya).

---

[48] Amīn, *Taḥrīr*, 172.

[49] Ibid., 179.

[50] This is ironic and perhaps another argument for ʻAbduh's involvement since Amīn himself criticized the involvement of the French courts in the divorce process in his first book.

MUḤAMMAD ʿABDUH

Indeed it is tempting to appropriate ʿAbduh as the quintessential supporter of codification and to read this support as a key function of modernist Islam, as has been done by others when discussing ʿAbduh.[51] By the time ʿAbduh was addressing issues of the expression of Islamic law against modern realities, he was a judge and the Grand Mufti of Egypt, a position he held until nearly his death in 1905. In this stage of ʿAbduh's life, he had long put behind him the political aspirations of al-Afghānī.[52] He reversed his position regarding the British and saw the need and utility of working with them as well as his own government and he had become overly concerned with reforming education for judges and for students at al-Azhar (a project he sought to dedicate the rest of his life to). He also began issuing fatwas that have become the source of study until today. It was in this very stage of ʿAbduh's life that he addressed the issue of codifying personal status law generally and sought to reform various aspects of divorce law specifically, which was an outgrowth of his study on the status of Sharīʿa courts at the end of the 19th century. This aspect of ʿAbduh's life and thought is unfortunately something that has not been explored in great length.[53] Even the most recent of works, Mark Sedwick's biography for example, lend too many pages to issues that are largely un-

---

[51] As Mark Sedgwick has observed, most people writing about ʿAbduh have been concerned with specific issues and angles, rather than treating ʿAbduh as a whole. Mark Sedwick, *Muhammad Abduh* (Oxford: Oneworld, 2010), xii.

[52] ʿAmāra, *al-ʿAmāl al-Kāmila lil Shaykh Muḥammad ʿAbduh*, 1:241; Sedwick, *Muhammad Abduh*, 57–59.

[53] A notable exception to this is the work of Ignac Goldziher *Die Richtungen Der Islamischen Koranauslegung* in which a section is dedicated to outlining ʿAbduh's interpretive methodology, largely taken from articles found in the *Manār* journal. In so doing, Goldziher describes how ʿAbduh eschewed the hard differences expressed by different schools of Islamic law. This led to ʿAbduh's anti-*taqlīd* position regarding fiqh matters and the need to find meanings and rulings directly from the original texts (the Qur'an and sunna) by way of *ijtihād*.

substantiated and did not have as much lasting impact as his various positions regarding certain Sharīʿa rulings.[54]

In the pages that follow, I will focus on ʿAbduh's writings as they relate to codification of personal status law, this will be the majority of the discussion, and his treatment of divorce issues, particularly the issue of a thrice-pronounced divorce counting as one, which will form the lesser of the two discussions.

ʿAbduh's Treatment of Islamic Law and Codification of Personal Status Law

Although ʿAbduh did not leave us with a written work on his legal methodology, this is not to say that he did not have a distinct perspective on interpreting, or re-interpreting Islamic law as the case may be. The challenge is that this theory needs to be gathered from his writings, particularly those written during his tenure as judge and Grand Mufti.

When ʿAbduh began to turn his efforts to addressing the need for legal reform in Egypt, he was also attempting to overhaul the system of education at al-Azhar. We know from ʿAbduh's own autobiographical account that he had an early traumatic experience with al-Azhar style learning. This came while a grammar-age student attending the al-Azhar schools in Ṭanṭa. ʿAbduh described that while attending a class on the *Ajrumiyya*, a 14th century grammar text composed by Ibn Ajrūm (d. 723/1323), the teacher was constantly using advanced technical terms that none of the students had studied or heard of before. Therefore, the class was completely unintelligible to ʿAbduh and he learned nothing. This incident caused ʿAbduh to forgo education altogether and run away

---

[54] Both Sedwick and Kedourie lend too many pages to discussing ʿAbduh's affiliation with Free Masonry and attempting to define him as a "free-thinker" who was at best an agnostic. These types of comments pass over the important discussions ʿAbduh had on various aspects on Islamic law and stem from a general distrust of the Islamic legal tradition that assumes anyone thinking outside the box to be a closet atheist. See Ellie Kedourie, *Afghani and 'Abduh: an essay on religious unbelief and political activism in modern Islam* (Berkeley: University of California Press, 1966), 20, 22, 63–65; Sedwick, *Muhammad Abduh*, 19–21, 35, 114.

until he met his maternal uncle who slowly re-directed him back to school. It is interesting that 'Abduh continued to reference this incident and the trauma of this learning process lasted, by his own account, for the rest of his life.[55] This was for him a critical reason why educational reform was desperately needed at al-Azhar. 'Abduh's main contention was that the education of the 'ulamā' was too scholastic, relying on endless glosses composed in the later period of the Sunnī tradition. This caused students to be flooded with technical jargon, in much the same way he was, that detached the subjects being studied from reality and application. 'Abduh also felt there was a need to revive earlier texts of the formative period for publication and study and this related directly to the study of Islamic law. He worked with scholars in North Africa, for example, to acquire manuscripts of the Mudawwana of the Mālikī school in order to publish a critical edition.[56] This is also the reason why he opted not to re-print Ibn 'Arabī's *al-Futuḥāt al-Makiyya*. Not because he was against Sufism as some authors have argued, but because the market was saturated with these types of work, and void of earlier works.[57] His discussions of legal matters, as we will see below, reflect this attitude of using earlier writings of jurists (Qadī Abū Bakr ibn al-'Arabī [543/1148] features frequently in 'Abduh's writings) as well as pro-ijtihād jurists like al-Shawkānī.

---

[55] Amāra, *al-'Amāl al-Kāmila lil Shaykh Muḥammad 'Abduh*, 3:192–193.

[56] Ibid., 2:362–363.

[57] According to dictionaries of published works of the late 19th century and early 20th century, the *Futuḥāt al-Makiyya* was a popular book. See for example Joseph Sarkīs, *Mu'jam al-Maṭbū'āt al-'Arabiyya wa'l Mu'āraba*. Keeping in mind 'Abduh's dedication to Sufism, ('Amāra, *al-A'amāl al-Kāmila lil Shaykh Muḥammad 'Abduh,* 3:193) he commented to Riḍā that not only is the *Futuḥāt al-Makiyya* easy for him to read, but that he had experienced many of the spiritual states mentioned in the work (Riḍa, *Tarīkh al-Ustādh al-Imām*, 1:929). It is unlikely, therefore, that his refusal to publish the work stemmed, like Riḍā makes it seem, from a negative view of the book. Rather, it was most likely a sentiment that the market had become saturated with those types of work and new ones need to be published. See Riḍa's comments cited in: Hourani, *Islamic Thought*, 150.

'Abduh's theory of Sharī'a was a function of his overall view of Islamic history and its cycles of growth and decay. 'Abduh viewed the formative period of Islam, a period that he stated lasted until the 'Abbāsids came to power in 750/1261, as a period in which Greek knowledge and other ancient wisdom came to the Arabs. The Arabs, having already Arabized Islam, mimicked this with Greek knowledge and wisdom.[58] This changed, however, when the 'Abbāsids adopted non-Arab Turkic troops for their protection and worldly gain transferring Islam to foreigners (*'ajam*).[59] These foreigners, in 'Abduh's narrative, approached Islam with a roughness and ignorance (*khushūna wa jahl*) and were the cause of many foreign elements seeping into Muslim practices, which themselves caused a gap between the ruling class and the 'ulamā'.[60] In addition to this lamentable syncretism, 'Abduh's main argument was that this introduced a stunting of intellectual growth (*jumūd*) which spread to every aspect of Islamic life and thought. In relation to law the effects of this *jumūd* were to make the Sharī'a and its rulings difficult on people and society.[61] This caused people to slowly leave the Sharī'a, and more importantly, reduced the number of people who actually understood how Islamic law was to be understood and applied. On this latter point, 'Abduh commented that:

> Contemporary 'ulamā' do not concern themselves with improving the nation. They have confined their knowledge to the commentaries, glosses, and meta-glosses of ancient texts. They are ignorant of anything else as if they are not of this world, not even of the people of this universe. Rather, they live on the periphery of society.[62]

'Abduh's understanding of Islamic history and the onset of jumūd as an endemic problem amongst the 'ulamā' relates to his eight principles upon which is build Islamic thought and by which one

---

[58] Muḥammad 'Abduh, *Islām Dīn al-'Ilm wa'l Madaniyya* (Cairo: Dār al-Hilāl, n.d.), 132.

[59] Ibid. This is a reference to non-Arabs.

[60] Ibid., 133.

[61] Ibid., 138.

[62] Amīn, *Muḥammad 'Abduh*, 102.

can access the primary sources of Islam.[63] Of these principles, three are pertinent to this discussion. The first of these principles is that when literal readings of a text run counter to reason one must advance reason over literal meanings. Although this relates largely to ʿAbduh's methodology of Qur'anic exegesis, it finds its way in his legal interpretative methodology as well. When asked, for example, to issue a fatwa concerning the correct belief of the flood of Noah (i.e. is it a literal world-wide flood, or not), ʿAbduh held that the meaning of the historic flood event should be restricted by science and reason arguing that, "it is incumbent upon all who believe not to deny any literal meaning of a Qur'anic verse or Prophetic tradition which contains sound chains of narration unless one adduces a rational proof (*dalīl ʿaqlī*) that demonstrates the literal meaning is not meant."[64] The second principle of note is ʿAbduh's claim that Islam completely inverted the structure of religious authority and destroyed existing religious establishments. Islam established in their stead the word of God (the Qur'an) and the teachings of the Prophet (ḥadīth and sunna). Again, when it comes to law ʿAbduh wrote and lamented on how the glosses of the late period caused people to replace the original sources of Islam as authoritative. Therefore, ʿAbduh put a premium on directly deriving rulings from the Qur'an and sunna. The last principle is that social welfare (maṣlaḥa) and the welfare of the hereafter are always combined in Islam. This is to say that Islam offers a balance of this worldly and otherworldly concern with each action that is legislated. Therefore, it is not possible for the Sharīʿa to command to-

[63] ʿAbduh's eight principles are: (1) Reason begets faith, (2) advancing reason over literal meanings when literal meanings of texts counter reason, (3) staying away from apostazing (*takfīr*) one another, (4) Contemplating God's work in the universe, (5) inverting the structure of religious authority, (6) protecting calling others to Islam (*dʿawa*) in order to offset civil strife, (7) inter marriage, and (8) advancing human health above religion. ʿAbduh, *al-Islām Din al-ʿIlm wa'l Madaniyya*, 95–109.

[64] Riḍā, *Tārīkh al-Ustādh al-Imām*, 1:667.

wards an action that would cause harm in this world, as this is not what the Sharīʿa has been set up to do.[65]

While ʿAbduh identified one of Islam's unique traits as having inverted the religious authoritative establishment, he grew to hold a slightly different view towards the political one. Before ʿAbduh's exile from Egypt he was politically active following the example of his teacher Afghānī. In this sense he was very much against the British occupation and the weak Egyptian government that allowed it. Upon his return to Egypt, however, his perspective towards both the British and the Egyptian regime changed. While ʿAbduh opined very strongly that Islam is built on a refusal of all other laws that violate the Sharīʿa, he saw that the political establishment was necessary for the enforcement of the system and its laws, including the Sharīʿa.[66] Therefore, the Sharīʿa itself affords legitimacy and civil power (*al-madaniyya*) to the political establishment.[67] It is only by the state that the Sharīʿa can be applied, a comment he also made in assessing the state of the Sharīʿa courts.[68] Although ʿAbduh did not use the term al-siyāsa al-sharʿiyya, I understand his comments here to be precisely his view on the topic and one that echoes the arguments of al-Minyāwī in the previous chapter.

In the year 1899 Muḥammad ʿAbduh was appointed to the position of Grand Mufti of Egypt. As part of this appointment he was to lead a committee that was tasked with inspecting the Sharīʿa courts. To better inform himself of the actual state of the courts he set out in the summer of 1899 traveling the entire country inspecting every branch and office of the Sharīʿa courts. By November of the same year he compiled his report and recommendations. This report, preserved for us in his collected works, provides one of the

---

[65] ʿAbduh, *al-Islām Dīn al-ʿIlm wa'l Madaniyya*, 108. The example ʿAbduh gives is not having to make ablutions with freezing water in order to be in a state of ritual purity for prayer. Some of ʿAbduh's commentators like al-Kaylānī reference this line of thinking to al-Shāṭibī's concept of maṣlaḥa. See: Shams al-Dīn al-Kaylānī, *al-Imām Muḥammad ʿAbduh* (Cairo: al-Ahlī li'l Ṭibāʿa wa'l Tawzīʿ, 2001), 34.

[66] ʿAbduh, *al-Islām Dīn al-ʿIlm wa'l Madaniyya*, 16, 100.

[67] Ibid., 102.

[68] This is a topic that will be discussed below.

most valuable windows into how the Sharīʿa courts actually functioned in Egypt at the turn of the 20th century. ʿAbduh's general observations of the Sharīʿa courts indicate that they were frequented by all different classes of Egyptians, not just lower class peasants.[69] These litigants, despite their social background, placed a lot of trust in the Sharīʿa courts, more so than the Mixed courts.[70] Even though the Mixed courts were established to handle cases of foreign nationals, Egyptian national litigants frequented the courts since the jurisdiction of the Mixed courts applied anytime when at least one litigant was a foreign national. It is conceivable and highly probable that Egyptian merchants and business leaders would have had a familiarity with these courts at this time alongside their own experiences in the Sharīʿa courts. In addition to the trust people had of the Sharīʿa courts, the courts dealt with sensitive family matters, the core of personal status law, and ʿAbduh reminded his readers that this gave the Sharīʿa courts a rare power to either be the source of great assistance, or the cause of great ruin.[71]

ʿAbduh's main objective in the report was to provide a detailed account of the inner workings of the courts, the problems with the personnel of the courts, and offer recommendations to make them better. ʿAbduh found the level of training of both the scribes and the judges to be sub-optimal. As a minimum, ʿAbduh claimed that judges need to have an intimate knowledge of Islamic law and its details to be able to properly adjudicate cases.[72] This requisite knowledge also applies to scribes as far as ʿAbduh was concerned. He observed that they could barely write and had no knowledge of Islamic law whatsoever. ʿAbduh also saw that deficiency in training manifested in other ways. For example, he observed that many cases ended by mediation and reconciliation (ṣulḥ) between the parties instead of actually being tried in a court by a judge. For ʿAbduh, this lack of training was a result of the poor educational methodology of al-Azhar, a theme he never let go

[69] Tucker's works, however, focuses largely on lower class peasants. Tucker, *Women in nineteenth-century Egypt.*

[70] ʿAmāra, *al-ʿAmāl al-Kāmila lil Shaykh Muḥammad ʿAbduh*, 2:213–214.

[71] Ibid.

[72] Ibid.

of throughout his life.[73] He argued that not only should the 'alimiyya degree be a prerequisite for being a judge, but that future judges should also have practical training and apprenticeships in the courts.[74] This is similar to his general critique of his contemporary 'ulamā' not having training in applying their area of expertise and receding to periphery of society.[75]

'Abduh's greatest complaints, however, refer to the way the law was actually dealt with in the Sharī'a courts. Judges lack of proper Sharī'a training was coupled with their strict and almost blind adherence to Ḥanafī rulings and procedures. For 'Abduh, this led to great delays in rulings that caused more harm than good, a topic I discuss in the next section. In other writings, 'Abduh commented on the problems of adhering to just the Ḥanafī school of law and specifically relying on Ḥanafī sources written in the later period.[76] In the context of the Sharī'a courts, 'Abduh saw a dire need to rely on all four schools of sunnī law in order to find appropriate rulings for situations, like the issue of a thrice-pronounced divorce. This eclectic approach (read talfīq) needed to go beyond the letter of the law and aim for the spirit of law in the same way as the early Imāms of the four Sunnī schools did.[77] 'Abduh's example in this regard is the undue hardship and time lost in following the Ḥanafī procedure in trying a case when the defendant is absent or missing. This is particularly damaging to poor women, often times the plaintiffs seeking to redress monetary rights taken from them by absent husbands, in which their literal daily bread depended on a speedy judgment.[78] Since 'Abduh saw current judges of the Sharī'a courts as ill trained to be able to delve into the depths of the legal schools to find these nuanced rulings, they must be aided, he argued, by the process of codification. While he recognized that this process was taking place in Egypt in the area of

---

[73] Ibid., 270–271.

[74] Ibid., 222.

[75] These are comments he made to the then Shaykh al-Islām in Istanbul. 'Amāra, *al-'Amāl al-Kāmila lil Shaykh Muḥammad 'Abduh*, 1:881–883.

[76] Riḍa, *Tārīkh al-Ustādh al-Imām*, 1.2:943–944.

[77] 'Amāra, *al-'Amāl al-Kāmila lil Shaykh Muḥammad 'Abduh*, 2:244–245.

[78] Ibid., 2:243–247.

personal status laws, he cited the lack of care and attention in producing a full code with procedures; something that the Ottoman 'ulamā' accomplished when drafting the Majalla.[79] 'Abduh saw the process of codification of personal status laws to be the exclusive domain of the 'ulamā' and to be a necessary step in light of the great social catastrophe (*'umūm al-balwā*) that had befallen Muslims.[80] As for the various court procedures and structures, this task belonged to the State to handle by way of government decrees (*lawā'iḥ*). One of 'Abudh's criticisms was that the codification up until that point had the State interfering with what was really the jurisdiction of the 'ulamā'.

These themes concerning Islamic law and reform was something that 'Abduh continued throughout his tenure as Grand Mufti. 'Abduh was outspoken for the need to tackle the intellectual stagnation (jumūd) that had befallen the 'ulamā' and their treatment of the Islamic sciences, law included. The brief interpretive points that 'Abduh offered in his report on the Sharī'a courts are also found in his collection of fatwas. On several occasions 'Abduh was adamant that strict adherence to the Ḥanafī school in matters of personal status was untenable. Not only did he see some of the later works of the Ḥanafī's as problematic, but he found some of the positions of the Ḥanafī school, issues of divorce for example, causing social problems. The majority of his collected fatwas, however, were based on standard Ḥanafī rulings. It is common to find him answering a question with the words, "what is commonly narrated from Imām Abu Ḥanifa is…"[81] However, he would often leave the source vague by writing, "what is common in the books of

---

[79] Ibid., 2:249. It should be remembered that 'Abduh taught the *Majalla* while living in exile in Beirut and was well versed in this text. See: Riḍwān al-Sayyid, "al-Imām Muḥammad 'Abduh wa'l Iṣlāḥ fi'l Awqāf wa'l Maḥākim al-Shar'iyya" in *al-Imām Muḥammad 'Abduh Mi'at 'Ām 'ala Raḥīlihi,* eds. Ibrāhīm al-Bayyūmī Ghānim and Ṣalāh al-Dīn Elgawhary (Cairo: Dār al-Kitāb al-Miṣrī, 2009), 613–614.

[80] 'Amāra, *al-'Amāl al-Kāmila lil Shaykh Muḥammad 'Abduh*, 2:271.

[81] 'Alī Jumu'a ed., *Fatāwā al-Imām Muḥammad 'Abduh* (Cairo: al-Jam'iyya al-Khayriyya al-Islāmiyya, 2005), 19.

fiqh…"[82] And yet there are other fatwas, like the Transvaal Fatwa, in which 'Abduh went directly to the primary texts of the Qur'an and ḥadīth to extrapolate meanings himself, then to demonstrate that his deduction has support from other *mujtahid* imams of the past.[83] 'Abduh applied this eclectic approach, coupled with his theory of codification when it came to issues of divorce, particularly the issue of a thrice-pronounced divorce counting as one divorce, not three, and it is to this issue that I now turn.

'Abduh's Discussion of a Thrice-Pronounced Divorce Counting as One

As early as 1881 Muḥammad 'Abduh wrote about marriage and polygamy, defending and explaining both institutions from an Islamic-legal perspective.[84] These topics, in addition to issues of women's seclusion, education, and divorce practices, became the subject matters of Amīn's books, mostly Taḥrīr al-Mar'a, discussed above. The similarity of Amīn's discussion of marriage and polygamy to the articles written by 'Abduh nearly a decade earlier gives more credence to the earlier discussion of 'Abduh's influence on Amīn. Writing about these topics in 1881 means that 'Abduh was amongst the first from both intellectuals and 'ulamā' to identify and address the difficulty women in Egypt faced, often times as a direct result of certain Islamic practices. In these early articles 'Abduh put his interpretative methodology to work to argue from an Islamic perspective how one can find solutions. To do this, 'Abduh attempted to go beyond the often-dry transactional language that is used in manuals of fiqh to describe marriage. He spoke out against descriptions of marriage being understood solely as contractual rights for men to sexually enjoy their spouses and rather brought the argument back to the Qur'an, as he often did in his fatwas on this subject matter, to argue that the Qur'an states clearly that marriage is based on mutual love and respect.[85] 'Abduh also openly

[82] Ibid.

[83] Ibid., 250–253.

[84] 'Amāra, *al-'Amāl al-Kāmila lil Shaykh Muḥammad 'Abduh*, 2:66–69, 76–81, 88–93.

[85] Ibid., 2:70–75.

acknowledged the dangers of divorce on women as well as the detrimental effects that multiple divorce pronouncements have.[86] As for the practice of polygamy, ʿAbduh argued that the Islamic ideal is for a man to take only one wife, not multiple wives as the practice of taking multiple wives is due to a need, not simply for pleasure. He also stated that the ruler has the right to disband the practice all together if it continues to create problems within society.[87] To support his claim, he reminded his readers that the rulings of Islamic law are not singular, but numerous and must be considered together. In other words, ʿAbduh here hinted towards the concept of undo harm (*ḍarūra*) and that were a certain implementation of a ruling to cause ḍarūra, the Sharīʿa itself would legislate its disbandment from the highest levels of political authority.

ʿAbduh's real contribution to the discussion of divorce, his influence on Taḥrīr al-Mar'a notwithstanding, came as he began his tenure as Grand Mufti of Egypt, not from these early articles. In the year 1900 the Ministry of Justice submitted a formal request for a fatwa (istiftāʾ) to address the problems of divorce in Egypt amongst Muslims. As was argued in the sections of divorce in Taḥrīr al-Mar'a and as was to be argued in the explanatory note to Law 25 of 1929 thirty years later, ʿAbduh highlighted that divorce in Islam is primarily a function of need and this means that, naturally, it can be abused and cause social problems. He then acknowledged that divorce indeed had become a problem in Egypt causing great harm to women and families. According to ʿAbduh, this necessitated a Sharīʿa solution by function of the concept of ḍarūra. This is itself something that is legislated directly from the Qur'an and sunna and, according to ʿAbduh, not something in which ijtihād is needed. Furthermore, the theory of ḍarūra, established clearly and considered from within the confines of the Ḥanafī school, necessitated and legislated that other opinions be sought from other schools. In other words, for ʿAbduh the Ḥanafī school itself, the rulings of which have provided an environment where these social ills have developed in the first place, allowed the taking of other positions from other schools to correct social problems that arise.

---

[86] Ibid., 2:80.

[87] Ibid., 2:86.

Therefore, 'Abduh argued that to take a non-Ḥanafī position regarding these matters is to follow the Ḥanafī School. Since the main problem laid out in both the question and the answer dealt with women whose husbands had been absent for a lengthy period of time (*ghā'ib*), 'Abduh easily found a solution by adopting positions from the Mālikī school. He further bolstered this by statements made by Shaykh al-Azhar and the Mālikī Muftī of Egypt.[88] 'Abduh concluded this discussion by offering eleven codes that he recommended be legislated into the personal status codes of Egypt to the formalize divorce process by introducing aspects of the state into the process, allowing for various levels of absentee statuses for missing husbands. This meant, as in marriage for example, an authorized person (*ma'dhūn*) would be the only person to initiate the divorce process. The next level would involve a judge whose main task in the divorce process was to warn the husband of the consequences of the divorce were it to be enacted.[89]

AḤMAD SHĀKIR

Aḥmad Shākir had an early exposure to the ways of the 'ulamā' and the issues they had to deal with in a changing, modernizing world. He was the son of Shaykh Muḥammad Shākir (1866–1939), known for his position as deputy to the muftī Mahdī al-'Abbāsī and later himself chief judge (*qāḍī al-qudah*) of Sudan. Aḥmad Shākir wrote that his father was one of the greatest influences on him alongside those he mentioned as "good 'ulamā'" consisting of Jamāl al-Dīn al Afghānī, Muḥammad 'Abduh, and Rashīd Riḍa.[90] In addition to this early, familial influence and instruction, Shākir received an al-Azhar education from the very beginning of his formal schooling.[91] This means that he attended al-Azhar affiliated institutions from

[88] Ibid., 2:666 Although 'Abduh does not mention them by name, I believe them to be Shaykh Ḥassūn al-Nawwāwī and Shakyh Muḥammad 'Illaysh respectively.

[89] Ibid., 2:667–669.

[90] Aḥmad Shākir, *al-Kitāb wa'l Sunna Yajibā an Yakūnā Maṣdar al-Qawānīn fī Miṣr* (Cairo: Dār al-Kutub al-Salafiyya, 1986), 7.

[91] When the name Shākir appears throughout this study, unless otherwise noted, it will refer to Aḥmad Shākir.

grammar school all the way until he completed his ʿālimiyya degree. Subsequent to the completion of his formal education, Shākir was appointed as a judge in the Sharīʿa courts in which he served with distinction until 1951, four years before the abolishment of these courts in Egypt. Holding this position in the late 1940s and early 1950s means that Shākir was amongst the last generation of ʿulamāʾ to serve in the courts. It also means that he witnessed their closing (which took place in 1955) before he died in 1958. These turbulent times for the Sharīʿa courts fueled his writings concerning the need for ijtihād, reform, and specifically codification of Islamic law. So troubling did he find the situation in Egypt, he wrote to King Saʿūd saying there is no hope in Egypt holding on to its Islamic legal system and the only hope left in the Muslim world was the nascent kingdom of Saudi Arabia.[92]

Shākir was concerned with the encroachment of secular, European law on Islamic law and the slow displacement of the latter by the former. He was emphatic throughout his career that European law could not replace Islamic law. He even went so far as to declare that this could be seen as an act of disbelief (*kufr*).[93] For Shākir, codification, amongst other tools, became a means to prevent this and he wrote extensively to articulate his point. In this regard, it is easy to confuse his critique of secular European codes as a stance against the process of codification of Sharīʿa, a point I expand on in the next section.

Shākir's intellectual output also contained two other areas that will find their way in the analysis of his view of codification generally and the issue of a thrice divorce pronouncement counting as one specifically. The first was his great interest in reviving the study of ḥadīth. He dedicated much time to providing critical editions of canonical collections of ḥadith, his most famous being his work on the *Musnad* of Imām Aḥmad ibn Ḥanbal (d. 241/855).[94] Secondly, he was very keen on bringing classical works that have been given little attention to a wider audience by providing new print editions

---

[92] Shākir, *Taqrīr ʿan Shuʾūn al-Tʿalīm waʾl Qaḍāʾ*, 20–21.

[93] Aḥmad Shākir, *Ḥukm al-Jāhiliyya* (Cairo: Dār al-Istiqāma, 1992), 29.

[94] Aḥmad Shākir ed., *Musnad al-Imām Aḥmad ibn Ḥanbal*, 19 vols., (Cairo: Dār al-Ḥadīth, 1995).

accompanied with extensive notes and commentary. While the majority of these works belong to the genre of ḥadīth studies,[95] others belong to the world of law and legal theory.[96]

Aḥmad Shākir's View of Islamic Law and Codification

Aḥmad Shākir had a tremendous amount of respect for Islamic law and his passionate defense of Sharī'a reflect this as well as his criticism of how the 'ulamā' had come to treat it. There was always a difference for Shākir between what the sources of the law say and the way they have been interpreted by many generations of 'ulamā'. Although Shākir respected the generations of scholars that came before him, his father's and grandfather's generations in particular, he criticized their staunch allegiance towards their own school of law to the exclusion of all other opinions. It is this tribal mentality, argued Shākir, that allowed their understanding and application of Sharī'a to stagnate. In turn, this rendered the 'ulamā' unable to adapt to new situations and apply interpretive methodological tools to derive new rulings, his definition of ijtihād.[97] Shākir claimed that this led the 'ulamā' of previous generations to be unable to cope with the changing trends of Egypt and the government's desire to modernize its legal system. To support this notion Shākir narrated a similar story to the one Rashīd Riḍa narrated in his *Tarīkh al-Ustādh al-Imām* that the 'ulamā' were given an opportunity to codify an Islamic legal system based on the four sunnī schools, but refused citing that this would lead to a type of eclecticism (talfīq) that is not permitted as it would render a particular action invalid by all schools from which opinions are taken and pieced together.[98] Shākir did not provide us with a source for this story and since it is slightly different than Riḍa's version, for example Riḍa does not mention their refusal on the grounds of talfīq, it is difficult to

[95] Some of these works include: Aḥmad Shākir ed., *Alfiyyat al-Suyūṭī fī 'Ilm al-Ḥadīth* (Cairo: Maktabat al-'Ilmiyya, n.d.); Aḥmad Shākir ed., *al-Bā'ith al-Ḥathīth Sharḥ Ikhtiṣār 'Ilm al-Ḥadīth* (Cairo: Dār al-Turāth, 2003).

[96] The most well-known being: Aḥmad Shākir ed., *al-Risāla li Imām al-Shāfi'ī* (Beirut: Dār al-Kutub al-'Ilmiyya, n.d.).

[97] Shākir, *al-Kitāb wa'l Sunna*, 5–7.

[98] Shākir, *al-T'alīm wa'l Qaḍā'*, 62–63; Shākir, *al-Kitāb wa'l Sunna*, 6–7.

prove that Shākir is quoting him. However, veracity and citation aside, Shākir's view was that the 'ulamā' had failed, not because they were not good people, but because their approach to Islamic law was fundamentally flawed. Part of the problem for Shākir was that some 'ulamā' saw the various schools of law independently, rather than collectively. To view the Sharīʿa collectively is a function of moving away from a strict view of taqlīd of one specific school and moving towards a more eclectic approach to Islamic law. Only then could appropriate rulings be found to form the code of personal status laws. Shākir, however, went further to dispute the concept of legal consensus (ijmāʿ) all together and to say that such a legal construct is difficult to conceive of in the first place and therefore not binding.[99]

Many of Shākir's comments on codification emerge from his lengthier discussions on the tensions between European secular law and Islamic law. Shākir saw this tension as a dangerous notion since his view of the Sharīʿa was that it is much larger and wider than common law. In fact, Shākir's opinion was that the Sharīʿa is *above* civil law and this is why, from a philosophical point of view at least, the latter must be derived from the former, not the other way around.[100] It is clear that in these comments Shākir was also commenting on the type of codification that was occurring within the civil code, a process that gained great momentum in the late 1940s.[101] While this process of codification is not the subject matter of this study, it is nonetheless important to be aware of it in as much as Shākir pays attention to it in deciphering its impact on codification of personal status law. In his observations, Shākir commented many times on the "accidental overlap" that newly adopted Western codes had with Sharīʿa.[102] For him, this was not a reason why another legal system should be accepted nor deemed to be compatible with the Sharīʿa. Rather, it is the law that must take and be informed by the Sharīʿa (*iqtibās al-qawanīn min al-sharīʿa*), a

---

[99] Aḥmad Shākir, *Niẓām al-Ṭalāq fī'l Islām* (Cairo: Maṭbaʿa al-Nahda, 1354 AH), 100–103.

[100] Shākir, *al-Tʿalīm wa'l Qaḍā'*, 84.

[101] This period is covered in: Ziadeh, *Lawyers*, 135–147.

[102] Shākir, *al-Tʿalīm wa'l Qaḍā'*, 78; Shākir, *Ḥukm al-Jāhiliyya*, 35.

phraseology that continues to appear today in discussing the relationship between law and Sharīʿa. Shākir offered a more active process of codification that should take place to protect and preserve Islamic law as the source of Egypt's emerging legal system. Acknowledging that this process is by no means simple, Shākir said that individual ijtihād is not sufficient nor is it possible since the task is enormous. Instead, Shākir offered what he termed a process of collective ijtihād (ijtihād ijtimāʿī).[103] This process would first entail ʿulamāʾ re-examining various rulings of Shārīʿa against interpretive tools, legal maxims, and actual ratio-legis found in the Qurʾan and sunna. Once it has been established what exactly the "correct" Sharīʿa position is on various issues, the committee would work with experts in western law to provide an equally exhaustive study of western secular legal systems. Once this is complete, the committee should then be able to choose from the secular codes those positions that do not counter what has already been established as correct Sharīʿa positions.[104] Without this collective-ijtihād, Shākir argued that the Muslim world would lose its Islamic identity.

Aḥmad Shākir and Divorce Laws

The codification of Egyptian marriage and divorce laws was very much a public affair. As early as 1916 Aḥmad Shākir wrote on the need to codify marriage and divorce laws with specific attention given to re-interpreting the primary texts on controversial issues.[105] When law 25 of 1929 was completed, both the text of the law and its explanatory note appeared in the official Egyptian government newspaper, *al-Waqāʾiʿ al-Miṣriyya*, and people were very vocal on their approval or disapproval of the law. Aḥmad Shākir was amongst those showing general support and he commented on it in

---

[103] Shākir, *al-Tʿalīm wa'l Qaḍāʾ*, 81–82.

[104] Ibid.

[105] Shākir mentions that he first commented on this topic in an article written in the *al-Ahrām* newspaper on March 16, 1916. See: Shākir, *Niẓām al-Ṭalāq*, 55.

a newspaper article.[106] Even though he offered the committee codifying the law suggestions and additional codes to improve the law, Shākir continued to comment on this issue dedicating an entire work to the topic, Niẓām al-Ṭalāq fi'l Islām, in 1936 into which he incorporated his previous article as well as lengthier discussions on the subject matter. He also followed this work with a brief comment on a divorce case in his 1941 work *Abḥāth fī Aḥkām*. However, it is Shākir's Niẓām al-Ṭalāq fi'l Islām that offers the most comprehensive commentary on this issue and therefore it will form the bulk of the discussion below.

While there is no clear indication that Shākir was part of the committee that codified the law in 1929, he did play an active role in that he was an accomplished Sharī'a court judge at the time dealing with both the social issue of divorce as well as the impact of interpreting the law in adjudicating these cases. There is no ambiguity that Shākir welcomed this law as a step in the right direction, but a small step since he felt it did not go far enough.[107] Shākir, like 'Abduh before him, was concerned with how this law was implemented, not just the theoretical and legal arguments behind it. For example, in commenting on a court case involving a thrice-pronounced divorce in his 1941 work, he wrote that there is no point to law 25 of 1929 if husbands continue to circumvent legal statues through other means.[108] He was certainly concerned with the social implications of the law on women and families as well. One of his main reasons for writing such an extensive work on the subject even though the law had already been codified and implemented in the Sharī'a courts is the story his father related to him of how al-Mahdī refused to offer a woman in need a legitimate position from the Mālikī school regarding a divorce from her husband who had abandoned her.[109] However, these concerns seem to trump a greater one that Shākir had and that was the issue of abso-

---

[106] Shākir mentiones that he wrote an article on this subject in the *al-Muqattam* newspaper on March 16, 1929. Aḥmad Shākir, *Abḥāth fī Aḥkām* (Cairo: Maṭba'a al-M'ārif, 1941), 104.

[107] Shākir, *Niẓām al-Ṭalāq*, 115.

[108] Shākir, *Abḥāth fī Aḥkām*, 101.

[109] Shākir, *Niẓām al-Ṭalāq*, 9–10.

lute ijtihād.[110] Shākir opens his discussion with the claim that he is both a mujtahid and a *salafī*.[111] This self-definition meant that Shākir was engaging in a form of ijtihād that is not confined by one of the four schools or any school of law for that matter, known as ijtihād *muqayyad*. This type of independent reasoning, known as absolute or *muṭlaq*, involves a return to the original sources and to re-interpret them, *in spite* of the arguments of jurists over many generations. I will show in the next chapter how this claim will run Shākir into a great deal of trouble with other 'ulamā' like al-Kawthārī and al-Muṭī'ī.

The discussion of a thrice-pronounced divorce in Islamic law is based on two primary texts: one is known as the ḥadīth of Rukāna in which the Companion Rukāna divorced his wife in a thrice-pronounced divorce, regreted this act, and complained about this to the Prophet of Islam who informed him that this only counted as one, revocable divorce and that he could re-marry his wife.[112] This ḥadīth is based on the narration of the Companion Ibn 'Umar. The second text involves 'Umar ibn al-Khaṭṭāb as Caliph abrogating this ruling and making the thrice-pronounced divorce count as an irrevocable divorce pronouncement.[113] This text is narrated by Ibn 'Abbās. The assumption of the majority of the jurists is that these two narrations build on one another and that 'Umar only changed the ruling because the original ruling had been abrogated (*mansūkh*), and the abrogator (*nāsikh*) is usually cited as the consensus (ijmā') of the Companions to the actions of 'Umar. In other words, since none of the Companions publically disagreed with Umar's actions, there must have been an implicit understanding that the ruling of the Prophet had been abrogated and 'Umar was carrying this out. Shākir interpreted 'Umar's change in a differ-

---

[110] It is important to note that Aḥmad Shākir was not a supporter of Qāsim Amīn and saw his writings to be the cause of much laxity in religion. See: Aḥmad Shākir, *Kalimat al-Haq* (Cairo: Dār al-Kutub al-Salafiyya, 1408 AH), 60.

[111] Shākir, *Niẓām al-Ṭalāq*, 4. I discuss this term in chapter 3.

[112] For a full citation of the ḥadīth of Rukāna see: Shākir, *Niẓām al-Ṭalāq*, 39.

[113] Ibid., 42.

ent manner than the rest of the jurists who discussed this issue, however. His understanding of 'Umar's change was that it was a function of 'Umar's obligations as a political ruler afforded to him by the concept of al-syāsa al-shar'iyya to punish people who have become too lax in their approach to marriage and divorce.[114] Shākir's argument is strengthened by the text itself in which 'Umar says, "people have hurried an issue in which there was deliberation, perhaps we should make the act count."[115] Shākir also claimed that there were disputes amongst the followers of the Companions (tābi'ūn) proving that this issue was not settled within the first generation of Muslims. Therefore, 'Umar's change was not a change in the ruling, but rather a function of him being the ruler of the community. As non-Arabs became Muslim and entered into the rapidly expanding community, and as these texts were being transmitted, Shākir claimed that statements such as "divorced three-times" began to be interpreted as a thrice-pronounced divorce, and therefore were accepted as such and misunderstood generation after generation in this manner.[116] It should be remembered that 'Abduh had similar arguments of the negative effects non-Arabs had in the rise of taqlīd.[117]

This relates to another one of Shākir's main arguments regarding the linguistic implications of a thrice-pronounced divorce. He argued that this has been largely misunderstood from early generations also as a function of non-native Arabic speakers accepting a false linguistic construct. Shākir reminded his readers that to understand divorce is to understand that it is first and foremost an annulment of a contract. Since marriage is a contract, it is governed by the same general conditions of contracts as understood by the Sharī'a. Therefore, once a man utters a divorce pronouncement, the annulment of the marriage contract has taken immediate effect. Adding a number to this annulment, i.e. to say that this contract is annulled two or three times, makes no sense, as the contract is al-

---

[114] Ibid., 79–81.

[115] Ibid.

[116] Ibid., 81–83.

[117] See pp. 95–96 above.

ready void with the first pronouncement.[118] Shākir acknowledged that others, most notably al-Ṭaḥāwī (d. 321/933) and most certainly a native speaker of Arabic, had argued that non-permissible "exits" or "annulments" of acts of worship have effect. For example, were one to be in prayer (*ṣalāt*) and were one to leave this act of worship with other than the normal closing *salam*,[119] these exit acts would have effect and therefore nullify the prayer. Ṭaḥāwī argued that this is the same for divorce. If one were to dissolve their marriage through a nonconventional and non-legislated means, this dissolution would have legal effect. It is understood by extension that a thrice-pronounced divorce would have effect. Shākir rejected this line of thinking claiming that it is an error in analogy to compare acts of worship (*ʿibādāt*) like prayer to contractual agreements (*muʿāmalāt*) like marriage and divorce.[120]

Shākir acknowledged that in Islamic law issues of gender relations are usually dealt with firmly and strictly (*al-aṣl fiʾl abḍāʿ al-taḥrīm*). He understood that this is a factor that arises in establishing divorce rulings as well. However, he did not see that this legal maxim applied in the situation of the thrice-pronounced divorce since there are other factors to consider. Throughout his writing, Shākir made frequent references to Ibn Taymiyya and his student Ibn al-Qayyim in their discussions of the ḥadīth of Rukana and the legal issue of the effect of a thrice-pronounced divorce. Even though both of them supported the conclusion that a thrice-pronounced divorce counted as one, Shākir found great objections with the fact that Ibn al-Qayyim claims this is an issue of debate, implying there is an o seempposing valid opinion that a thrice-pronounced divorce had effect.[121] Because of Shākir's argument above, he concluded that it is impossible both linguistically and textually that a thrice-pronounced divorce could count and have effect. For Shākir, the

[118] Shākir, *Niẓām al-Ṭalāq*, 47.

[119] This is a reference to concluding both canonical and supererogatory prayers by saying *al-salāmu ʿalaykum* to the right and to the left. See: Nuh Keller, *Reliance of the Traveler* (Beltsville: Amana Publications, 1994), 144 (f8.47).

[120] Shākir, *Niẓām al-Ṭalāq*, 18.

[121] Ibid., 51–52.

dispute between the Companions and their followers was never about this issue, but rather about consecutive divorces in one menstrual cycle, proving Shākir's conclusions.[122] Furthermore, Shākir claimed that social issues and pressures forced other 'ulamā' to capitulate. He applied this claim to Ibn Ḥajar al-'Asqalānī (d. 852/1449) and his discussion of the Rukāna ḥadīth in *Fatḥ al-Bārī*. Ibn Ḥajar's conclusion regarding this issue was that there must have been an abrogator (nāsikh) that 'Umar and some of the Companions knew to the exclusion[123] of the others and therefore a thrice-divorce pronouncement has full effect.[124] Ibn Ḥajar concluded with the following sentence that caused Shākir to doubt his intentions, "I have prolonged this section due to the confusion of those who have asked me repeatedly about this issue."[125] Without providing any rationale, Shākir concluded that this is an indication that Ibn Ḥajar was forced to engage in a polemic against the school of Ibn Taymiyya and that he secretly did not believe in this position. Shākir went on to provide some details, similar to his above line of argumentation, regarding the strength and weaknesses of various primary texts related to this issue. However, like his rejection of Ibn Taymiyya's and Ibn al-Qayyim's claim that there is another valid opinion, Shākir claimed that to seed that there is, is to understand that the Companions formed a consensus (ijmā') on the issue. Shākir rejected the conventional understanding of ijmā' saying it was not possible to conceive of and extremely difficult to actually take place. He further argued against what Ibn Rushd (d. 595/1198) termed silent and passive consensus (ijmā' *sukūtī*).[126] To bolster his argument, Shākir quotes from an Imāmī scholar, Ibn

---

[122] Ibid., 53.

[123] Meaning that it took a certain amount of time for this ruling to spread due to the spreading out of the Companions during the Caliphate of 'Umar.

[124] Quoted in: Shākir, *Niẓām al-Ṭalāq*, 91–94. Ibn Ḥajar's original discussion can be found here: Ibn Ḥajar al-'Asqalānī, *Fatḥ al-Bārī bi Sharḥ Ṣaḥīḥ al-Bukhārī*, 14 vols., (Cairo: al-Maktaba al-Salafiyya, 1400 AH), 9:275–278.

[125] Ibid.

[126] Ibid.

Wazīr (d. 840/1436), in claiming that real *ijmā‘* can only be concerning necessarily known facts from religion (*al-ma‘lūm min al-dīn bi'l ḍarūra*) since only this can bring certainty (*yaqīn*) which is the purpose of consensus in the first place. Any other issue can only be based on high-probability (*ẓann*), which cannot be the basis of binding consensus.[127]

Aḥmad Shākir's conclusion regarding the issue of a thrice-pronounced divorce was that both narrations (the divorce of Rukāna and the change made by 'Umar) are completely sound (*ṣaḥīḥ*) texts. However, unlike those jurists in the past who had the same opinion, Shākir went further to deny that a thrice-pronounced divorce ever had effect except under the Caliphate of 'Umar for certain socio-political reasons. According to this idea, Shākir welcomed law 25 of 1929 as a relief for what he described as a "nightmare."[128] However, writing as a practicing Sharī‘a court judge, Shākir continued to find problems with marriage and divorce as husbands were circumventing the law by claiming their divorce pronouncement was preceded by two others and therefore the current one represented the final, irrevocable divorce pronouncement. Likewise, many of the civil workers authorized to process marriage and divorce did not believe in the codified law and inclined to find a thrice-pronounced divorce to have effect one way or another. Shākir's legal solution to these continued problems was to offer 24 additional codes that would not allow a divorce pronouncement paired with a condition to have any effect, to render as null and void a divorce unless it is properly witnessed, and not allowing divorce to have effect for women undergoing their menstrual cycle.[129]

Aḥmad Shākir saw, like those before him, great problems with marriage and divorce in Egypt and the difficulty certain positions of the Ḥanafī school caused in adjudicating these cases. Unlike those before him, however, Shākir was dealing with both the declining influence of the Sharī‘a courts as well as the growing influence of European laws upon the National courts. Codification of

---

[127] Ibid., 102–103.

[128] Ibid., 115.

[129] Ibid., 138–140.

personal status laws for Shākir was a necessary process to advance Sharī'a in light of the changing reality, but it was also a process that would allow 'ulamā' to re-think and re-interpret issues that had been passively accepted for generations. In attempting to delve into the details of the issue of a thrice-pronounced divorce, Shākir demonstrated the extent and potentials of his use of interpretive tools. Not only did he challenge the legal opinion (*far'*), but he also challenged accepted and often times agreed upon interpretive tools (uṣūl). As I will demonstrate in the next chapter, these claims did not go unchallenged.

CHAPTER 3. THE COUNTER ARGUMENT: 'ULAMĀ' AGAINST CODIFICATION OF PERSONAL STATUS LAW

This chapter marks a new direction in this study as the discussion turns to 'ulamā' who disagreed with both the concept and actual act of codification of Islamic law. In the earlier chapters, particularly chapters 1 and 2, I discussed a common approach where codification was both theoretically and operationally promoted and defended, but from different vantage points. In this chapter and in the next and final one, I will discuss the other side of the argument: those who found codification both theoretically and operationally problematic. Accordingly, it is important to be reminded of the three important variables that constitute the process of codification as defined throughout this study: ijtihād, talfīq, and al-siyāsa al-shar'iyya. Although the 'ulamā' of the previous chapter shared a general approach to these three issues, they were often times from different intellectual camps and hailed from different time periods. This chapter brings this distinction into sharper focus as we deal with two *'ālim*s who were contemporary of one another, but very much the opposite of one another in their approach to articulating a 20th century intellectual-Islamic paradigm. Rashīd Riḍa is often described as a reformer and modernists 'ālim of the 20th century, while Zāhid al-Kawthārī is remembered for his conservatism and defense of the classical approach. Yet, despite these basic ideological stereotypes, they both shared the same conclusion of the dangers of codification of Islamic law and what it entailed from both a process point of view and the role of the 'ulamā' in shaping it. They arrived at this conclusion, however, by means of different arguments and positions.

MUḤAMMAD RASHĪD RIḌĀ

Muḥammad Rashīd Riḍā (d. 1935) is often remembered as the student and chief biographer of Muḥammad 'Abduh. Riḍa was no doubt instrumental in introducing 'Abduh and his reform thought to a wider public, particularly in the immediate years following 'Abduh's death. Yet, like 'Abduh who grew from his early relationship with Afghānī, so did Riḍa grow intellectually to formulate his own perspective and school of thought on various matters confronting 20th century Muslim thinkers. After all, he continued to be intellectually active for three decades after his teacher's death in 1905. While 'Abduh migrated towards education reform and a wider approach to applying Sharī'a in a changing world, Riḍa's approach became focused on the implications that changing geopolitics had on Islam as a state and a legal system.[1] Therefore, while he certainly had a perspective on the mechanics of reforming Islamic law (his voluminous fatwa collection attests to this), at times he appeared to be more concerned (or perhaps equally concerned) with the changing political structure of the Muslim world and the implications this had on Islamic law. In other words, while Riḍa spent a great deal of time demonstrating how Islamic law could remain relevant, he spent even more time (particularly in his later years) concerning himself with articulating the kind of political environment that is needed to have Islamic law operate and thrive in the first place.[2]

One of Riḍa's main themes was to demonstrate Islam's relevance in the modern age. His phrase, "*al-Islām ṣāliḥ li kull zamān wa makān*" is ubiquitous in his legal responsa and other writings, particularly those I examine in the pages that follow. One of the main tools he argued for to keep Islam's relevance, especially legally, was to combat a rigid sunnism and revive a more pristine approach to Islam, an approach that is often termed salafism. Qasim Zaman

---

[1] See pp. 92–93 above.

[2] A good overview of Riḍā's discussion is: Mahmoud Haddad, "Arab Religious Nationalism in the Colonial Era: Rereading Rashīd Riḍā's ideas on the Caliphate," *Journal of the American Oriental Society* 117, no. 2 (1997): 253–277.

makes the point that while the term salafism or salafi could take on a wide array of meanings, particularly as they relate to current usage, there is a clear and basic definition that relates to the thought of Riḍā. Zaman states that "[T]he term salafi is also used for, and by, those who reject the authority of the medieval schools of law and insist on an unmediated access to the foundational texts as the source of all norms."[3] Zaman continues to say that this "denotes an approach to Islam that was anchored in the foundational texts and in the examples of the 'pious forbears' – the salaf – as contrasted with understandings of Islam 'distorted' by centuries of legal, theological, and mystical debates, self-serving 'ulamā', and despotic rulers."[4] This does not mean that Riḍā categorically ignored the debates of the medieval period or even works written by scholars that hailed from this era, in fact he not only relied on these works to make his point, he was known to publish and revive some of these writings he found significant for his overall reform agenda. I understand Riḍā's salafism to mean that he did not acquiesce that all issues were necessarily settled through the filters of classical Islam, and that many issues are still open to debate, particularly issues that define the boundaries of normative Islam. In other words, Riḍā was comfortable rejecting medieval interpretations, as well as accepted forms of legal and interpretive authority that have come to define normative sunnī Islam. Accordingly, there is a perceivable shift in Riḍā's thinking from a pure scholastic exercise of reinterpreting particular Sharīʿa positions in light of shifting modern mores to addressing the larger issue of the causes of intellectual stagnation amongst the 'ulamā'.

It should also be kept in mind that Riḍā lived during a time that was marked by great political change and upheaval in the Muslim world. A common theme for him was European colonial interests encroaching on the sovereignty of Muslim nations. For Riḍā this translated into a fundamental change in the dynamics of the traditional "circle of justice" and a direct threat to the central role of the 'ulamā' in the formation of the state and the protectors of

---

[3] Muhammad Qasim Zaman, *Modern Islamic Thought in a Radical Age* (Cambridge: Cambridge University Press, 2012), 7.

[4] Ibid.

Islamic law.[5] The 'ulamā's role was also threatened by the rise of the secular legal field in Egypt combined by the rise of the National courts and the demise of the Sharī'a courts. There are three critical issues that influenced his thinking on this topic: the loss of the Ottoman Caliphate, British colonial influence over Egypt, and the closing of the Sharī'a courts.

Riḍa's foray into the issue of the Islamic state was a reaction to the Turkish National Assembly stripping the Caliphate of temporal powers in 1922, relegating the office to a ceremonial, pseudo-religious one.[6] Riḍā's commentary on the incident elicited several articles that he published from December 1922 to May 1923 in his news-journal al-Manār. These serialized articles eventually formed the majority of his book *al-Khilāfa wa'l Imāma al-'Uẓmā*, which provides his most comprehensive treatment on the role of the 'ulamā' in the state and legislation.[7] Riḍā was agitated by the notion that the Caliphate could be considered simply ceremonial or spiritual in function, *al-khilāfa al-rūḥiyya* in his exact language. Riḍā saw the Islamic state as the backbone of Islam and the source of sovereignty for Muslim nations. The key to preserving this backbone was a two-pronged approach: reviving the Caliphate and ensuring the 'ulamā' take their proper place as regulators of legislation. Therefore, for Riḍā, the Caliphate is more temporal than spiritual, more executive than ceremonial.[8] The loss of the Caliphate, a historical event that officially took place in 1923, but considered already dead by Riḍā with the decree of 1922, meant the loss of the structure that ensures Islamic law remains relevant and in force legislatively. In fact, Riḍā's entire argument against codification hinged on this very point. In an early formulation similar to Hallaq's theory of the effects of the modern state on Islamic law discussed in the intro-

[5] See note 68 in the introduction.

[6] The original 1922 tract of the Turkish Grand National Assembly is the *Hilafet ve Hakimiyet-i-Milliye*. Quoted in: Kerr, *Islamic* Reform, 164.

[7] I have relied on the following edition for Riḍā's work on the Caliphate: Wajīh al-Kawtharānī ed., *al-Dawla wa'l Khilāfa fi'l Khiṭāb al-'Arabī Ibbān al-Thawra al-Kamāliyya fī Turkiyyā* (Beirut: Dār al-Ṭal'iyya li'l Ṭibā'a wa'l Nashr, 1996; hereafter *al-Khilāfa*).

[8] Kerr, *Islamic Reform*, 179.

duction, Riḍā feared that both the Sharīʿa and the ʿulamāʾ would be completely cast out by result of the loss of the Caliphate, and Islamic law as we know it would come to an end. Rather than focus solely on Islamic law's relevance to modern occurrences, something his fatwa collection demonstrates, Riḍā also focused on reviving the Islamic state and in so doing carved out a new, and perhaps unprecedented, role for the ʿulamāʾ.

Riḍā's position on the Ottoman Caliphate, it must be admitted, is a bit contradictory. In commenting on the 1922 edict, Riḍā spared no time in condemning not only the Kelmalist movement, but also the Ottomans themselves whom he equated with colonial forces occupying parts of the Muslim world.[9] He took an extremely limiting view of who rightfully can claim the office of the Caliphate, arguing for the classic definition that only people from the house of Quraysh would claim the title, and in so doing criticized the legitimacy of not only the Ottomans, but the ʿAbbāsids and the Umaayds as well.[10] At the same time, in his recommendations for modern Islamic legislation, something I discuss in detail below, he cited a process nearly identical to the Ottoman process in forming the Majalla and called for the "proper Islamic ruler" to form a digest of Islamic law.[11] One possible explanation for this contradiction is that Riḍā, like other ʿulamāʾ before him, took for granted the Islamic state structure that existed and the nominal connection of a nation like Egypt to the Sublime Porte. This provided an intact system, granted very weak and ailing, that allowed, if only theoretically, the sort of influence of the ʿulamāʾ Riḍā advocated for. The encroachment of the secular movement in Turkey and its echoes throughout the Muslim world must have signaled to Riḍā that what one might have thought was an Islamic system was no longer and a new way of thinking must be developed to provide the needed political substrate for Islamic law to continue its role. One might argue that such a commentary is irrelevant in this current discussion, however, the perception of the ʿulamāʾ towards what the aspects of al-siyāsa al-sharʿiyya are functioning often times determined how

---

[9] Riḍā, *Khilāfa*, 85.

[10] Kerr, *Islamic Reform*, 168.

[11] Riḍā, *al-Manār* 22 (1902): 866.

they viewed certain related matters. For example, Makhlūf al-Minyāwī's perception was clearly that the legitimate Imām (in his case the Khedive of Egypt) asked him to engage in a comparative legal exercise in order to adopt a modern code, something he defended. For others, like Riḍā, the perception was different and so too were the conclusions.

The second major issue that influenced Riḍā's perspective on codification was European colonization and occupation of Muslim lands, particularly Egypt. Riḍā saw Egypt not as an isolated case, arguing that large parts of the Muslim world followed a similar fate.[12] Riḍā saw this as a political as well as moral problem and a form of Divine punishment for Muslims leaving God's religion.[13] Like Shākir and other salafi figures of the early to mid-20th century, Riḍā cozied up to the nascent Saudi Kingdom as one of the few beacons of light, the "last hope" to preserve the Islamic state structure and by default the role of the 'ulamā'.[14]

The loss of the Caliphate and the foreign occupation of Egypt directly influenced Riḍā's perspective on a third issue, the closing of the Sharī'a courts and the wave of legal reform that struck Egypt in the early 20th century. While the dangers and implications of the loss of the Caliphate in the mid-1920s towards the 'ulamā' were largely theoretical, the dwindling jurisdiction of the Sharī'a courts in Egypt and the encroachment of legal reforms on personal status laws, the last stronghold in the Egyptian judiciary of Islamic law, were real and actual. In Riḍā's main articles relating to this, articles I discuss below, Riḍā reacted to suggestions made by British to the Egyptian government, suggestions that came before the formation of the various committees of personal status laws, to link Sharī'a courts to the National ones by way of judges from the latter sitting on the former with the power of oversight.[15] If Riḍā was sensitive to the undermining of the 'ulamā' from government, it should

---

[12] Riḍā, *al-Khilāfa*, 84.

[13] Riḍā, *al-Wahhābiyūn wa'l Ḥijāz* (Cairo: Maṭba'at al-Manār, 1344 A.H.), 2–3.

[14] Ibid, 6, Riḍā likens Muḥammad Ibn 'Abd al-Wahhāb to the "reviver of the age", *mujadid al-'aṣr.*

[15] Riḍā, *al-Manār* 23 (1922): 540; *al-Manār* (8) 1899:117–121.

come as no surprise that he took issue with a suggestion he assumed came from Egypt's British overseers, and a function not of Egypt's Muslim monarch deciding what is best for his people, but a directive from Britain to undermine Islamic law. Riḍā argued that if the Sharīʿa courts and its jurisdiction were merged with the National courts, the Sharīʿa would no longer exist and the ʿulamāʾ would be completely cut off from legislative matters.

Like the issue of the Caliphate and foreign occupation, Riḍā used this issue as a springboard to talk about legal reform and also the revival of ijtihād in conjunction with his formulation of a new concept of siyāsa and the Islamic state. The Islamic state, one of Riḍā's main topics throughout his later life, is the recurring theme and the reason, as I will demonstrate, he rejects codification of Islamic law.

MUSLIM UNITY AND THE ISLAMIC STATE

Riḍā's writings dealing with matters of the Islamic state stemmed mostly from his concern with the disunity of the Muslim world at the turn of the 19th century. This disunity was a direct cause of the lack of legitimate Islamic leadership (his critique of the historical manifestation of the Caliphate) and the effects of a rigid medieval Islam that has been inherited blindly (Riḍā's definition of taqlīd) and had slowly weakened the Muslim body politic over the last several centuries. For Riḍa unity, both political and religious, was a necessary corollary to restoring a true and pure Islamic political leadership.[16] In this section and the next, I will discuss Riḍā's theory of the Caliphate (what he terms *al-imāmā al-uẓmā*), which itself informs his theory of al-siyāsa al-sharʿiyya. This will allow for another discussion around his opinions of Islamic law with a focus on his perspective on ijtihād, taqlīd, and talfīq, all with the aim of

---

[16] I use the word pure as a reference to the traditional Sunnī requirements that the Caliph be from the tribe of Quraysh. Riḍā seemed, at times, to be concerned with the Caliphate being pure and adherent to classical definitions. For classic qualifications of the Caliphate/Imāma see: Juwaynī, *al-Ghiyāthī*, 254–264; Muhammad Ibn Ḥabīb al-Māwardī, *al-Aḥkām al-Sulṭāniyya* (Cairo: al-Maṭbaʿat al-Ḥalabī, 1973), 6.

providing a clear understanding of Riḍā's opposition to codification of Islamic law.

Riḍā's rejection of the notion of a spiritual Caliph offered by the Turkish National Assembly in 1922 was based on his understanding that the Caliph's position in both the political structure and the wider society he governs is that of both an interpreter of God's law as well as its chief enforcer. This assumes that Islamic law reigns supreme legislatively and that both religious matters (ʿibādāt) and worldly matters (muʿāmalāt) conform to the Islamic legal tradition.[17] Riḍā believed in this function to the extent that at one point he even denied the spiritual function of the office altogether.[18] Riḍā strengthened such a sentiment by arguing that most of the issues dealing with governance and worldly matters (muʿāmalāt) are themselves ijtihād matters, as opposed to matters of ritual and worship (ʿibādāt), which are largely agreed upon amongst the jurists (i.e. matters of ijmāʿ) and contain little opportunity for ijtihād.[19] Similar to al-Minyāwī arguing for the necessity of political order and for the Caliph to sit at the top of this order, Riḍā saw the Caliph as necessary for society (what he termed as an individual obligation – *farḍ ʿayn*); and since ijtihād was naturally a part of governance, the Caliph must be a mujtahid who is steeped in Islamic law with the ability to extrapolate new rulings as new events occur. The discussion of the Caliph, for both Riḍā and some of his classical interlocutors, is more about the position itself: who qualifies, and how he is chosen, than it is about the structure of the government the Caliph is to oversee. Riḍā argued, as did other con-

---

[17] It is important to note here that Muslim jurists would argue that both realms are religious in the sense that Divine law (Sharīʿa) has a say in both kinds of matters. I, however, make a distinction between religious and worldly matters since while in theory both areas are governed by Islamic law, the state and various other forces have often played an active role in regulating the latter.

[18] Kerr, *Islamic Reform*, 179. This may have been an issue that Riḍā oscillated on since in his work on the Caliphate he argues for a form of spiritual-politics. Riḍā, *al-Khilāfa*, 52.

[19] Riḍā, *al-Manār* 10 (1901): 368. As for Riḍā's discussion on *ijtihād*, this will come in the subsequent section.

temporaries like Muṣtafa Ṣabrī (d. 1954) that Islamic law had not laid down definitive rulings on government formation only definitive moral directions. This theory, one must assume, is predicated on the notion that once a true *mujtahid*-Caliph came to power such minutiae would sort themselves out since Islamic law would remain relevant (one is left to wonder how) and fully enforced. Even though Riḍā's analysis of the state of the Muslim world at the turn of the 19th century led to an articulation of the need for a revival of the Caliphate, at the heart of this was essentially an argument for a revival of an ijtihād-based approach to Islamic law.

Riḍā's Caliph is not a position born from a vacuum, but rather the result of a specific process. Unlike modern democracies where people elect officials, either directly or through proxies such as electoral colleges, to represent them, the Caliphate is selected by an elite group of people known as ahl al-ḥall wa'l 'aqd, literally the people who loosen and bind. While Islamic jurists and political theorists have discussed the important role that this elite group plays in statecraft, there has never been a consensus on exactly who is a member.[20] What is clear in discussions of this group, however, is that the 'ulamā' were a part of it: either entirely or partially. Riḍā joined his classical interlocutors in commenting on this topic by commenting on Qur'an 4:59's text, "O you who believe, obey God, and obey the Messenger and those of you who are in authority; and if you have a dispute concerning any matter, refer it to God and the Messenger if you are believers in God and the Last Day. This is better and more seemly in the end", and particularly the phrase "those in authority." Riḍā's conclusion on the matter was straightforward: "those in authority" is a clear reference to ahl al-ḥall wa'l 'aqd and the opinions of those who constitute this group forms a legal, binding consensus for the rest of the Muslim community.[21] Riḍā's conclusions, while straightforward, have implications that

---

[20] Zaman has an excellent treatment of this debate outlining the three possible interpretations of this group. See: Zaman, *Modern Islamic Thought*, 47–55.

[21] Rashīd Riḍā, *Tafsīr al-Qur'an al-Ḥakīm al-Mushtahir bi Tafsīr al-Manār*, 12 vols., (Cairo: Dār al-Manār, 1947–54; hereafter *Tafsīr al-Manār*), 5:182.

are necessary to highlight within the context of the current discussion. As Zaman points out in his discussion on Riḍā's commentary of this verse, Riḍā offered a genealogy of 'Abduh's own thinking on this topic in which he had formulated a conception of the ahl al-ḥall wa'l 'aqd that included a wider segment of the society, not just the 'ulamā'.[22] Riḍā claimed that 'Abduh held this view privately thinking he was alone in his conclusions until he read a similar interpretation in al-Nisabūrī's Qur'anic exegesis. I too share Zaman's conclusion that this notion is problematic given the available print edition of al-Nisabūrī's work during both 'Abduh and Riḍā's time. One possible explanation of this, and one that is not too uncommon throughout Islamic legal history, is that one is better served by grounding an independently arrived at opinion in classical sources than claim to have broken with tradition.[23] At times Riḍā maked this point, but in reverse order. For exmaple, in his *al-Muḥāwarāt Bayn al-Muṣliḥ wa'l Muqallid* he claimed that while he shared Ghazalī's opinion on taqlīd, he arrived at such an opinion independent from Ghazālī, obviously to demonstrate his scholastic abilities.[24] His discussion of this opinion, however, is entirely established by quoting directly from Ghazālī's *al-Qiṣṭās al-Mustaqīm* not his own argumentation.[25] This could mean that both 'Abduh and Riḍā felt their conclusion of an inclusive definition of ahl al-ḥall wa'l 'aqd of which the 'ulamā' are a part as opposed to the more classic definition of al-Rāzī who argued for an exclusive definition of the 'ulamā' as the "prince of the princes" was potentially controversial. Zaman interprets this episode as an attempt by Riḍā to

---

[22] Zaman, *Modern Islamic Thought*, 47–52.

[23] One classic example of this is when a particular *mujtahid* makes a claim that they have reached the level of absolute (al-*ijtihād* al-muṭlaq), but their independent *ijtihād* has produced the same result of a mujtahid from the past. Al-Suyūṭī was one such jurist to make this claim. See: Jalāl al-Dīn al-Suyūṭī, *al-Radd 'ala man Akhlada ilā al-'Ard wa Jahila anna al-Ijtihād fī Kul 'Aṣr Farḍ* (Beirut: Dār al-Kutub al-'Ilmiyya, 1983); Jalāl al-Dīn al-Suyūṭī, *Taqrīr al-Istinād fī Tafsīr al-Ijtihād* (Alexandria: Dār al-D'awa, 1983).

[24] Riḍā, *al-Manār* 10 (1901): 362.

[25] Ibid.

wrestle power away from the 'ulamā'.[26] This is certainly a logical conclusion and a valid implication to Riḍā's theory. However, Zaman's argument concerns the implications of the discussion as it relates to *ijmā'* and in this regard, Riḍā did advocate, as did Shākir, for a more institutional, forum-based consensus process.[27] However, I think that there is a different set of implications as this discussion relates to statecraft and political authority.

It is important to remember Riḍā's original goal in engaging in the discussion of ahl al-ḥall wa'l 'aqd: to regain a proper Islamic political environment where Islamic law can govern and remain relevant, all with the goal of regaining Muslim political hegemony. As I have already stated, the goal is to give more agency to both the Sharī'a and the 'ulamā', not less and not divided. Riḍā defined the Caliphate almost exclusively in terms of its relation to Islamic law. He never mentioned other traits such as physical fitness requirements.[28] The most ubiquitous of his traits is that the Caliph be a mujtahid and must exercise this ability alongside the 'ulamā'. In reality, Riḍā argued, any potential Caliph would not likely be an actual mujtahid and therefore, the real seat of legislative power sits with "those in authority" whom Riḍā said is obligatory for the Caliph to follow.[29] Riḍā also acknowledged that those who form the elite group of ahl al-ḥall wa'l 'aqd are not necessarily the most knowledgeable (i.e. in matters of law).[30] What he did not say explicitly is that the 'ulamā' are the most knowledgeable ones within the group and since his entire definition of the Caliphate is but a mere function of it carrying out ijtihād and instituting Islamic law, it is only the 'ulamā' who have any real agency from amongst the ahl al-ḥall wa'l 'aqd and who ultimately retain the power to appoint and depose the Caliph. The 'ulamā', then, are the only ones that can

---

[26] Zaman, *Modern Islamic Thought*, 50.

[27] Ibid., 51 and pp. 106–107 above.

[28] To fulfill the physical fitness requirements, the Ottomans held a ceremony of the girding the sword of Osman. For details of this ceremony see: "New Sultan Breaks Moslem Traditions," *New York Times*, May 11, 1909.

[29] Riḍā, *Tafṣīr al-Manār*, 5:187.

[30] Riḍā, *al-Khilāfa*, 59.

keep the "circle of justice" intact. My understanding of this interpretation is also aided by acknowledging the changing dynamics of Egyptian society in the first half of the 20th century. By the time Riḍā was writing, the elite of society were already military leaders, editors of leading newspapers, business leaders, etc., but the 'ulamā' had lost significant standing. His adoption of al-Nisabūrī's inclusive definition of ahl al-ḥall wa'l 'aqd was, I believe, a way to bring the 'ulamā' back to power, not to wrestle power away from them. In other words, Riḍā is acknowledging the changing structure of Muslim societies in the early 20th century and arguing that the 'ulamā' deserve a seat at the table; in reality his view of both the Caliphate and the process by which the Caliph is to govern has very little to do with the other groups of his definition of ahl al-ḥall wa'l 'aqd.[31]

RIDA AND CODIFICATION OF ISLAMIC LAW

There should be no doubt that for Riḍā the Sharī'a plays a central role in governance. To demonstrate this, he offered four main principles that he said should regulate the interaction between the two: the Qur'anic and sunnaic texts (i.e. naṣṣ), legal consensus (ijmā' of the people who loosen and bind as defined by Riḍā), and general principles laid out in the first two.[32] The need for a mastery of Islamic law and the centrality of these four principles in governance are the key in Riḍā's understanding of both the Islamic state and Muslim unity. He did not concern himself with the form of the Islamic state and argued that a plurality of systems of government could fulfill these necessary points.[33] To further facilitate the supremacy of Islamic law as executed through the office of the Caliph, Riḍā argued that it is incumbent upon the Caliph to enact "a book of legal rulings (aḥkām) based on deep legal principles, appropriate for modern times, easy to apply, and rulings that have no

---

[31] I admit that this conception is perhaps ill conceived as the worldly power constituted in the other groups forming the *ahl al-ḥall wa'l 'aqd* could render the *'ulamā'* irrelevant at any point in time, which is precisely what continued to happen in Egypt vis-à-vis the treatment of the state towards al-Azhar.

[32] Riḍā, *Tafsīr al-Manār*, 5:187.

[33] Ibid., 5:189.

dispute concerning them."[34] He also said that a book of Islamic legal principles is needed alongside this to prove the Sharīʿa's viability and relevance to modern times.[35] Although this sounds like an endorsement for codification, I will argue in this section that it is not. While such a digest of law is needed to facilitate Muslim unity through adherence to a uniform Islamic law, Riḍā was also quick to point out that both the system and the Caliph himself must submit ultimately to the Sharīʿa since it is the Sharīʿa, the commands of God and His Prophet, that retain all sovereignty.

To understand Riḍā's opinion on codification of Islamic law generally and personal status law specifically, it is important to keep in mind two important facts: one, this study has offered a very specific definition of codification of personal status law outlined in the introduction. Therefore, it is important to make a distinction between Riḍā's opinion of this specific process of codification versus his endorsement of the need to provide a manual of easy access to Islamic law in modern times, what I will argue below is essentially a consolidation of law, not codification. The second is that I have been defining this specific process of codification as containing three important variables: ijtihād, talfīq, and al-siyāsa al-sharʿiyya. Therefore, it is best to take these one-by-one and analyze what Riḍā thought on each of them before deviling into his arguments against codification.

Ijtihād

It will come as no surprise that Riḍā, like other modernist and reform thinkers of the mid-20th century, was a strong supporter of ijtihād. While many others highlighted the importance of ijtihād as a continual functioning facet of Islamic law, Riḍā articulated not only the need for ijtihād as a form of Muslim unity, something we saw in the preceding section, but also as the only way to actually apply Islamic law in the first place. As strong as his defense of ijtihād, so too was his denunciation of taqlīd. Like ʿAbduh who argued that taqlīd seeped into Muslim thought during the times of

---

[34] Riḍā, *al-Manār* 4 (1902): 866.

[35] Riḍā, *al-Khilāfa*, 103–4.

the 'Abbāsids causing intellectual stagnation, so too did Riḍā argue that *taqlīd* was the direct cause of the splintering of the Muslim world along the fault lines of sectarianism, thus leading to Muslim political fragmentation.[36] For Riḍā, taqlīd does not offer a paradigm of a "full Islam" since it leaves out clear directives to contemplate the Divine message and the universe.[37] Those who lived up to this directive, the truly enlightened, were the great Imāms of the past as well as the select (*khawāṣṣ*); taqlīd was not befitting of their stature.[38] Surely the 'ulamā' that Riḍā discussed as playing an important role in statecraft as well as the Caliph himself cannot be bound by imitating others and must be able to exert their own effort to correctly interpret the Qur'an and sunna.

Riḍā's Muslim-unity-through-ijtihād paradigm is guided by ten principles he lays out in his Muḥāwarāt, four of which are pertinent to this discussion:[39]

1. *Acquired knowledge ('ulūm kasbiyya) is difficult to grasp and in need of ijtihād. Later generations have a better chance of understanding these difficult issues as they can rely on the formation of ideas and explanations of previous generations.*

While he does not directly state it, Riḍā obviously saw himself as well as those he promoted through his writings like Amīr Shakīb Arslān (d. 1946) as inheritors of a golden age and in an appropriate place to shed light on such issues that might have been obfuscated in the past. Riḍā not only stretched traditional modes of authority like qiyās and maṣlaḥa, but he also offered, like 'Abduh, new readings to issues and supported non-orthodox opinions, like a thrice-pronounced divorce counting as one.[40]

---

[36] Riḍā, *al-Manār* 4 (1902): 571.

[37] Ibid., 285.

[38] Ibid,, 275.

[39] Ibid., 207.

[40] While not my focus in discussing Riḍā, he did in fact comment rather favorably to this issue and used it as an example of the flexibility of the Sharī'a. See Ibid., 210–11. However, Riḍā used this as an example of *shūra* as a vehicle of legal authority over the verbatim text when deemed necessary by the *'ulamā'*.

2. *Understanding directly from the Qur'an and sunna is easier than accessing books of jurisprudence.*

The importance of the filters of legal reasoning of the jurists, what one may be inclined to refer to as classical Islam, is something that Riḍā seems uncomfortable with most of the time. I say most of the time since he is equally comfortable with reviving classical authors, such as Najm al-Dīn al-Ṭūfī (d. 716/1316), when these voices agree with his reform agenda. This is a manifestation of Riḍā's salafi thought in which a return to the original texts, itself linked to a return to the formative period of Islam, guides his approach to legal interpretation.

3. *God has criticized taqlīd as have the imāms*

Riḍā uses certain verses from the Qur'an, such as 43:23 "And even so We sent not a warner before you into any township, but its luxurious ones said: we found our fathers following a religion, and we are following their footprints," to outline how blind imitation was the downfall of sinful peoples in the past. The blind imitation that the Qur'an mentions, in Riḍā's usage, is equated to perpetual ignorance. Likewise, the great imāms of the formative period of Islam were equally critical of more technical meanings of taqlīd, what might be thought of as following the juridical conclusions of another scholar.

4. *Pure Islamic law has wide boundaries and is flexible, but the schools of Islamic law created differences and narrowness*

This point is more of a historical reference than the others. As mentioned in number two above, Riḍā was a salafi thinker who saw a return to the formative period necessary to avoid the challenges and differences presented by the classical schools of Islamic law. Rather than see the schools of laws as a necessary filter through which one should access the original sources, something a more conservative thinker like al-Kawtharī would argue as I illustrate below, Riḍā saw these filters as limiting. He saw the discussions of the various legal schools leading to intellectual isolation in Islamic law creating artificial differences, whereas the formative period was much more open and fluid. In his theory on the Caliphate, Riḍā argued for an approach to the schools of Islamic law that viewed and treated them as one school and allowing for differences of legal opinion to signal the breadth of Islamic law, not its narrowness.

Islamic law is usually discussed as containing two broad sections: one dealing with acts of devotional worship (ʿibādāt) containing legal discussions on purity, prayer, fasting, alms giving, and pilgrimage, and a second section dealing with transactions (muʿāmalāt) containing discussions of and not limited to, marriage and divorce, custody, business transactions, court cases, and sections on the Caliphate. To make his point thoroughly, Riḍā discussed the implications of ijtihād/taqlīd in both areas. He agreed with some of his classical interlocutors that acts of worship are fairly standardized containing very little room for interpretation and/or ijtihād. However, he did not label following of such positions as a form of taqlīd since, he argued, taqlīd is a function of ijtihād.[41] Rather, such positions and rulings are simply common practice and a form of following the directives laid out in the primary sources. The realm of transactions, and specially court decisions, however, is quite the opposite and is completely the realm of ijtihād and interpretation.[42] Recalling Riḍā's discussion of the Caliphate, it is the realm of transactions and court cases where the vast majority of statecraft takes place. It is the realm of public interest and therefore not a place where society benefits from imitation. It needs, rather, fresh analysis and legal extrapolation, since this way, Riḍā argued, is the way of enlightenment and the way of unity.

Of course, Riḍā's negative opinion of the schools of legal thought, the historic embodiment of taqlīd and the premier institution of Islamic law, would be cause for many to attack him. How could over a thousand years of legal scholarship be discarded and how can the juristic thinking of so many centuries not prove useful to understanding legal imperatives as outlined in Islam's primary texts? There are two main ways that Riḍā navigated this difficult position to defend his opinion on ijtihād. The first is that he claimed the great imāms never wanted their schools to be codified

---

[41] Ibid., 368. Taqlīd is a function of ijtihād since if one is not able to perform itjihād regarding a certain topic, the only option left is to follow (taqlīd) an opinion of a mujtahid on that certain topic. However, in the matter of acts of devotional worship, Riḍā saw no ijtihād was needed since these matters were already settled.

[42] Ibid.

and followed by others in the first place. They engaged in a pure form of ijtihād and they wrote the results of their ijtihād for others to benefit from, but not necessarily to imitate. This is how he read the story of Imām Mālik and Harūn al-Rashīd that I discussed in the introduction.[43] He also listed many statements of the early imāms, particular Aḥmad Ibn Ḥanbal, that bolster his claim of the low opinion they had of taqlīd, implying, not stating, that ijtihād is the preference. The other way Riḍā navigated the authority of the schools of law was to offer a new reading to the concept of maṣlaḥa (the common good). While this is a topic that deserves to be treated on its own as Riḍā's opinions of maṣlaḥa impacted generations of legal thinkers after him, I will limit my discussion to those aspects of this topic that influence his opinions of ijtihād and the current discussion. Riḍā followed the 8th/14th century al-Ṭufī in his understanding that the common good takes precedence as a form of legal authority over consensus (ijmāʿ). In addition, while Riḍā argued that the goal of acts of devotional worship was to follow the original meaning of the primary texts, the goal of the other realm of Islamic law was to base rulings on the common good, even if they go against both verbatim readings of the primary texts and the consensus of the legal schools.[44] Therefore, even were one to hold the opinion of the importance of the legal schools and legal consensus, matters of the modern age must conform to what is best for the common good and this trumps the authority of the schools.[45]

Talfīq

In his discussions on the Caliphate as well as ijtihād, Riḍā argued for the "making of the legal schools one" in their treatment.[46] His

---

[43] See pp. 17–18 above.

[44] Riḍā's treatment of maṣlaḥa can be found in his comments in his reprint of al-Ṭufī's treatise on the topic: Riḍā, *al-Manār* 9 (1906): 745–70; *al-Manār* 4 (1902): 859–64. For an excellent treatment of the topic of the common good one should read: Zaman, *Modern Islamic Thought*, chapter 4.

[45] Conservative thinkers like al-Kawtharī do not let such claims go unanswered, as I will discuss in the following section.

[46] Riḍā *al-Manār* 4 (1901): 365.

logic was that since all the Imāms essentially agree on the core principles of religion (uṣūl *al-dīn*), their schools are essentially one since they are of the same religion (dīn) differing only in minor legal issues. Therefore, and here I extrapolate on his argument, all schools and legal opinions are part of the same religious paradigm and can be chosen from equally. Riḍā defended talfīq after an action has occurred which means that after a person engages in an action that is deemed not to conform to a particular school of law, if it is found that this action conforms to another opinion, then the action is valid. He also defended the formation of new rulings, like the thrice-pronounced divorce counting as one, which he openly defended, arguing that one cannot criticize legal positions about which there is legitimate scholarly debate.[47]

Since much of the debate around the process of codification of personal status law related to the Ḥanafī school, Riḍā was also keen to dispute the claim made by some Ḥanafī jurists that talfīq was not permitted outside one's own school. Riḍā argued that in fact the entire Ḥanafī school is itself based on talfīq and an amalgamation of the views of several mujtahid Imāms, and that the differences between them are at times greater than the difference between Imām Abū Ḥanīfa himself and the other schools.[48]

In short, Riḍā was concise and direct in his defense of legal eclecticism and argued that, fundamentally, Islamic law is expansive and flexible, much more at least than the schools of jurisprudence that have come to define it.

Al-siyāsa al-shar'iyya

As I mentioned at the beginning of the section of Riḍā above, the majority of the second half of Riḍā's life was consumed with the changing geo-political landscape of the Muslim world. He was particularly moved to tackle this issue in light of the loss of the Caliphate in the 1920s. In his discussion of such matters, all within the purview of al-siyāsa al-shar'iyya, Riḍā came to see codification of

---

[47] Ibid., 207. Of course, the issue of a legitimate debate is itself debatable and a subject that drew much criticism towards Riḍā's claims, particularly from al-Kawtharī.

[48] Ibid., 365.

personal status law (and Islamic law in general) as not only an anathema, but a tool of the European occupation of the Muslim world and therefore a major threat to the sovereignty of Muslim governments and the ʿulamāʾ. While he was a great champion of the revival of ijtihād and the permissibility and even necessity of talfīq, two of the most important tools in the codification process, he equally argued that the essential relationship between the Caliphate and ijtihād could only take place under certain political conditions; conditions he believed did not exist in Egypt at the turn of the 20th century.

From the time of the Napoleonic invasion of Alexandria in 1798, Egypt had been home to various foreign influences (particularly European), both direct and indirect. As early as the time of Khedive Ismāʿīl, whom I discussed in chapter 1, the issue of legal reform and the need for codification as its twin was a common topic that elicited commentary from the ʿulamāʾ. Yet, Riḍā did not seem to mind this or interpret these reforms as a form of colonization since, I assume, there was some semblance for him of an Islamic system of government, even if, as I argue above, this was taken for granted. In his later writings, however, Riḍā criticized these colonial governments. The loss of the Caliphate put this particular political situation into focus for Riḍā and he believed that proxy Muslim governments were just as repugnant as their European overlords. Since Riḍā saw the Caliph as an executive position, and one directly linked to the interpretation and execution of Islamic legal positions, Islamic law, as it relates to matters of the state, can only be applied through this office and in close relationship to the ʿulamāʾ who, as discussed above, are the most important members of ahl al-ḥall waʾl ʿaqd.

This is Riḍā's understanding of the relationship between Islamic law and a needed Islamic political system. What, however, is his understanding of the nature of law itself? He saw a clear distinction between secular law (qānūn) and law based on religion (Sharīʿa). Since the realm of secular law overlaps with his notion of transaction law within the Sharīʿa (muʿāmalāt), and since transaction law must be based on itjihād and not taqlīd, only an Islamic political system that links ijtihād to law can produce proper jurisprudence which secular law certainly is not.[49] Secular laws (qānūn) are for Riḍa a product of human development, not of Divine origin.[50] Riḍā seems to have held this view even if the outcome was the same in the two systems.[51] For example, while he upheld the Sharīʿa position that a thrice-pronounced divorce counts as one, revocable divorce, based on his itjihād and use of talfīq, he rejected this same conclusion as coming from the committee of personal status law. He even refused to comment on the proposed personal status code at all when asked since this would, in his opinion, acknowledge the legitimacy of the process in the first place.[52] This line of argumentation implies that, for Riḍā, a change occurs when a Sharīʿa ruling is taken from its Islamic legal context (of which the political system is essential) and rendered into a code which is, as discussed in the introduction, a product of the state. This change cuts off the law from its Divine origin, from the authority of the naṣṣ, and makes it into a product of human efforts where human reason, not Divine principles and ijtihād, govern. This is almost verbatim the argument put forth by both Hallaq and Messick as to the negative effects of codification upon Islamic law. Riḍā conclud-ed, as they do, that codification, thus defined, would render the Sharīʿa dead.[53]

Throughout Riḍā's extensive writings, he made reference from time to time to the need of offering a code or manual of Islamic

---

[49] Riḍā, *al-Manār* 23 (1922): 543.

[50] Ibid., 544. This argument emerges from Riḍā's conversation with Bakhīt al-Muṭīʿī on his use of the word qānūn. I do not read this episode simply as Riḍā making a linguistic suggestion to Muṭīʿī that the committee of personal status should rename the code to *al-Majalla al-Sharʿiyya fi'l-Aḥkām al-Shakhṣiyya*, but rather I interpret this as Riḍā making a clear philosophical distinction between the two systems.

[51] At one point he says that most new personal status laws do not violate the Sharīʿa. See: Riḍā, *al-Manār* 30 (1930): 783.

[52] Riḍā, *al-Manār* 20 (1918): 405.

[53] Riḍā argued that the closing of the Sharīʿa Courts meant an end of the Sharīʿa and a total reliance on the secular National courts. See Riḍā, *al-Manār* 2 (1899): 120.

law.[54] In his dialogue with Muṭīʿī he even argued that if the committee simply changed the name from qānūn to "*al-majalla al-sharʿiyya fi'l aḥkām al-shakhṣiyya*" it would be an acceptable form of codification.[55] Does this not mean, then, that he accepted the concept of codification of Islamic law? It is clear from his opinions on ijtihād and talfīq as well as outlines of the roles to be played by the ʿulamāʾ and the Caliph that he did argue for a code of Islamic laws. However, the fact that the actual codification that took place was not a majalla of law, but a secular code of law (qānūn) meant for Riḍā that it did not take place in the proper political context. Had he argued that the exiting political structure in Egypt was essentially Islamic in nature and that the function and role of the Caliph was found in the head of the Egyptian government, then he would have most likely agreed with the codification process, perhaps in a manner similar to Shākir. I say most likely because when Riḍā commented on the need for the Caliph and his cohorts of ʿulamāʾ to offer a simple manual of Islamic legal codes to be used throughout the state, he did not seem to endorse a complete codification, i.e. changing the form and substance of the law as outlined by Bentham, but rather advocated for a digest of law along the lines of the Ottoman Majalla, hence his use of the word majalla rather than taqnīn. In light of this, it would be more appropriate to consider his endorsement as a call for a consolidation of Islamic law, and not a codification. In either case, as this last point remains theoretical, Riḍā did reject the codification of personal status law in Egypt even though in different places he arrived at the same fiqh-based conclusions.

In Rashīd Riḍā we have a very good example of the importance al-siyāsa al-sharʿiyya plays in the process of codification. Bentham and other early proponents of codification argued that the process of codification could only take place under direction of the state since it is the state that provides the power to enact the law, while it is the use of existing legal traditions that provides its legitimacy as law. While Riḍā was famous for his use of ijtihād and use of talfīq, he was equally against the deteriorating Islamic politi-

[54] Riḍā, *al-Khilāfa*, 103–4; Riḍā, *al-Manār* 22 (1902): 866.

[55] Riḍā, *al-Manār* 23 (1922): 544.

cal structure since it too is needed to provide the necessary context for codification and consolidation of Islamic law in the first place. Therefore, not only are the outcomes of the codification process important to analyze, but so too the process and mechanism of codification itself.

MUḤAMMAD ZĀHID AL-KAWTHARĪ

For those who study Islamic intellectual trends of the 20th century, the idea of Zāhid al-Kawtharī (d. 1951) and Rashīd Riḍā appearing in the same chapter as agreeing on a certain topic might seem strange. While Riḍā represented a modernist and reformist Islam built on the idea that new thinking is needed to keep Islam and the Sharī'a relevant, al-Kawtharī represented the opposite, arguing that a taqlīd-based Islam as articulated in the four canonical sunnī schools of law is sufficient to answering difficult questions and the source of authoritative interpretation of the primary sources. However, while such a broad notion might indeed have merit and veracity, as this study has demonstrated thus far, the world and thinking of the 'ulamā' is much more intricate and nuanced. On this topic and countless others, figures from "opposing" intellectual paradigms have found a common conclusion, if argued from opposite perspectives.

Al-Kawtharī was one of the most well-known 'ulamā' of the early to mid-20th century. He served as a deputy to Shaykh al-Islam Muṣtafa Ṣabrī and was exiled with him to Egypt with the collapse of the Ottoman Empire. While this ended al-Kawtharī's political career, it placed him on a different trajectory that gained him international fame as a highly accomplished 'ālim and a defender of a more orthodox sunnī Islam against an onslaught of secular and reform thinking.[56] In the field of Islamic law he commented on the new direction that 'ulamā' like Aḥmad Shākir and Rashīd Riḍā were promoting and in the process attacked both the process and results of legal codification.

---

[56] For biographical details on al-Kawtharī's life, see: Aḥmad Khayrī, *al-Imām al-Kawtharī* (Cairo: Maktabat al-Azhariyya lil Turāth, 1999).

THE ANTI-REFORM ARGUMENT

I have made a point throughout this study to avoid using the term traditional Islam although it is my personal opinion that it is a more suited term than classical Islam, the late sunnī tradition, or any other variation.[57] By choosing the term classical Islam, I refer to both a time and a methodology. As for the time of the classical period, I borrow slightly from Alexander Knysh who defines the period of the "later Islamic tradition" as being the intellectual activity between the 7th/13th–10th/16th centuries.[58] I certainly agree with beginning at the 7th Islamic century as this represents the time when the formative period of ḥadīth collection and Islamic law came to an end and saw the formation of canonical works in both sciences. However, there were important contributions to the Islamic sciences after the 10th/16th centuries, as Wael Hallaq has shown, and both Riḍā and al-Kawtharī use 'ulamā' and writings from the post 10th/16th centuries to argue their points against codification.[59] Therefore, I think it is more accurate to say the time between the 7th/13th–10th/16th centuries represents the classical period while the time period between the 10th/16th–13th/19th centuries refers to the late sunnī period. As for the methodology of the classical Islamic period, it is a reference to a cohesive approach to the primary

---

[57] By avoiding the word tradition, I am attempting to avoid being forced to engage in the term vast genealogy and its deep meaning as used by the likes of Alasdair MacIntyre and others, which, while important discussions, would take the conversation down too many foreign paths from the current subject matter. See: Alasdair MacIntyre, *After Virtue* (Indiana: University of Notre Dame Press, 2007); Alasdair MacIntyre, *Three Rival Versions of Moral Enquiry* (Indiana: University of Notre Dame Press, 1990).

[58] Alexander Knysh, *Ibn 'Arabi in the Later Islamic Tradition* (New York: State University of New York Press, 1999), 4.

[59] Some of these figures are discussed in Wael Hallaq, "Was the Gate of *Ijtihād* Closed?", International Journal of Middle East Studies 16 (1984): 3–41. Of particular interest are Shawkānī's opinions. A good source regarding him and his thought is: Bernard Haykel, *Revival and Reform in Islam: the Legacy of Muhammad al-Shawkani* (Cambridge: Cambridge University Press, 2003).

sources, their treatment through key interpretive Islamic disciplines, and the acceptance of a certain understanding of the boundaries of authority and orthodoxy. One Egyptian source from the 10th/16th century defined these boundaries in rhyming verse:

> *Mālik and the rest of the Imāms as well as Abu'l Qāsim (al-Junayd) are the guides of this nation,*
> *It is likewise obligatory to follow (taqlīd) the guided, scholars have stated in a clear way*[60]

A 19th century commentator on this line, Ibrahīm al-Bayjūrī, argued that the definite article *al* in the word *al-a'immah* is a clear reference to the four sunnī Imāms, i.e. Mālik Ibn Anas, Abu Ḥanīfa, Muḥammad al-Shāfi'ī, and Aḥmad Ibn Ḥanbal, and that their schools of law must be followed in practice. Al-Bayjūrī acknowledged that some scholars have allowed the following of other mujtahid Imāms outside these four, but one cannot do this in matters related to legal responsa.[61] Al-Bayjūrī's reasoning for this is that the legal works of other imāms were not compiled and redacted in the same manner as the four canonical schools. Therefore, they represent incomplete legal thought, possible for certain circumstances, but not for wide use by the community, and certainly not in any official capacity.

This text and its commentary are not unique in their articulation of the boundaries of legal-orthodoxy throughout the classical period. In reading through these legal discussions, one can usually find opinions that lay beyond the four sunnī schools. However, there was very little use of these positions in practical matters. An example from this study is Aḥmad Cevdet offering two non-canonical opinions as potential solutions, but never actually using

---

[60] The author of these verses is Ibrahīm al-Laqqānī (d. 1041/1632) and the poem is entitled *Jawharat al-Tawḥīd*, which is a 144 rhyming verse poem on basic sunnī creed. It is typically referenced and studied with a commentary and/or gloss. See Ibrahīm al-Bayjūrī, *Tuḥfat al-Murīd 'ala Jawharat al-Tawḥīd* (Cairo: Dār al-Salām, 2006), 247–251.

[61] Ibid. Meaning that one could follow non-orthodox opinions as needed, but official fatwas cannot be based on these opinions.

or codifying them in the Majalla.[62] This is one of the reasons why the discussion of talfīq is so important to the debates of codification of personal status laws. A question that lingers regarding talfīq is whether or not the legal construct of eclecticism was meant to present a theoretical exercise in normative sunnī law, or was it meant to be a practical tool applied to complex legal situations?

Be that as it may, al-Kawtharī was a leading proponent of defending classical Islam and its approach against two main threats: Muslim reformists like Aḥmad Shākir and Rashīd Riḍā as well as secularists who sought to do away with Islam's influence upon Egyptian institutions, especially legal institutions. As it relates to this current discussion of codification of personal status law, Kawtharī's anti-reform stance contains four fundamental arguments:

Argument 1: Against Uniting the Schools of Islamic Law

It is common in Egypt today and at academic conferences hosted by al-Azhar University to find the concept of *taqrīb* or bringing closer together various branches of the Islamic sciences and most especially bringing together sunnī and shi'a schools of law.[63] Whether it is discussions reconciling the thought of Ibn 'Arabī with mainstream sunnī orthodoxy, or conferences outlining the definition of Muslim orthodoxy by demonstrating the acceptability of shī'ī jurisprudence, the approach of uniting and comparing what are traditionally considered independent fields is a theme very much still in vogue. In al-Azhar classes, both university and public lessons, it is not uncommon to find reference to Shī'ī legal works and positions as acceptable legal solutions, but rarely used in fatwas per al-Bayjūrī's warning examined earlier.[64] However, calls for

[62] Ḥaydar, *Durar al-Ḥukkām*,1:9.

[63] One of the most popular of such efforts and one led by senior al-Azhar officials is the Amman Message. See: HRH Ghazi Bin Muhammad Bin Talal, *True Islam and the Islamic Consensus on the Amman Message* (Amman: n.p., 2006).

[64] As it relates to the current discussion, the Egyptian law on inheritance adopted a Ja'farī position of allowing bequests to one's inheritors without the permission of the other inheritors, which goes against the sunnī position that such an act is forbidden by the ḥadīth narrated by al-

bringing Sunnī schools of law closer, not to speak of overtones of shī'ī thought, were not common discourse before the 1950s. While there were indeed those 'ulamā' of the classical period who considered all the schools of law as one school with varying degrees of rulings, 'Abd al-Wahhāb al-Sha'rānī's *al-Mizān al-Kubra* being one such example, as we saw in the previous chapter, it was not until Muḥammad 'Abduh that a four-sunnnī school approach was taken with national fatwas. And it was not until the likes of Muḥammad al-Marāghī (d. 1945) and Maḥmūd Shaltūt (d. 1963) that the concept of "bringing together" the schools and including Shī'ī thought became an openly discussed topic.[65]

The argument for bringing the schools of law closer together, often deduced from the arguments of its opponents, was an attempt to bring unity to the Islamic sciences and religious factions who were often perceived as being against one another in addition to provide a broad definition of orthodoxy, as is best articulated with the Amman Message. The general sentiment of this approach is to demonstrate that since all schools of law essentially are the same, and one does not need to be confined by them in deriving new rulings.

Al-Kawtharī rejected this position because he argued that the schools of Islamic law were already close in nature as they hail from the same intellectual and interpretive paradigm.[66] To be precise, al-Kawtharī continued, the rulings of the four sunnī schools of law are two-thirds the same, with only a third containing unique

---

Bayhaqī, "there is no bequest for inheritors." For a discussion of this law see: 'Alī Jumu'a, *Fatāwā al-Bayt al-Muslim* (Cairo: Dār al-Imām al-Shāṭibī, 2009), 324–327. For the text of the Egyptian law see: Qadrī, *al-Aḥkām al-Sahr'iyya*, 4:1757–1758.

[65] An excellent work that discusses Shaltūt's reform program and his efforts in bringing schools of Islamic thought closer is: Kate Zebri, *Maḥmūd Shaltūt and Islamic Modernism* (Oxford: Clarendon Press, 1993), 24–6, 150, and 172. For the rapprochement efforts of al-Azhar, see: Rainer Brunner, *Islamic ecumenism in the 20th century: the Azhar and Shiism between rapprochement and restraint*, trans. Joseph Greenman (Leiden: Brill, 2004).

[66] Zāhid al-Kawtharī, *Maqālāt Kawtharī* (Cairo: Dār al-Bashā'ir, 1998), 101.

and truly different positions.[67] Therefore, there is not only no need to bring them closer since this is a *fait acompli*, the method of bringing the schools closer is based on false assumptions and faulty source texts.[68]

One byproduct of the argument for uniting the schools of law is the notion that there is a difference between fiqh, which in this case can be thought of as the historic, intellectual output of the schools of law, and the Sharīʿa, which is often associated with being "true religion". At one level al-Kawtharī accepted that there is such a demarcation and that the schools of law are indeed "man-made". However, al-Kawtharī cautioned against bifurcating the two, as the schools of law are essential for understanding the Sharīʿa. His main critique of this argument was that it seemed to destroy the edifice of fiqh which he maintained was essential to understanding not only *what* the primary sources say, but equally important *how* they have been understood in the past. This understanding, it should be noted, is not the understanding simply of jurists, but rather the understandings of the mujtahid Imāms of the various schools that lived at different times throughout history. So, while the schools of law are man-made in one sense, they are the repository *par excellence* of orthodoxy and legal authority.

One tangible way al-Kawtharī's opinion on this argument played out in the codification story is in his condemnation of opinions based on direct quotation of Companions or their Followers as became common with Egypt's personal status codifiers.[69] This sort of argumentation for Kawtharī cuts these statements off from their interpretive context, a context only provided by the schools of law, which catalogue the argumentations of the mujtahid Imāms, not just their conclusions, as well as represent the redaction of

---

[67] For a list of historical sources that Kawtharī uses to make this claim see: Ibid.

[68] In one particular case, al-Kawtharī demonstrated that an entire argument used to make this point is itself based on a false and weak ḥadīth. Ibid., 95.

[69] See for example the explanatory note to law 25 of 1929, pp. 72–75 above.

these positions over time.[70] To use the language of codification, these opinions disregarded the juristic discussion of the classical period, which is essential to not only understanding the law, but plays a central role in forming legal authority.

There is little doubt that al-Kawtharī's anti-reform stance necessitated the defense of the al-madhāhib al-fiqhiyya. Whereas Egyptian legislators sought to codify personal status laws by going back to original Islamic texts, al-Kawtharī argued that one cannot access such texts without reading them through the opinions and redactions of the schools of law. Since al-Kawtharī was also a strong proponent of *taqlīd*, he said that one should not access all the opinions and arguments on a given subject in a particular madhhab, but rather suffice with the conclusive, authoritative opinion on said matter as this represents the redacted position of a particular school.[71] It appears that al-Kawtharī was less interested in proving that a certain inherited fiqh position was right or wrong, than submitting to the centuries of legal reasoning that instead produced opinions that yielded a high probability of accuracy.

Argument 2: The Schools of Law and the Limits of Orthodoxy

Al-Kawtharī's position on classical Islamic law represents a conventional, institutional definition of orthodoxy. Similar to the verses of al-Laqqānī described above, al-Kawtharī saw Islamic orthodoxy as residing within classical institutions, particularly the schools of law and orthodox Sufi orders. However, for al-Kawtharī there were strict definitions and limits to this authority. Regarding law, al-Kawtharī agreed with al-Laqqānī's opinion of there being only four Sunnī schools of law with little exception. While al-Kawtharī himself was a supporter of the Zaydī school, he spoke of the dangers of Shīʿī thought in general and the deficiency of other weaker Sunnī schools like the *Ẓāhirī* school.[72] For al-Kawtharī the inclusion

---

[70] Al-Kawtharī, *Maqālāt*, 114.

[71] Ibid., 115.

[72] Ibid., 102. Al-Kawtharī thought highly of the Zaydī school of law in Yemen and wrote an introduction to *al-Rawḍ al-Naḍīr fi Sharḥ al-Majmūʿ al-Fiqhi al-Kabīr* (See: Zāhid al-Kawtharī, *Muqadimāt al-Imām al-Kawtharī* [Damascus: Dār al-Thurayya, 1997], 405–484). While he defended this

of these "schools" in the definition of orthodoxy, and indeed in the formulation of codified laws of personal status was a direct threat to what he termed "inherited fiqh," by which he meant orthodoxy. The "inherited fiqh" of al-Kawtharī is not a system of rules and opinions that one follows blindly, but rather the cataloguing and careful redaction of sophisticated legal reasoning throughout the centuries. The schools of law become the filters through which one can interpret the primary sources of Islam and therefore represent the limits and horizons of orthodoxy. In this regard, as al-Kawtharī spoke out against the uniting of the schools of law, he equally spoke out against the other extreme of doing away with the schools of law altogether; what he termed *lā madhhabiyya.* This approach, common during al-Kawtharī's time in discussions by secular minded lawyers such as Aḥmad Ṣafwat, argued against "outdated" opinions and "archaic" terminology, and pressed for a reformation and reinterpretation of orthodoxy to cope with the modern world. Needless to say, al-Kawtharī saw this type of approach as extremely dangerous.[73] Whether taking other schools of law and equating them with canonical schools, or simply taking random opinions found throughout Islamic legal traditions, Kawtharī saw both paths as a form of neo-Mu'tazilism and a modern manifestation of placing human reason ahead of revelation and classical sunnī methodology. Al-Kawtharī's understanding of Islam, what I have likened to classical Islam, argues for a more submissive approach, an approach found in Sufism where one adheres to a safer mode of practice by avoiding laxity in legal matters.[74]

Argument 3: *Taqlīd* and *Talfiq*

Accepting the authority of the four Sunnī legal schools also means, in most cases, accepting a certain amount of reverence and defer-

---

school as a legitimate one, he argued that it was essentially a manifestation of the Ḥanafī school. Regarding the Ẓāhirī and Ja'farī schools, al-Kawtharī argued that the former's rejection of *qiyās* and the latter's lack of emphasis on the naṣṣ cast them outside of schools that can be used.

[73] At one point he likened such an approach to insanity (*junūn*). Al-Kawtharī, *Maqālāt*, 108.

[74] Ibid., 109.

ence towards them. In the space of jurisprudence and in the practice of the law, this deference takes the form of taqlīd. Even for highly accomplished jurists, no doubt we could consider al-Kawtharī to be such a figure, taqlīd is the ultimate sign of submitting to the authority of the mujtahid imāms and their legal reasoning as encapsulated and redacted over time. However, while this is a simple enough concept to grasp, it does lead to several open questions when it comes to application, and these questions refer themselves to one central question: what exactly are the limits of taqlīd? Is one necessarily obligated to follow one school to the exclusion of others, or can one follow the school they feel most comfortable with, *etc.*? In previous chapters I discussed how different supporters of codification discussed on the issue of taqlīd. From these discussions it should be clear that historically the boundaries of the schools were porous and legal sources often discussed "moving from one school to another" as a common theme. Yet, there were limits to such movements and these limits involved the possibility of a particular action being deemed prohibited by one's school (if strictly applying taqlīd) or by each school involved (if one were taking a discursive approach to following the schools of law, a practice termed talfīq). In moving from one school to another, the texts quoted by al-Minyāwī and others found throughout this study, argue that one could leave one's own school in a particular matter and follow another. Were one a Mālikī for example, they might, out of some necessity, follow the Shafiʿī school in making ablutions before prayer, then continue to follow the Mālikī school to pray two units of prayer. While some might consider this action a less scrupulous form of practice since the necessity of following another school could be subjective, it is technically not illegal. However, there is another more complicated form of talfīq in which one could conduct one action, ablution to follow the example above, and combine rulings from both the Mālikī and Shāfiʿī school in this same action. Such a *talfīq* could be considered invalid if both schools used in the performance of the action considered the particular action undertaken invalid.

It should be no surprise that al-Kawtharī did not agree with the concept of talfīq in the formulation of opinions and laws. He equated it to a reprehensible innovation (bidʿa) and something that should be avoided at all costs. While Kawtharī did not write extensively on the topic of talfīq, he did make specific comments against talfīq as it related to the committee of personal status law.[75] This is significant because it is highly unlikely that he denied the classical understanding of talfīq since there are strong sources, including Ḥanafī sources, which spoke of the permissibility of following other schools. His critique of talfīq, as I understand it, is limited to what he observed from the committee of personal status law, not the role of codification in general and its place in classical Islamic law, since he argued that they were producing laws that no established school of law legitimized and that these laws, argued under the rubric of talfīq, were essentially foreign to the body of Islamic jurisprudence. Rather, for al-Kawtharī, the permissibility of leaving one's school to follow another is a function of necessity (ḍarūra) as defined by the Sharīʿa and not by one's own whims and reasoning.[76] In the process of issuing legal responsa (iftāʾ) he cautioned against inundating people with the legal differences causing them to be confused and leading them, like the code of personal status laws, to opinions not sanctioned by any reading of the Sharīʿa.

Argument 4: On Maṣlaḥa

The last major argument in al-Kawtharī's anti-reform program, and very much in relation to the discussion of talfīq, is his treatment of the concept of maṣlaḥa, particularly the reading of al-Ṭufī on the subject as revived and discussed by Riḍā. Al-Kawtharī's basic premise in articulating the classical position on maṣlaḥa is that there is a sovereignty of the text (naṣṣ) and while there is certainly an act of reading and interpreting the text(s), there is ultimately an act of submission and deference to its meaning. His critique of both Shīʿī and Ẓāhirī approaches to Islamic law is that they lack a total reverence and preponderance towards the primary Islamic texts. His treatment of maṣlaḥa followed the same general pattern. The concept of the public good can only be defined within the context of the Sharīʿa, like the concept of ḍarūra, and cannot be defined by rational or worldly efforts.[77] To do so would place human reason,

---

[75] Ibid., 96.

[76] Zāhid al-Kawtharī, *al-Ishfāq fī Aḥkām al-Ṭalāq* (Cairo: Maṭbaʿa Majalat al-Islām, n.d.), 3.

[77] Al-Kawtharī, *Maqālāt*, 201.

and potentially human whim and caprice, above the authority of the naṣṣ al-Kawtharī also argued that al-Ṭūfī's position on maṣlaḥa carried theological complications as it assumes that God, in laying out the parameters of law in the Qur'an, did not know and does not know what is in the general good for mankind.[78] A conclusion al-Kawtharī found unacceptable.

Incidentally, al-Kawtharī's main example of how following al-Ṭufī's opinion could lead to a problematic legal outcome was the issue of divorce, which I discuss in detail in the next section. For al-Kawtharī, the rise of divorce in Egypt, and elsewhere in the Muslim world for that matter, was not a legal problem that needed certain legal answers, but fundamentally a moral one. As I discuss in the previous two chapters, supporters of codification held that allowing a thrice-pronounced divorce to count as one, revocable divorce solved the societal problem. However, for al-Kawtharī such a legal argument, one he finds completely incorrect, only *encourages* rather than *discourages* divorce, ultimately having the opposite effect than the original intent of the codified law.[79] In addition, this sort of legal thinking causes an overall weakness to how the Sharī'a and the Sharī'a courts were perceived, a concern that colors his entire opinion towards the codification process.[80]

As mentioned at the beginning of this section, al-Kawtharī did not write extensively about codification even though he lived during the time of the codification of personal status law. Rather, he was more vocal on the changing nature of the Sharī'a courts, their waning power, and the encroachment of secular law upon its jurisdiction. On this last point, al-Kawtharī was specifically vocal about the dressing of western law in Islamic garb.[81] Part of this encroachment for al-Kawtharī was the language used in the codification process such as qānūn and niẓām. However, and in much the same way as Riḍā, one cannot associate the Sharī'a (a divine source) with common law (a man-made system of rules). Therefore, the issue for al-Kawtharī was not simply one of vocabulary since the

---

[78] Ibid., 200.

[79] Ibid., 201–202.

[80] Al-Kawtharī, *Ṭalāq*, 4–5.

[81] Ibid.

law (qānūn) and, therefore, a code of law, stems from human legal reason, and it cannot be used to replace Islamic law, or Sharī'a rulings in the adjudicating of cases. He therefore had a philosophical position against codification. So far as the three main variables of codification, it is clear from the preceding discussion what he thought about ijtihād/taqlīd and talfīq, however, he was relatively silent on the role of the state and the 'ulamā' in statecraft. His opinions on the first two give us a clear indication that codification was theoretically not compatible with Islamic law. As for the specific reasons why, he did not support codification, a discussion on his critique of a thrice-pronounced divorce counting as one will suffice.

AL-KAWTHARĪ AND THE ISSUE OF A THRICE DIVORCE PRONOUNCEMENT

The Egyptian law of personal status was amended in the year 1929 with law 25, which codified, amongst other things, a thrice-divorce pronouncement counting as one, revocable divorce. Aḥmad Shākir's work defending this law, which I discuss in chapter 2, was published in 1946 and al-Kawtharī's work critiquing Shākir's book and arguing against law 25 of 1929 was published in 1956, twenty-seven years after the law was codified and in operation throughout the Egyptian judiciary. While both Shākir's work and al-Kawtharī's work deal with the mechanics of codification, the fact that they were written much later than the actual process of codification speaks to an important theme I discuss in the introduction. Codification is not simply limited to the technical act of codifying the law but must also include the juristic discussion of the law and code, what I term the intellectual footprint, surrounding the entire process, even if such discussions take place after a particular law is codified. This is one such example.

Al-Kawtharī's work discussed in this section is very important as it tackles the mechanics of codification and, according to him, demonstrates the flaws and ultimate incompatibility of codification, and the particular issue of a thrice-pronounced divorce counting as one, with Islamic legal norms. Aḥmad Shākir provided very specific discussions on why he supported the ruling of a thrice-pronounced divorce counting as one, revocable divorce. Likewise, al-Kawtharī responded in kind against this position and in so doing leaves us with one of the richest discussions of the mechanics of codification of Islamic law.

Orthodoxy and the Limits of *Ijtihād*

In the previous section I discussed al-Kawtharī's concern with defining and limiting the boundaries of orthodoxy to the four canonical schools of Islamic law. In similar fashion, his main criticism of the opinion of a thrice-pronounced divorce counting as one, revocable divorce is that it upholds "un-orthodox" legal opinions from "un-orthodox" legal schools of the past. Al-Kawtharī not only levied this attack against this specific opinion, but also maintained throughout his writing that this is one of the main weaknesses of the reform platform; i.e. having to rely on heterodox jurisprudence. Al-Kawtharī acknowledged that this specific opinion has existed in the past, particularly by Ibn Taymiyya, Ibn Ḥazm, and al-Shawkānī, however he deemed these jurists unreliable and therefore impermissible to follow. For example, he regarded Ibn Taymiyya as a liar and unreliable for stating other than what he preached.[82] Regarding al-Shawkānī, Kawtharī said that he simply followed the ḥadīth grading provided by Ibn Ḥazm whom he considered overall weak and wrong in this issue.[83] Al-Kawtharī also wrote against Shawkānī's understanding of the use of "twice" in the Qur'an to mean two "separate" pronouncements using the argumentation provided by the famous Mu'tazalite al-Zamaksharī (d. 1144/1731).[84] However, al-Kawtharī referred this discussion to the word's treatment in Sunnī sources, like Bukhārī (d. 256/870), Shāfi'ī, and al-Jaṣṣāṣ (d. 370/980) who all argue that "twice" includes a two-time divorce in one pronouncement. Kawtharī's biggest argument was that Bukhārī included this verse under the chapter heading, "Those who have permitted a three-fold divorce with one pronouncement."[85] The opinions of Ibn Taymiyya, al-Shawkānī, and Ibn Hazm and

---

[82] Al-Kawtharī, *Ishfāq*, 37. Kawtharī said that Ibn Taymiyya's grandson attested that his grandfather was duplicitous in his position on the thrice-pronounced divorce.

[83] Ibid.

[84] Qur'an 2:229.

[85] Al-Kawtharī, *Ishfāq*, 38–39.

their ratio legis, according to al-Kawtharī, have no legal effect since they violate the consensus (ijmāʿ) "of those whose opinion truly counts."[86] Therefore, al-Kawtharī on the one hand affirmed that these legal thinkers in fact held this position, the same position used to codify law 25 of 1929, but he argued on the other hand that these are aberrant opinions as they violate the authority of legal consensus.

Al-Kawtharī's opinion on what opinions count and what opinions do not count is highly significant and relevant to this discussion. For al-Kawtharī, the practice of itjihād is limited and restrictive. He relied on Ḥanafī sources to argue that there were no more than twenty mujtahids from amongst the Companions. Of the estimated 100,000 Companions that lived, this means approximately .02% of them were mujtahids.[87] Therefore, for al-Kawhtarī, ijtihād is a difficult level of legal reasoning to achieve and, as we saw in Riḍā's discussion of ahl al-ḥall wa'l ʿaqd, only the opinions of the mujtahids count towards consensus and the building of legal opinion within a school of law. To follow an aberrant opinion, therefore, is simply idle argumentation (khilāf) and not scholarly debate and divergence (ikhtilāf).[88] While al-Kawtharī cited a few of the key ʿulamāʾ whom Shākir used to form his opinion, his particular discussion of Ibn Taymiyya is most significant since it was Ibn Taymiyya's opinion, as transmitted by his loyal student Ibn al-Qayyim, that was quoted in the explanatory note of law 25 of 1929.[89] It is also the opinion of Ibn Taymiyya that is used in legal responsa today in Egypt to defend a thrice-pronounced divorce

---

[86] Ibid., 29.

[87] The number of total Companions is a subject of debate and various biographical dictionaries of the Companions have different totals. A round approximation used is that there were reportedly 100,000 Companions when the Prophet of Islam conquered Makkah. For a full discussion of this topic, one should consult: ʿAlī ʿIzz al-Dīn Ibn Athīr, *Usd al-Ghāba fī Maʿrifat al-Ṣaḥāba*, 7 vols., (Cairo: Majala Kitāb al-Shaʿb, 1970), 1:9–19; :Abd al-Barr al-Qurtubī, *al-Istiʿāb fī Mʿarifat al-Aṣḥāb*, 4 vols., (Beirut: Dār al-Kutub al-ʿIlmiyya, 1995), 1:9–31, 99.

[88] Al-Kawtharī, *Ishfāq*, 34.

[89] See my discussion of this law in chapter 1 above.

counting as one, revocable divorce.[90] These sources obviously consider Ibn Taymiyya to be a mujtahid, while al-Kawtharī, using internal sources of the Ḥanabalī school, considered him unreliable and legally insignificant.

Al-Kawtharī's concern with defending orthodoxy and classical Islam were not limited to attacking "aberrant" opinions, but also included, at times, attacking those within the orthodox classical paradigm who show any leanings outside this paradigm. For example, al-Kawtharī criticized Ibn Ḥajar al-'Asqalānī for including too many discussions in his commentaries. In this case including a discussion on this subject that some Companions held a view that a thrice-pronounced divorce counts as one, revocable divorce.[91] Al-Kawtharī found this a source of Ibn Ḥajar's scholarly "weakness". It did not seem to concern al-Kawtharī, for example, that this very topic seems to have been a legal discussion from a very early time and included people who he himself used in other places to uphold the classical legal paradigm.

The Ḥadīth of Rukāna and 'Umar's Decision

As demonstrated in Shākir's discussion of this issue, the ḥadīth of Rukāna and the subsequent decision of 'Umar to allow a thrice-pronounced divorce to have effect is at the heart of the debate surrounding the thrice-pronounced divorce. This ḥadīth contains three central issues: one, which I will not discuss here, is the linguistic significance of the word "thrice" (in Arabic *thalāthan*) which reformers like Shākir argued did not make linguistic sense and defenders of classical Islam like al-Kawtharī argued did make linguistic sense. The second and third issues, the ones I focus on in this section, relate to the ḥadīth's veracity and grading within the science of ḥadīth criticism, specifically *'ilm al-jarḥ wa'l t'adīl*, as well as the meaning and legal ramifications of 'Umar's decision.

On the first of these two issues, the veracity of the Rukāna text itself, al-Kawtharī argued that its soundness, or 'ṣaḥīḥness', is

---

[90] 'Alī Jumu'a, *al-Kalim al-Ṭayyib: Fatāwa 'Aṣriyya*, 2 vols., (Cairo:Dār al-Salām, 2005), 1:389–90.

[91] Al-Kawtharī, *Ishfāq*, 28. For the original discussion by Ibn Ḥajar see: al-'Asqalānī, *Fatḥ al-Bārī*, 9: 274–78.

doubtful.[92] He also levied the same criticism of the text citing the decision of 'Umar to treat thrice divorce pronouncements as counting three, permanent divorces, rather than one, revocable divorce.[93] Rather than argue the defects and weakness of both texts, Kawtharī, as was his fashion, cited credible classic authorities to do his bidding: in this case Abu Bakr ibn al-'Arabī (d. 543/1148) from the Māliki school and Ibn Rajab the Ḥanbalite (d. 795/1393). Since both of these texts are weak in the face of stronger evidence involving stronger ratio legis as well as the authority of ijmā', al-Kawtharī concluded that the "difference of opinion" on this subject matter in fact represents idle-argumentation (khilāf), not legitimate-scholarly-debate (ikhtilāf). Therefore, there is no veracity or legal legitimacy to the claim that a thrice-pronounced divorce counts as one, revocable divorce and such an opinion, while in fact held by some jurists of the past, is completely baseless and false.

However, al-Kawtharī did not limit his discussion to a critique of the ratio legis of the three-as-one opinion or the ratio decidenti of the codifiers to codify this law. He rather continued to offer more support and evidence why the three-as-one opinion has no validity. Largely relying on Ibn Rajab's writings, al-Kawtharī offered ten key points to support his claim:[94]

1. *The opinion of Ibn 'Abbās, the narrator of the ḥadīth, has been established from other ḥadīth that he in fact supported 3 as 3. Therefore, this particular text contradicts the narrator's own opinion.*

Al-Kawtharī based this on Ibn Rajab's treatment of Tirmidhi's *Defects* and accordingly rated this particular ḥadīth as weak and defective based on this principle. The assumption here by al-Kawtharī is that Ibn 'Abbās could not have flip-flopped on this issue as this would be unbecoming of a Companion.

2. *Ṭāwūs (d. 106/713), one of the narrators from the generation of the followers of the Companions (tābi'ūn), has singularly transmitted this*

---

[92] Al-Kawtharī, *Ishfāq*, 33.

[93] Ibid., 43–51.

[94] Al-Kawtharī's points are very technical and I have chosen, therefore, to spell them out, as I believe they are highly pertinent to the current discussion. The following points are paraphrases of his points, and not exact translations.

ḥadīth while the other narrations contradict Ṭāwūs's text, rendering this ḥadīth defective.

Similar to the previous point, al-Kawtharī argued that this is another factor causing the ḥadīth to be weak and defective for use in forming a legal ruling.

3. *According to some ḥadīth critics, Ṭāwūs's son Abdullah (d. 132/749) lied about narrating this text on the authority of his father.*

Concluding that he is a defective narrator and therefore not reliable, causing the entire text to be weak and unusable.

4. *The specific wording of Ṭāwūs, "Abu al-Ṣahbā' (d. 62/681) has said" reflects a break in the wording of the ḥadīth.*

Again, another attempt by al-Kawtharī to demonstrate the unreliability of this particular narration and therefore its non-use in forming a Sharī'a ruling.

5. *If in fact the narrator is Abu al-Ṣahbā', the patron of Ibn 'Abbās, then he is a weak narrator. If he is another Abu al-Ṣahbā' then he is an unknown narrator, both leading to a weak and defective ḥadīth.*

This is similar to number 4 above and is an attempt by al-Kawtharī to drive more doubt to the text in question.

6. *In some of the variants of the ḥadīth, Ibn 'Abbās was asked to "bring forth some of your opinions" and it would be beneath him or any other Companion to be asked such a direct question and not answer with their true opinion.*

This demonstrates al-Kawtharī's reverence for the Companions and upholding a classical Sunnī position that all the Companions are just (*'udūl*) with regards to the transmission of ḥadīth texts.

7. *Even if this is Ibn 'Abbās' opinion, his dispensations are well-known.*

That is, this is not one of them.[95]

---

[95] This is my reading of this point as I find al-Kawtharī's treatment to be a bit vague. Another potential reading is that al-Kawtharī meant to say that Ibn 'Abbās's dispensations have caused problems and this is a known fact and therefore does not hold weight in scholarly disputes. One such example is Ibn 'Abbās' opinion that it is permissible to combine

8. *Regarding 'Umar's decision in the matter, it necessitates that he went against the Sharī'a using his own opinion.*

This assumes, of course, that there was binding consensus on the issue and that there was not a change in opinion as has been argued by other 'ulamā'.

9. *This last point would also necessitate that the Companions as a group did not have the Prophet of Islam serve as their judge in matters of contention.*

This is a reference to Qur'an 4:65 and al-Kawtharī put strict observance to the sunna as a source of legal authority above all else.

10. *As for the argument that 'Umar did this from a siyasa shar'iyya point of view, how could he go against the Sharī'a for the sake of siyāsa.*

Aside from the relevance of this point to the previous one, this also demonstrates al-Kawtharī's opinion on the limits of al-siyāsa al-shar'iyya as not something that trumps agreed upon tenets of the Sharī'a, but rather must conform to it. This is the same line of argumentation that he employed when dealing with the argument of al-Ṭufī on maṣlaḥa arguing that such an approach could "destroy" the Sharī'a.[96]

These arguments constitute al-Kawtharī's main proof that the texts used to support the claim that a thrice-pronounced divorce counts as one, revocable divorce are weak and defective. It is important to

---

canonical prayers for any reason outside of travel, sickness, and the like. He narrates a ḥadīth to this effect, but al-Tirmidhī says that this is one of the most popular examples of a sound ḥadīth that is unusable. See: Muḥyi al-Dīn al-Nawwawī, *Sharḥ Ṣaḥīḥ Muslim*, 18 vols., (Beirut: Dār al-Ma'rifa, 2006), ḥadīth 1626 (5:221); Abī 'Isa Muḥammad Ibn 'Issa bin Sawra al-Tirmidhī, *Sunan al-Tirmidhī*, 2 vols., (Germany: TraDigiital Stuttgart GmbH, 2000), 2:995–96.

[96] Al-Kawtharī, *Ishfāq*, 43. The only argument that al-Kawtharī did not respond to at length is the issue brought up by Shākir and others that there must have been an abrogation (*naskh*) of the original ruling and this abrogation was the cause of 'Umar's change. Al-Kawtharī said that this point is the weakest of all and the opinions of other scholars like al-Shāfi'ī suffice for a response.

note that al-Kawtharī never disputed the claim that this was an opinion held by the likes of Ibn Ḥazm, Ibn Taymiyya, Ibn al-Qayyim, and al-Shawkānī. In fact, al-Kawtharī at one point provided a logical tree of how the original ḥadīth stating, "A thrice divorce during the time of the Prophet was one" claiming that one of the logical readings is that a thrice pronounced divorce counted as one divorce, not three.[97] He therefore did not dispute that this is either a possible reading of the text or that this reading was actually held by some 'ulamā'. His point, however, was that such readings and interpretations are invalid because they necessitate a violation of the nodes of authority that constitute the skeletal structure of the entire Islamic legal discipline. The ramifications of this point are discussed in the next and final section.

Revisiting Consensus and Upholding Traditional Uṣūl al-Fiqh

If al-Kawtharī were asked directly regarding the permissibility of a thrice-pronounced divorce counting as one, revocable divorce, he would most likely respond by saying this is not possible since there is ijmāʿ that a thrice-pronounced divorce has full effect. This is not to say that the other arguments he presented, many of which I discuss in the previous two sections, are irrelevant to his decision-making process. Rather, they represent his thorough approach to providing a point-by-point rebuttal to the major arguments adduced by his opponents, most of which were used to support codification. However, discussions of ḥadīth criticism and nuances of the Arabic reading are not the main reason for al-Kawtharī that a thrice-pronouncement counts as three. The main reason is that Islamic law, as defined by al-Kawtharī, has already settled this issue and the consensus of the mujtahid imāms is binding; end of debate. In classical Islamic law, legal consensus (ijmāʿ) is a central and binding principle alongside the textual preference of the Qur'an and ḥadīth and the use of analogy (qiyās). While it is technically true that there is no consensus on consensus as others have argued against it, al-Kawtharī argued that those opinions and those 'ulamā'

---

[97] Ibid., 45–46.

simply do not count towards forming a legal consensus since they are not at the level of ijtihād. Of course this line of argumentation can become circular and is, in my opinion, the reason there is an increased amount of plurality in interpreting Islamic law in the modern context.[98] Indeed, 'ulamā' like al-Shawkānī and modernists like Riḍā and Shākir have argued against ijmā' as well as advocated for a wider usage of the public good (al-maṣlaḥa al-'āmma) to allow for more nuanced Sharī'a opinions to accommodate a particular modern predicament. However, al-Kawtharī completely rejected this as a form of insanity (*junūn*) that could lead to the destruction of the edifice of classical Islamic law.[99]

On the general issue of reforming Islamic law, al-Kawtharī argued that only the mujtahids can form and reform Islamic law since it is their opinions that count towards the creation of Islamic law in the first place. Al-Kawtharī upheld a narrow view of ijtihād that it is a difficult rank to achieve and statistically small historically in relation to other 'ulamā'-jurists. Reform and adaptation, then, became for al-Kawtharī a function of following the classical methodology of Islamic law and taking a morally cautious approach (*'azīma*) to ensure that one is submitting to the law and not having the law submit to one's desires and whims.[100]

---

[98] One modern author, Dr. 'Alī Jumu'a, the former Grand Muftī of Egypt, argues that the Egyptian code of personal status has taken the opinion of Ibn Taymiyya in arguing that a thrice pronounced divorce counts as one, revocable divorce citing the legal principle that it is permissible to follow a differing opinion when there is a scholarly debate on a given topic. See note 90 above.

[99] Al-Kawtharī, *Ishfāq*, 83–84; al-Kawtharī, *Maqālāt*, 101–102.

[100] Al-Kawtharī, *Maqālāt*, 109.

CHAPTER 4.
'ULAMĀ' ON THE FENCE: A SILENT MAJORITY?

This chapter turns to the final section of this study to analyze a very important, yet very difficult to define group of 'ulamā'. In the previous chapter I looked at 'ulamā' who were clearly against the codification of personal status law. Their negative position was established specifically vis-à-vis the tripartite definition I laid out in chapter 1 regarding codification of Islamic law. Since they found one or more of the variables unacceptable, they concluded that the codification experiment was fundamentally flawed and un-Islamic. In this chapter I turn to 'ulamā' who outwardly seem to have concluded that codification was problematic, but on closer look actually had a nuanced position; they accepted the theoretical process of codification of Islamic law, but often critiqued the result of the actual codification process. I ask the question in the title of this chapter if one can refer to this group as the silent majority of the 'ulamā', or not. While it is virtually impossible to verify this, there are no polls for example from the 1920s–1940s that measure the opinion of the 'ulamā', I believe that this was the position of many of them, a theme I turn to in the conclusion.

I have made it a point throughout this study not to follow a specific chronology when discussing the various 'ulamā'. However, it should be kept in mind that there certainly is a chronology of the codification process and this in turn had an actual impact on when certain opinions of the 'ulamā' emerged. This reality is very much in focus in this chapter, particularly with the first 'ālim I discuss, as reactions to the codification of Egypt's civil law emerged in the 1940s. While various laws of personal status were codified in the 1920s and 1930s, the massive overhaul of Egypt's civil code in 1948 was an opportunity, once again, for the 'ulamā' to comment on the viability, or lack thereof, of the codification project itself. This led to a conflating of both projects, codification of personal status laws and codification of civil laws, and discussions of the 'ulamā' during this time period typically touched on both at the same time. It is in these two crucial decades that many opinions emerged regarding codification of Islamic law that continue to inform how the 'ulamā' of today's Egypt view the topic.

While my focus throughout this study has been on the codification of personal status law, the topic of codification of civil law and the role Islamic law played in this codification occupied a great deal of the 'ulamā's legal discussions throughout the 1940s and 1950s, and it is almost impossible to exclude them in the current discussion. While not my direct focus, it is a subject that must be accounted for in order to understand the nuanced positions of the 'ulamā' discussed in this chapter. In light of this, therefore, it is important to provide an overview of the major events of the codification of Egypt's civil code throughout this time period as pertinent background information for the rest of this chapter.

THE LATE HISTORY OF THE CODIFICATION OF EGYPT'S CIVIL CODE

As mentioned above, the focus of this study has been the codification of Egypt's personal status law. One of the reasons for this focus, as I argue in chapter 1, is that personal status law and Sharī'a became synonymous in legal discussions in the mid to late 19th century and the first half of the 20th century. As personal status laws were exclusively based on Islamic law, such an assumption was natural. However, personal status laws were not the only body of law in which Islamic law played an important role. Laws relating to commercial transactions, torts, and criminal actions (what makes up the majority of the civil code) were all aspects on which the 'ulamā' and Islamic law had much to say.[1] Accordingly, the process

[1] A separate body of law and one that was almost completely dominated by Islamic law was religious endowments (*awqāf*). See Qadrī Pasha's *Qānūn al-'Adl wa al-Inṣāf lil qadā' 'alā Mushkilāt al-Awqāf*.

of codifying Egypt's civil law in the 1940s and the endless legal discussions regarding codification brought this to light.

Egypt's first civil code was drafted in 1883 and was used throughout the National courts, a parallel legal system to the Mixed courts that adjudicated cases of foreigners through its eclectic legal code.[2] The Treaty of Montreux in 1936 called for the abolition of the Mixed courts (they were officially closed in 1949), and as early as 1937 there were discussions of rewriting the civil code and merging all legal jurisdictions into the National courts.[3] One of the major figures to emerge in this discussion was 'Abd al-Razzāq al-Sanhūrī Pasha (d. 1971).[4] al-Sanhūrī's concern with Islamic law

---

[2] See note 25 of the introduction for sources on the Mixed courts.

[3] Ziadeh, *Lawyers*, 136.

[4] 'Adul al-Razzāq al-Sanhūrī's interest in codification hails back to one of his PhD dissertations he wrote in Paris in 1926 on the subject of the Islamic Caliphate. Sanhūrī expressed concern that some body was needed to fulfill the position of the Caliphate. He posited a type of Organization of Eastern Nations to take its place and by so doing prevent the vanishing of the legal basis of a ruling (known in Islamic law as *dhahāb maḥall al-ḥukm*). Sanhūrī argued that this could not be achieved without first reforming Islamic law. The significance of this theory is that Sanhūrī perceived his work on codifying Egypt's Civil law and later his similar work in Syria and Iraq as the beginning steps in the process of restoring the Caliphate and Islamic governance. Its significance for the discussion of codification is that while Sanhūrī's remit was to develop a new civil code based on the 1883 code, he equally relied on Qadrī Pasha's writings, particularly *Murshid al-Ḥayrān*, as well as certain analytical tools found within Islamic law to make sure that the new civil code was compatible and acceptable to the Sharī'a. For Sanhūrī's writing on the Caliphate see: 'Abd al-Razzāq Aḥmad al-Sanhūrī, *Le califat, son évolution vers une société des nations orientale* (Paris: P. Geuthner, 1926); 'Abd al-Razzāq al-Sanhūrī, *Fiqh al-Khilāfa wa Taṭawuriha li Taṣbaḥ 'Uṣba Umam Sharqiyya* (Cairo: Al-Hay'a al-Miṣriyya al-'Āmma lil Kitāb, 2013); Nādiya Sanhūrī ed., *al-Sanhūrī min Khilāl Awrāqihī al-Shakhṣiyya* (Cairo: Dār al-Shurūq, 2005), introduction. For the Islamic nature of Sanhūrī's code see: Enid Hill, "Al-Sanhūrī and Islamic Law: The Place and Significance of Islamic Law in the Life and Work of 'Abd al-Razzāq al-Sanhūrī, Egyptian Jurist and Scholar, 1895–

goes back to the 1920s when he wrote about the effects of the loss of the Caliphate and the need to introduce much needed reforms in Islamic law.[5] Both Qadrī Pasha's works in the late 1800s as well as al-Sanhūrī's writings provided key arguments for how Islamic law was treated and applied throughout the codification of civil law. It was at this moment in time that a renewed interest emerged in Islamic law with a call for Sharī'a to be respected as an international legal system that should be given the same attention as the European legal systems being used in the codification process. Many 'ulamā' like Shaykh Muḥammad Sulaymān (a judge in the supreme Sharī'a court), Aḥmad Shākir (whom I discussed in chapter 3), as well as Sayyid 'Abdallah 'Alī Ḥusayn al-Tīdī (the focus of the following pages) saw the reform of Egypt's civil code as an opportunity to reassert the role of Sharī'a in Egypt's legal system and have it serve as the basis of all laws.[6]

At the same time, there was another important issue that was emerging at this time that impacted the discussion of Islamic law's influence, or in this case lack thereof, in the Egyptian judiciary. In 1928 a then unknown Arabic teacher in the city of Ismā'īliyya began an organization that would change not only the discourse of Islam in Egypt, but throughout the Muslim world. Ḥasan al-Banna (d. 1949) established the Muslim Brotherhood with the purpose of filling in the many gaps created by the collapse of the Ottoman

---

1971," part I & II *Arab Law Quarterly* 3(1988). For Sanhūrī's use of Sharī'a tools in his code see: Bechor, *The Sanhuri Code,* 81–89.

[5] Ibid., specifically Enid, *al-Sanhūrī and Islamic Law*; Sanhūrī, *Fiqh al-Khilāfa.*

[6] Al-Sanhūrī was very clear that Islamic substantive law was one of the main sources of Egypt's Civil law, not just in its drafting, but as a continual guide for judges and courts. In addition, Islam as a religious identy has remained part of Egypt's constitutional language to identify Egypt as "an Islamic nation." See: 'Abd al-Razzāq al-Sanhūrī, *al-Wasīṭ fī Sharḥ al-Qānūn al-Madanī*, 10 Vols., (Beirut: Dār Iḥyā' al-Turāth al-'Arabī, n.d.), 1:45. Also see my discussion of Muṭī'ī below and the article two of the Egyptian constitution. See pp. 183–186 below.

Caliphate.[7] While originally focused on social issues, the Muslim Brotherhood quickly spread its activities to politics and, in some instances, armed conflict earning it the ire of the government. While the growth of this movement is outside the scope of this work, its relevance to the current topic is two-fold. The first is that it introduced a new Islamic voice to public commentary. Up until the 1920s the voice of Islam was almost exclusively that of the 'ulamā' represented largely by the al-Azhar. Even when non-'ulamā' were inclined to comment on Islamic topics, they usually aligned with an *'ālim* to make their case.[8] The rise of the Muslim Brotherhood meant that there was a new way, however, to comment on things Islamic and being an *'ālim* was no longer a prerequisite. The urge to actively participate in public and political life and to advocate for everything to be "based on the Qur'ān and sunna" allowed the Muslim Brotherhood to add a twist to the religious discourse in Egypt. No longer was the call for reform and modernization coming from al-Azhar 'ulamā' like Ṭahṭāwī and 'Abduh, there was now a vying voice that was gaining popularity. The second way that the Muslim Brotherhood impacted the discussion on codification was their commentary on Egypt's legal reforms. The movement did not remain a social service movement as originally intended. Its modus operandi was largely built on the methodology laid out by its founder and charismatic leader Ḥasan al-Bannā and later replaced by the ideology of Sayyid Quṭub (d. 1966). The idea behind the movement, in brief, was that Islam plays a private and public role (termed by Bannā *dīn wa dawla*).[9] It also urged a return to a more

---

[7] The most authoritative work on the Muslim Brotherhoods remains: Richard P. Mitchell, *The Society of the Muslim Brothers* (London: Oxford University Press, 1969). For the original writings of Ḥasan al-Banna one should consult: Ḥasan al-Bannā, *Majmū'at Rasā'il al-Imām al-Shahīd Ḥasan al-Bannā* (Beirut: Dār al-Andalus, 1965).

[8] In this study, I discussed in chapter 2 how Qāsim Amīn was closely aligned to Muḥammad 'Abduh in thought and in writing. See pp. 86–91 above.

[9] These principles can be found in his Bannā's writings: Bannā, *Majmū'at Rasā'il.*

pristine Islam often times referred to as salafism.[10] As the organization spanned out into politics, their critique of legal reforms was that they were simply not Islamic (and therefore inherently evil) and must be based solely on the Qur'an and sunna, not western laws and norms. This is significant for the purposes of this chapter since it is often easy to conflate the opinion of certain Muslim Brotherhood figures during this time as the voice of the 'ulamā'.[11] This is often times extended as well to the secondary literature where there is a ubiquitous absence of the 'ulamā's voice, a voice that I have concerned myself with exclusively throughout this study. In Ziadeh's treatment of this period, for example, the Muslim Brotherhood figures as the Islamic voice of conservatism and opposition to legal reform and modernization in general and the codification of personal status law specifically.[12]

There were three main committees established to draft the civil code. The first met in March 1936, the second in November

---

[10] Ibid. While this is usually the argument, a closer look will show that Bannā was more influenced by Sufism and Sufi organizational structures, which provided the framework for his social vehicles. The post-Bannā Muslim Brotherhood was, however, more inclined to salafism.

[11] I would argue that this significance carries until today where there is a confluence of the voice of Islamic political movements and the voices of the *'ulamā'*. In contemporary writings and discourse, there is often confusion of whose voice is really being discussed. Such is the issue I find with Bruce Rutherford's work on Egypt. He relies on the narratives of those who first wrote about modern Egypt as background material (P.J. Vatikiotis, Nathan Brown, Farhat Ziadeh, Afaf Lutfi al-Sayyid Marsot, and Nadav Safran), and therefore offers the same general story of liberals bringing the "light" of liberalism to the ancien régime of Islamic institutions. At its core there is still the basic narrative of the "triumph" of liberalism, the "defeat" of Islam, and the resulting secular (read un-religious) nature of both law and government. Furthermore, the Muslim Brotherhood emerges as the main opposition and holds a monopoly on the Islamic position in contemporary Egyptian society. See: Rutherford, Bruce, *Egypt After Mubarak: Liberalism, Islam, and Democracy in the Arab World* (Princeton: Princeton University Press, 2008), on and around page 30.

[12] Ziadeh, *Lawyers*, 135–147.

1936, and the third in May 1938. The code was finally completed in April 1942 and given a three-year review period.[13] The code was finally accepted on October 15, 1949. Throughout this entire process, however, none of the 'ulamā', even those who were inclined to support the process of codification, were present. There were no 'ulamā' present at the three-committee meetings, nor at the special Senate committee meeting convened on May 30, 1948 to discuss the proposed code. What is more, there seems to be almost no mention by Sanhūrī of the voices of opposition, be they form the 'ulamā' or the Muslim Brotherhood, to the codification process as a whole. This absence was noticed by one *'ālim* in particular and rather than remain silent, he took his pen to catalogue his concern and frustration at a lost opportunity to once and for all find a compatible relationship between modern law and Islamic law. His name was Sayyid 'Abdallah 'Alī Ḥusayn al-Tīdī (d. 1948).

SAYYID 'ABDALLAH 'ALĪ ḤUSAYN AL-TĪDĪ[14]

For the majority of his professional life, Ḥusayn served as a Sharī'a lawyer and was intimately familiar not only with the Sharī'a courts and issues of personal status law, but also other areas of law that were still being adjudicated by the Sharī'a courts.[15] At the same time he was trained in Leon, France, in French law and received a

[13] Ibid., 141.

[14] His name is usually rendered as Sayyid 'Abdallah 'Alī Ḥusayn without the name "al-Tīdī". Accordingly, I will cite him throughout this work as Ḥusayn.

[15] This is a very important point since many contemporary commentators posit that since the 20th century the *'ulamā'* have been far removed from worldly matters and are only familiar with matters of personal status law. See for example Hatem Bazian's article "Religious authority, state power and revolutions: Recent events in the Arab and Muslim world are redefining the role of religious scholars" http://www.aljazeera.com/indepth/opinion/2013/09/20139106443895282.html. Two useful sources that demonstrate the opposite are: Qasim Zaman, *The Ulama in Contemproary Islam: Custodians of Change* (Princeton, Princeton University Press, 2002); Qasim Zaman, *Modern Islamic Though in a Radical Age: Religious Authority and Internal Criticism* (New York: Cambridge University Press, 2012).

law degree in 1925. Not since the time of Ṭahṭāwī did such a combination exist amongst the Azharites making him highly skilled and unique amongst his peers.[16] This combination would prove its use and utility at the end of his scholarly life when the codification of Egypt's civil law reenergized discussions of codification of Islamic law throughout the country. Like many of his contemporary 'ulamā', Ḥusayn saw the civil code as an opportunity for the 'ulamā' to once again assert their influence on the judiciary and to have Islamic law play a more purposeful role in the formation of the civil code. As mentioned in the previous section, al-Sanhūrī did not include any of the 'ulamā' in his codification work and review. As would be expected, this bothered the 'ulamā' who took to writing in newspapers to complain.[17] Ḥusayn's *magnum opus*, what the bulk of this section focuses on, was composed largely as a reaction to the non-inclusion of the 'ulamā' from the codification process of the civil code. While he does not mention al-Sanhūrī by name, it is a fair assumption that the "legal reformer" Ḥusayn quotes and challenges is none other than al-Sanhūrī himself. Ḥusayn felt that al-Sanhūrī and others who took on the process of codification without consultation from the 'ulamā' were handicapped for not considering the following essential points:

French Law is Originally Based on Mālikī Fiqh

This is one of Ḥusayn's main points throughout his writings on codification. It is even one that seems to have caught the attention of other 'ulamā' as well.[18] Specifically, Ḥusayn confines this notion

---

[16] According to HRH Prince Ṭūsūn 'Umar, Ṭahṭāwī was the only Azharite to study a European legal system. See: Ṭūsūn, *al-Bi'thāt.*

[17] See Ziyadeh, *Lawyers*, 136–138, 143 for some examples.

[18] In the many letters his contemporary *'ulamā'* wrote in support of his *Muqāranāt* work, there is copious reference to the "fact" that French law is based on Mālikī law. I myself experienced this when interviewing a well-known contemporary Mālikī jurist, Shaykh 'Abdullah bin Bayya on Saturday June 8, 2013 at Tysons Corner, VA. I enquired about this notion and he said that it is a well-known fact and that he himself had tried to engage French jurists on this point, but it always seemed to anger them.

to areas of civil law, mainly matters of commercial transactions.[19] He does find many similarities in areas of personal status law, however there are equally as many differences which he clearly points out. Even though the French civil code has many sections dealing with personal status issues, Ḥusayn saw his comparative work as dealing primarily with civil law, not criminal or personal status. He did, however, provide full commentary on personal status issues as they are covered in the French civil code. The similarities, he argued, came in both the legal point, a particular French code corresponding with its equivalent ruling in Mālikī law for example, as well as the same ratio legis ('illa) for these points. It is in fact the ratio legis for Ḥusayn, much more than the legal point itself, which allowed him to conclude that nine tenths of French law was taken directly from Mālikī fiqh.[20] He defended this point even against detractors, like al-Sanhūrī who argued, in Ḥusayn's understanding, for the lack of influence and therefore the inferiority of the Islamic legal system towards the French system.[21] An important question that emerges from this discussion is why did Ḥusayn, then, have issue, as we will see, with the Egyptian codification project adopting large swaths of the French code? In other words, it is important to understand why Ḥusayn would have any problems with a code he himself argues was 90% based on Mālikī fiqh in the first place. One reason, and one I expand on below, is that such compatibility simply represents an accidental overlap and not a purposeful adoption of Islamic law. In other words, adopting French law, or any European legal system for that matter, means that Islamic law is not truly the *basis* for the Egyptian legal system.[22]

He did say that even in his travels he has seen French legal experts acknowledge the notion that *Mālikī* law heavily influenced French law.

[19] Sayyid 'Abdallah 'Alī Ḥusayn, *al-Muqāranāt al-Tashrī'iyya*, 4 vols. (Cairo: Dār al-Salām, 2006), 1:135–38.

[20] Ibid., 1:50, 61.

[21] Ibid.

[22] See note 6 above.

Foreign Occupation of Egypt

Ḥusayn argued that the fate of foreign occupation had befallen not just Egypt, but the majority of the Muslim world. There were those nations that were completely controlled by foreign military might, and only God, he lamented, could save these nations. However, there was a second type of occupation in which certain nations, Egypt being among them, were not completely under foreign rule, but heavily influenced by their foreign overlords. These nations, Ḥusayn demonstrated, had their own governments, parliaments, and legislators. They also had mujtahids (both sunnī and shīʿī, so he must have included Iran amongst these nations as well) that have the ability to make modern, relevant Islamic laws.[23] These nations could either break free and develop modern legal codes completely compatible with Islamic law, or, as the case with Egypt and its civil code project, become unknowingly occupied.

As with other ʿulamāʾ I have discussed throughout this study, the presence of foreign influences and occupation in Egypt was a cause for great concern. Specifically, as it relates to the topic of codification, the ʿulamāʾ often interpreted reform efforts of the Egyptian government in light of foreign directives. Ḥusayn, like others before and after him, saw the codification initiative as the potential for infiltration of western legal norms, which could stand in opposition to Islamic ones. There already were the Mixed courts of Egypt which had their own eclectic European based legal code causing consternation amongst the ulamāʾ, as well as foreign influences throughout the civil and criminal codes. This was also exaggerated through the establishment of foreign schools and, as a result, the proliferation of western education amongst the upper class, which, as Ḥusayn argued, created a wedge between the ʿulamāʾ, the caretakers of Islamic law, and the emerging, westernized civil society.[24] This amplified his argument that Egypt was in fact moving away from a Sharīʿa based legal system, what the famous Article Two of the civil code was meant to address, and becoming

---

[23] Ḥusayn, *al-Muqāranāt,* 1:56–57.

[24] Ibid., 1:36–38.

a nation run by foreign legal mores, all part, he was convinced, of a foreign plot against Egypt.[25]

Role of 'ulamā'

The process of codifying Egypt's civil code, unlike the codification of laws pertaining to personal status, largely precluded the 'ulamā'. Ḥusayn saw this as dangerous since, according to the classical exegesis of Qur'an 4:59, the 'ulamā' are the ahl al-ḥall wa'l 'aqd, meaning that without their involvement and consent, the legal system would have no religious legitimacy.[26] This led to the confused state of Egypt being an Islamic nation by identity, but non-Islamic in its [civil] legal code, thus isolating Islamic law to matters of personal status. Ḥusayn saw it as an obligation for the 'ulamā' to address this critical issue and demonstrate Islamic law's ability to cope with modernity and the capability of 'ulamā', like him, to deal with codification. Due to the failing state of education and huge foreign influence, Ḥusayn saw that this true reality of both Islam and the 'ulamā' was being lost.[27]

Ḥusayn mentioned that in 1936 Shaykh Muḥammad Sulaymān 'Ināra, the then vice chair of the High Courts, was the first to publicly call for the Sharī'a to be the basis for all of Egypt's laws. Aḥmad Shākir followed suit in 1942.[28] Ḥusayn saw his own work as a continuation of these calls and part and parcel of the Islamic-codification genealogy.

The Muqāranāt Work of Ḥusayn

The above themes constitute the main reasons why Ḥusayn composed the Muqāranāt al-Tashrī'iyya. However, despite its name, Ḥusayn's work is very different than the *Muqāranāt* work of Makhlūf al-Minyāwī, which I discuss in chapter 1. Ḥusayn's work is broader in focus, concerning itself with the entire French civil code, of which matters of personal status are a part. While al-

---

[25] Ibid.

[26] Ibid., 1:58.

[27] Ibid., 1: 61.

[28] Ibid., 1:76.

Minyāwī focused on finding overlaps and points of compatibility, often times leaving large sections without commentary, Ḥusayn provided a true comparison with clear references to the ratio legis used by both legal systems, and in some cases the Justinian code as well. Therefore, while al-Minyāwī skipped many sections, most likely since those sections were not compatible with Mālikī law, Ḥusayn did a more thorough job of commenting and comparing article by article.

Likewise, while both works claim to compare Mālikī law to French law, it is important to understand what exactly their sources were. As I stated in chapter 1, there is a high likelihood that al-Minyāwī did not know French.[29] We also know from his work that he relied on al-Ṭahṭāwī's Arabic translation of the Code Napoleon printed in Egypt. Ḥusayn, however, relied on two French legal sources printed in 1922.[30] While the essence of the law is the same, Ḥusayn was clearly looking at a more modern version of French law and accessing the works in their original language, not a translation. That notwithstanding, both scholars come to a very similar conclusion regarding the distinct similarity of French law to Mālikī fiqh.

Ḥusayn, it must be remembered, was primarily writing as a reaction to the codification of Egyptian civil law and role, or lack-thereof in his opinion, of Islamic law in the process. He makes this clear in his introduction.[31] An important question that arises is why should I include his work in this study that focuses exclusively on codification of personal status law? The answer is twofold. Even though he uses the French civil code as his basis for analyzing French law, he comments extensively on laws of personal status law since the French code covers these laws. About one fourth of his work (nearly an entire volume) deals with commentary on the codification of personal status law. Secondly, Ḥusayn's work is rich

---

[29] See p. 48 above.

[30] Ḥusayn lists both sources as *Mukhtaṣar Uṣūl al-Qānūn al-Madanī* by Rene Fawani and *al-Majmū'a al-Ṣaghīra li Dalūz* by Henre Bordeaux, yet I have been unable to track down the original French. See Ḥusayn, *al-Muqāranāt*, 1:30.

[31] Ḥusayn, *al-Muqāranāt*, 1:49.

in the discussion of the basis of European law and the basis of Islamic law and the impact of codification on both legal systems that to not include such a discussion within this study would be to fall short of my mark: analyzing the opinions of the 'ulamā' towards codification of personal status laws specifically and Islamic law generally.

Ḥusayn and the History of Legal Reform in Egypt

Unlike the other 'ulamā' found in this study, Ḥusayn made it a point to discuss his interpretation of the history of legal reform in Egypt up until his time. Perhaps this is due to the fact that he was a contemporary to so much rapid change in the National courts and the civil code. Nonetheless, as an heir to earlier legal reforms that came to define Egypt's modern judiciary and as a witness to the final push to solidify the laws of Egypt into one, national code, his history offers us a unique perspective to the thinking of the 'ulamā' during the middle of the 20th century.

Ḥusayn's view of Egypt is that up until 1856 Islamic law was the only legal system used throughout Egypt for all legal jurisdictions. This was replaced in 1856 when Khedive Ismā'īl complied with the Imperial Ottoman Humayūn Decree introducing non-Sharī'a court systems. The move away from Islamic law was advanced with the establishment of the Mixed courts in 1863 and this, in Ḥusayn's opinion, marked the first "aggression" against the Sharī'a and, by extension, the 'ulamā'.[32] This wedge increased since the creation of the Mixed courts created a vacuum in Egypt's legal system. Foreigners could have their cases heard in an advanced court (the Mixed courts), but Egyptian nationals had little recourse to an effective, national legal system. This problem was addressed with the establishment of both the national civil code and National courts to adjudicate cases in 1883 and 1889 respectively.

For Ḥusayn, this history of legal reform led to two main outcomes. The first was the limiting of Islamic law qua Islamic law to

[32] Ibid., 1:41–43.

matters of personal status,[33] and the second was the association of the 'ulamā' to "men of religion" meaning for Ḥusayn a notion that the 'ulamā' only dealt with "religious" issues and therefore had no connection to worldly affairs.[34] For Ḥusayn this posited a dichotomy that relegated religion to private, personal matters and labeled it as something unfit to for matters of this world, and most especially, unfit for jurisprudence. This isolation and relegation of Islamic law and the 'ulamā' is furthered by three conclusions Ḥusayn argued legal reformers arrived at:

1. Previous legal systems, all of which were based on Sharīʿa were in complete disarray.
2. Islamic law was not unified, and up until the mid-19th century three main schools of sunnī fiqh were being used to adjudicate cases (Ḥanafī, Mālikī, and Shāfiʿī) concurrently.
3. Islamic jurisprudence and legal thought became stagnant and its creative growth halted in the late sunnī period.[35]

Ḥusayn rejected these conclusions and offered a different interpretation for the plurality of Islamic law. Ḥusayn interpreted the various schools, not as an indication that there is no uniformity and therefore confusion in Islamic law, but rather a sign of the richness of legal commentary and interpretation of the primary sources. He argued that no legal system emphasizes the letter of law without recourse to human reasoning and that the different schools of Islamic law are precisely human reason exercised by the 'ulamā' of the various schools of Islamic law.[36] He also argued, as I will discuss in detail below, that the Sharīʿa is very much alive and that there is no limit to ijtihād. The problem with renewal in Islamic

[33] Ibid. I discuss the limiting of Islamic law to personal status law in the introduction.

[34] Ibid., 1:44.

[35] Ibid., 1:45.

[36] Ibid., 1:46. As I have argued in the introduction, this diversity is equivalent to the juristic discussion that is so central to the codification endeavor. See pp. 12–13 above.

jurisprudence, he argued, is that the works of Islamic law are too sophisticated and beyond the reach of western legal experts.[37]

Ḥusayn's main problem with the history of legal reform in Egypt, however, was more philosophical in nature. He saw a major contradiction between Egypt claiming to be an Islamic state (according to its constitution), yet not having the Sharī'a as the supreme source of law as is indicated by al-Sanhūrī's second article.[38] Ḥusayn's interpretation of the Qur'anic verse 5:44 is that Islamic law is to be applied to both governors and the governed, without exception.[39] Therefore, one cannot rightfully place custom or any other legal system over the Sharī'a.

ḤUSAYN AND AL-SANHŪRĪ

Throughout his writings Ḥusayn never mentions al-Sanhurī by name. We know, however, and in large part due to the work of the edited version of the Muqāranāt, that Ḥusayn targeted Sanhūrī as his main antagonist in the fight to keep Islamic law influential in the formation of Egypt's new legal system, specifically the codification of the civil code.[40] Much of this antagonism rests on the critical issue of ijtihād. Ḥusayn saw much of al-Sanhūrī's arguments based on the notion that ijtihād in the latter generations; a period unfortunately not specifically defined by either al-Sanhūrī or Ḥusayn, waned and ceased to be exercised.[41] This led to a stagnation of Islamic law and therefore its irrelevancy in the modern period, a conclusion Ḥusayn was quick to point out many, including certain European jurists, shared.[42] As would be expected, Ḥusayn argued the exact opposite, namely that Islamic law continued to be relevant not only because it is not true that ijtihād was not practiced amongst the later generations of Muslim jurists, but also be-

---

[37] Ibid., 1:47.

[38] Ḥusayn interprets al-Sanhūrī's article two as an open invitation to leave Islamic law altogether. Ibid., 1:54.

[39] Ibid., 1:57

[40] See pp. 158–163 above.

[41] Ḥusayn, *al-Muqāranāt*, 1:52.

[42] Ibid., 1:61.

cause the door to ijtihād is always open.[43] Furthermore, the notion that Islamic law became stagnant and unable to renew itself since its internal process for doing so, i.e. ijtihād, no longer is practiced had become such a staple narrative of those who felt Islamic law was unable to be a key player in Egypt's new civil code. It led to the narrative, a narrative Ḥusayn blames al-Sanhūrī for propagating, that Islamic law is altogether backward and inapplicable for Egypt's modern codification process.

In his discussion of the Qur'an as a primary source of legislation, Ḥusayn explained the piecemeal revelation of the text and how, in the process, certain rules and regulations evolved (he uses the prohibition of alcohol as an example). His point in this discussion is that all legal systems, not just Islamic law, unfold themselves over time and in this journey, there is an evolution of legal thinking. In the world of Islamic law, therefore, one cannot properly interpret the primary texts (i.e. both the Qur'an and the sunna) without being a mujtahid, and one can only achieve this rank if they are versed in certain legal and interpretive subjects:

1. Personal traits that include being of mature age and intelligent.
2. Knowledge of: ratio legis of Sharīʿa rulings, the sciences of the Arabic language, jurisprudence methodology, rhetoric, rulings found in the primary texts, matters of legal consensus (ijmāʿ), abrogated rulings, reasons for revelation (*asbāb al-nuzūl*), conditions of texts being narrated by (*tawātur*) or singularly (*aḥād*), texts that are sound (ṣaḥīḥ) and weak (*ḍaʿīf*), and the conditions of those who transmit texts.[44]

---

[43] Ibid., 1:52, 61. Ḥusayn arguing that *ijtihād*'s door is always open is a reference by him to the narrative used by secular Egyptian jurists during his time that the gates of *ijtihād* had been closed by the *ʿulamāʾ* in later centuries.

[44] Ibid., 1:67. Tawātur is a concept that Bernard Weiss defines as "the recurrence of recitation of a text on a scale sufficient to give rise to the knowledge that the text recited is fully authentic." See: Bernard Weiss, *The Spirit of Islamic Law* (Athens: The University of Georgia Press, 2006), 49.

His conditions for ijtihād lead to two conclusions. The first is that these are conditions that can actually be fulfilled as opposed to a theoretical claim, and one who has them must practice ijtihād openly, and one who does not have these traits needs to follow those who do, i.e. taqlīd. The second conclusion is that law as such is a dynamic body of knowledge that is constantly in need of evolution. This is true of secular law (qānūn) and of Islamic law (sharī'a) alike. This constantly evolving body of knowledge is therefore in constant need of explanation and elucidation vis-à-vis changing circumstances in order for it to be relevant and to continue to live; otherwise it weakens and dies.[45] And since this process, i.e. the process of ijtihād, never ceased within Islamic law and is continually practiced, Islamic law as such is very much alive and, more importantly, relevant.

In addition to arguing for the possibility and necessity of ijtihād of Islamic law, Ḥusayn also argued that the code al-Sanhūrī was relying on, i.e. the French code,[46] was itself based on Islamic law, specifically Mālikī fiqh, further proving, in Ḥusayn's opinion, that Islamic law is not only relevant and valid for modern legal purposes, but that it is already playing a direct role in the formation of Egypt's civil code. This argument, backed by his claim that nine tenths of the French code is compatible with Mālikī fiqh, concluded for Ḥusayn that whether al-Sanhūrī or any secular jurists liked it or not, they were in fact dealing with Islamic law in the formation of the new civil code of Egypt.

In his short but poignant discussion of Sanhūrī, Ḥusayn also commented on the overall role, or lack thereof, of the 'ulamā' in

---

[45] Ibid., 1:52. I should note here that this is almost verbatim my understanding of Jil's "juristic discussion" which I analyze in the Introduction.

[46] We know that al-Sanhūrī used dozens of western civil codes to form the Egyptian civil code and did not rely only on the French code. Ḥusayn also makes another significant mistake when he says that the Mixed courts of Egypt were based on French law. However, in a follow up letter to al-Azhar leaders, Ḥusayn complains that one of the main problems of the new civil code is that it is an amalgamation of sixteen civil codes. Ḥusayn, *al-Muqāranāt*, 1:74; 4:1656–58.

the codification of the civil code. We know that none of the 'ulamā' were part of the various committees to produce the civil code. We also have no evidence that Ḥusayn specifically was part of the committee to oversee the codification of personal status laws. Ḥusayn was quick to dispel the notion that the 'ulamā' have been silent on this subject and demonstrated that there were those, like himself, who had risen to the challenge, and since these 'ulamā' are essentially the people "who loosen and bind", they are an integral part of the legislation process. To make this point clear, Ḥusayn sent copies of his opus to various contemporary 'ulamā' asking for their feedback during his lifetime. These letters, preserved as an appendix in the edited version of the al-Muqāranāt, demonstrate that this group of 'ulamā' supported his notions that they have an important role to play in the codification discussion. Ḥusayn also demonstrated through these letters that he is not the only one capable of making a positive impact in Egypt's new civil code.

Much of what Ḥusayn accused al-Sanhūrī of, al-Sanhūrī did not actually say. In fact, al-Sanhūrī was very much a proponent of Islamic law's needed revival in order for it to take its proper role in international jurisprudence.[47] He also did not have anything against using Islamic law as a basis for his own civil code project.[48] It is also likely that the many writings of al-Sanhūrī written before 1948 were accessible to Ḥusayn. Therefore, the question to be asked is why did Ḥusayn interpret al-Sanhūrī as not only antagonistic towards Sharī'a, but a proliferator of the negative narrative of Islamic law as dead and irrelevant? I believe the answer lies not in Ḥusayn's interpretation of Sanhūrī's writings, but in his interpretation of al-Sanhūrī's actions. By not including the 'ulamā' in the committee for the formation and review of the civil code, especially Ḥusayn who was so focused on this issue and made this concern public knowledge, 'ulamā' like Ḥusayn were only left to conclude that al-Sanhūrī sought to usurp the right to interpret the Sharī'a from the world of the 'ulamā', those who alone can "loosen and bind", to the world of secular lawyers who, like Qadrī Pasha in the previous

[47] See sources on al-Sanhūrī in note 4 above.

[48] Al-Sanhūrī defended his use of Islamic law and its absolute importance in his codification process. Al-Sanhūrī, *al-Wasīṭ*, 1:45.

century, had some training in Islamic law. Whether knowingly or unknowingly, al-Sanhūrī's omission was interpreted by Ḥusayn as a serious rupture in the system of al-siyāsa al-shar'iyya and presented a threat to the crucial role that the 'ulamā' played up until the middle of the 19th century, a role that was no doubt waning.

ḤUSAYN AND THE TRIPARTITE DEFINITION OF CODIFICATION

If Ḥusayn was so against al-Sanhūrī's codification project, how can one claim that he was a supporter of the codification of Islamic law? I believe that to ascertain this, one must make a distinction between the codification of Islamic law as such and the codification of Egypt's civil code that was undertaken by Abd al-Razzāq al-Sanhūrī. I believe that a rejection of the latter, a specific process taking place at a specific point in time, does not equate with a rejection of the former, a more theoretical position that is cast upon the entire body of Islamic law qua Islamic law. I also believe, as mentioned in the previous section, that Ḥusayn's rejection of the al-Sanhūrī project was not due to a theoretical problem with the codification of Islamic law, nor even necessarily with al-Sanhūrī's conclusions. Rather, it had to do with the sidelining of the 'ulamā' in playing a role in interpreting the Sharī'a and subjecting the newly drafted civil code to a Sharī'a review. Ḥusayn himself argued that the definition of law (*qānūn*) is simply a collection and ordering of all legal rulings (aḥkām in his language) and their legal conditions (shurūṭ) in one volume. According to this understanding, this term applies to the Qur'an itself.[49] This is significant since the understanding that the 'ulamā' had of qānūn is part and parcel of their opinion towards codification (taqnīn). That is to say that codification of Islamic law for Ḥusayn is simply rendering the Sharī'a in the same form and structure as law (qānūn) and not necessarily an altering of its substance.

---

[49] Ḥusayn, *al-Muqāranāt*, 1:80–81.

Al-siyāsa al-sharʿiyya

Although Ḥusayn may have taken issue with elements of the Egyptian government, particularly the legislative branch, he was on the whole highly supportive of the overall political structure. He never posited, like Riḍā for example, that there was to be one expression of an "Islamic state" and completely accepted the historical plurality and manifestations of various Islamic body politics.[50] He was not so much concerned with the mechanics of the state as he was concerned with what principles and constitutional laws the state itself was based on. In this regard he was comfortable making a distinction between *tashrīʿ samāwī* and tashrīʿ *waḍʿī* to imply that it is natural that the day-to-day affairs of the state and its institutions would run according to rules and regulations set by the government.[51] Such laws as the need to keep records, filing systems, the order and upkeep of infrastructure, etc., are laws that are needed to make the state run and since the Sharīʿa at a macro level calls for the establishment of a state, it has legitimized such laws.[52] However, the constitutional laws, what he terms qānūn niẓām al-ḥukm, must be based exclusively on the Sharīʿa and it is this that gives legitimacy to the state and its civil laws. These constitutional laws, according to Ḥusayn, are based on clear texts found in Islam's primary sources and are immutable, timeless principles that must be adhered to without exception. His main objection to al-Sanhūrī's project was that it was based not on the Sharīʿa, but French law. Even though Ḥusayn made a compelling argument through the al-Muqāranāt that the overwhelming majority of French law is compatible with Mālikī fiqh, and even though he viewed al-Sanhūrī as adopting this code for Egypt's civil code, his objection was that the civil code should be based on Islamic legal principles and not the accidental overlap one European legal code may have with Islamic common law.

Ḥusayn also posited that there are laws that change with time and circumstance according to the wellbeing of society at large

---

[50] Ibid., 1:77.

[51] Ibid., 1:81.

[52] Ibid., 1:104–105.

(maslaḥa). These laws require two things: The first is people who have been authorized by the state to enact and enforce these laws, implying that this is a fundamental right of a legitimate state, a description he believes applies to Egypt. The second is that these laws are in need of changing (he likens this to the process of ijtihād) in order to maximize the wellbeing of society. These changeable, enacted, and enforced laws, however, are not to violate constitutional laws, which are, in Ḥusayn's opinion, based solely on clear texts and principles laid out in the Qur'an and sunna.

Ḥusayn's conclusion on this subject is that when the correct political and legal process is applied, there is not only no problem with codification of Islamic law, there is no discrepancy between manmade civil laws and the Sharī'a.[53]

Ijtihād and *Taqlīd*

Ḥusayn was an al-Azhar trained 'ālim before he received his secular legal training in France. His three works answering questions related to law and theology in the Mālikī, Shafī'ī, and Ḥanafī schools attest to the breadth of his knowledge in Muslim substantive law (furū').[54] These works demonstrate that, as might be expected, Ḥusayn typically stayed within the confines of the sunnī schools of law in answering questions. In matters of personal status for example, the primary focus of this study, Ḥusayn rarely left the standard relied-upon opinion of each school in answering questions. For example, on the subject of a thrice-pronounced divorce in his work on Mālikī furū', he acknowledged that such a divorce has full effect.[55] However, for the Shāfi'īs this subject depends on the intention of the husband issuing the pronouncement.[56] On the topic of

---

[53] Ibid., 1:81.

[54] Ḥusayn, Sayyid Abdallah, *al-Ajwiba al-Fiqhiyya fi'l Madhhab al-Sāda al-Shāfi'iyya* (Cairo: al-Maktaba al-Maḥmūdiyya al-Tujāriyya, n.d.); Ḥusayn, Sayyid Abdallah, *al-Ajwiba al-Khafīfa fi'l Madhhab al-Imām Abī Ḥanīfa* (Cairo: al-Maktaba al-Maḥmūdiyya al-Tujāriyya, 1958); Ḥusayn, Sayyid Abdallah, *al-Ajwiba al-Tīdiyya fi'l Madhhab al-Sāda al-Mālikiyya* (Cairo: al-Maktaba al-Maḥmūdiyya al-Tujāriyya, 1965).

[55] Ḥusayn, *al-Ajwiba al-Tīdiyya fi'l Madhhab al-Sāda al-Mālikiyya*, 103.

[56] Ḥusayn, *al-Ajwiba al-Fiqhiyya fi'l Madhhab al-Sāda al-Shāfi'iyya*, 133.

the divorce pronouncement of a drunkard, he held that for the Mālikīs it does not count as a true divorce[57] (the opinion chosen by the code of personal status law),[58] while for the Ḥanafīs it does count and have full effect.[59]

These types of answers, and essentially any section one reads in these three books on substantive law, would lead to the conclusion that Ḥusayn was a proponent of taqlīd over ijtihād. However, the case is very different when one reads his comments on the subject in the al-Muqāranāt. He talked openly about the conditions that need to be fulfilled to reach the rank of ijtihād adding no disparaging comment that such a level is impossible to reach. He also wrote that ijtihād is an open issue that needs to be practiced by those who are qualified.[60] The only limitation he put on ijtihād was that it could not take place against a clear text (naṣṣ) of the Qur'an and sunna.[61] Ḥusayn also demonstrated his own ijtihād throughout the al-Muqāranāt work. In discussing the difficult topic of inheritance across religions, i.e. a Muslim inheriting from non-Muslim relatives, a topic that is usually treated as a source of legal consensus (ijmāʿ) against such an act, he offered a nuanced interpretation. Ḥusayn argued that one could treat the Abrahamic faiths (Judaism, Christianity, and Islam being the three main religions in Egypt at the time of Ḥusayn's writing) as one *milla* or religious community to allow for interfaith inheritance.[62] Also, in discussing the fatwa of Shaykh Muḥammad ʿIllaysh (d. 1299/1881) on the issue of women's gold bracelets and potential alms on them, he argued that the customs of the 1940s had varied greatly from the time of ʿIllaysh and the ruling should therefore reflect this.[63] His ijtihād also worked in reverse. That is to say he often times used the tactics of ijtihād to defend an Islamic legal position against modern concerns

---

[57] Ḥusayn, *al-Ajwiba al-Tīdiyya fi'l Madhhab al-Sāda al-Mālikiyya*, 100.

[58] ʿAbd al-ʿĀṭi, *al-Mabādi' al-ʿĀmma*, 125; Geuthner, *Revue Des Études Islamiques*, 137–153.

[59] Ḥusayn, *al-Ajwiba al-Khafīfa fi'l Madhhab al-Imām Abī Ḥanīfa*, 167.

[60] Ḥusayn, *al-Muqāranāt*, 1:52.

[61] Ibid., 1:66.

[62] Ibid., 4:1378.

[63] Ibid., 4:1465.

by analyzing the evidence for such a position and tackling modern critics. For example, he defended the marriage age of the Egyptian code of personal status and argued *against* raising it to be compatible with the French code.[64] The point to be made here is that Ḥusayn did not take for granted positions of the sunnī schools of law by way of taqlīd and instead employed ijtihād in a serious way to defend the codification of Islamic law and by so doing demonstrated that the Sharīʿa is applicable in every time and place.[65]

Did Ḥusayn's position regarding ijtihād change from writing his first three works on substantive law in face of the realities of the codification of Egypt's civil code, or was he, in some fashion, representing the same position, but in different settings? I believe that the answer is the latter. I understand Ḥusayn's first three works discussed in this section briefly to be works written within the context of a singular school's substantive legal tradition. There would be no reason, therefore, to argue against a particular ruling as being too stringent or being archaic and not applicable with regards to modern norms. Rather, the point of these books was to offer standard rulings to questions students might have regarding them. The situation changes, however, when one asks for a fatwa, implying that one is seeking an answer for the here and now, a practical ruling to be applied against modern realities. This is where his al-Muqāranāt falls and this is why he took a different approach towards ijtihād and other issues. I also find after clear examination that Ḥusayn supported this exact notion in his three *Ajwiba* books making a clear distinction between answering questions of substantive law and issues of iftā'. In answering questions on Mālikī rulings regarding divorce, for example, he wrote that when a mufti is introduced, they must take into consideration custom (*'urf*) as the application of these rulings can change with circumstance.[66] His al-Muqāranāt, therefore, should be considered a large application of this very notion.

---

[64] Ibid., 1:165.

[65] Ḥusayn, *al-Muqāranāt*, 4:1668.

[66] Ḥusayn, *al-Ajwiba al-Tīdiyya fi'l Madhhab al-Sāda al-Mālikiyya*, 103.

Talfīq

In line with his use of ijtihād outlined above, Ḥusayn's treatment of talfīq is very similar. In his works on Muslim substantive law, when discussing a particular school of law, he did not bring in others' opinion in answering questions in which there is a legitimate legal debate (khilāf). For example, in answering questions on a divorce pronouncement associated with a number, i.e. "I divorce you twice, or thrice", he answered strictly according to the rulings of each school (Mālikī, Shāfiʿī, and Ḥanafī). He did not offer footnotes, for example, citing another school's legal opinion. As I argue above, this is not an implicit argument against talfīq, but rather an adherence to the genre of writing within the confines of a particular school of law. When it came to his al-Muqāranāt, however, Ḥusayn had a different attitude towards legal eclecticism and practiceed it openly.

Ḥusayn explicitly stated that any code of law for Egypt should be based on the Sharīʿa.[67] He never made a point that the code must be based on a specific school of law (madhhab), but rather the law's basis must stem from Islamic law, not European law. To make this point clear, and to demonstrate that a law based on the Sharīʿa is different than a law based on a specific school of law (the madhhab being an interpretation of the Sharīʿa), Hussayn offered from time to time eclectic legal answers other than the standard Mālikī opinion his opus claimed to offer:

1. He supported talfīq in the marriage process by offering the opinions of all four schools of sunnī law in discussing issues such as: allowing a woman to marry herself to a man, the non-necessity of having a legal guardian conduct the marriage contract, etc. Rather than offering the opinions of Mālikī jurists only, what he did in *al-Ajwiba al-Tīdiyya fi'l Madhhab al-Sāda al-Mālikiyya*, in the al-Muqāranāt he offered the full gambit of legal opinions.[68]
2. The majority of sunnī jurists hold that a woman's legal guardian (*walī*) must be a non-marriageable, male relative

[67] Ḥusayn, *al-Muqāranāt*, 1:79–80.

[68] Ibid., 1:164.

(*maḥram*). However, when discussing this issue as it relates to personal status law, Ḥusayn said, "it is permissible for the walī to be a woman in the school of Abī Ḥanīfa."[69]

3. In complicated matters relating to personal status law, Ḥusayn typically offered the breadth of legal opinions on the matter. It is no surprise that on the topic of a thrice-pronounced divorce he did the same. In his work on Mālikī substantive law, Ḥusayn clearly stated that a divorce pronouncement accompanied by a number has effect.[70] In discussing the matter in the al-Muqāranāt, however, he allowed a thrice-pronounced divorce to count for one, revocable divorce pronouncement.[71] Since he ascribed this to a unique opinion amongst the Mālikīs, this represents a form intra-madhhab talfīq.

The point to be made here is that Ḥusayn used legal eclecticism when it came to apply Islamic law to modern legislation. As long as he was able to ground a legal point in an argued Islamic legal context, the law became *based* on the Sharī'a and therefore applicable for Egypt's legal needs.

THE INCOMPATIBILITY OF FRENCH LAW FOR MUSLIM PERSONAL STATUS ISSUES

Ḥusayn's major claim throughout his al-Muqāranat was that French law, specifically the sources he looked at, was 90% compatible with Mālikī law for the simple reason that the former is based on the latter. While the main function of his al-Muqāranāt project was to challenge Sanhūrī's process of codifying the civil code, the French code of law itself contained many sections related to matters of personal status law. While there is no denying that the articles of the French code Ḥusayn analyzed bear a resemblance to Mālikī law, even if it is not satisfactorily established that French legal sources took from Mālikī substantive law. However, when Ḥusayn dis-

[69] Ibid., 1:170.

[70] Ḥusayn, *al-Ajwiba al-Tīdiyya fī'l Madhhab al-Sāda al-Mālikiyya*, 103.

[71] Ḥusayn, *al-Muqāranāt*, 1:261.

cussed the relationship of French personal status laws to Islamic law, he found French law grossly incompatible with Islamic legal norms. Whereas French laws related to civil issues could be reconciled with Mālikī legal reasoning, Ḥusayn demonstrated this rather effectively throughout his work, he argued that such is not the case with French laws related to personal status. It is not surprising, then, that the 10% of French law that is not compatible with the Sharīʿa, in Ḥusayn's opinion, are in fact the laws of personal status. Specifically, laws pertaining to marriage and divorce.

Husayn's critique of these laws can be summarized in the following three themes:

The Financial Relationship Between Husband and Wife

A major theme Ḥusayn observed throughout the French legal discussion of marriage was that a wife's financial independence, i.e. her own wealth and property, was neither protected by the law, nor were these individual holdings kept private after marriage.[72] Legal independence is not something unique to Mālikī substantive law, and, as Ḥusayn pointed out is something that the four sunnī schools of law agree on.[73] This financial independence is also not vitiated by marriage and, according to legal consensus amongst Muslim jurists, this carries through marriage and even after marriage seizes either by death or divorce.[74]

Gender Mixing

Like many jurists of his time, Ḥusayn took great offense to what he saw as, "lax sexual mores" of Europeans. Unlike many of his contemporary, he at least had lived in France for several years and would have seen gender interactions amongst the French first hand. As it relates to the law, Ḥusayn criticized the French notion of the engagement period. While such a pre-marriage period theoretically exists in Islamic marriage custom, legally speaking it has no effect on the relations between the engaged couple. The only thing

[72] Ḥusayn, *al-Muqāranāt*, 1:158.

[73] Ibid.

[74] Ibid., 1:235.

according to the Sharī'a that makes gender mixing and sexual relations licit is the marriage contract itself. Before that, all forms of interaction fall under the illicit. For Europeans, or more specifically in Ḥusayn's case the French, the notion of gender mixing generally and the engagement period specifically as one manifestation of this concept, leads, in Ḥusayn's opinion, to a highly promiscuous society, which, according to the Sharī'a, is an anathema.[75] Rather than prolonging this strictly non-legally binding period, Ḥusayn argued that couples should marry at an earlier age rather than wait. This was one of his main reasons for opposing the proposed law to raise the minimum marriage age in Egypt.[76] Ḥusayn, rather surprisingly, held the view that marriages officiated before the legal minimum age is sound *(jā'iẓ shar'an)*, but has no legal effect (i.e. through the state). Couples, therefore, incur no moral sin and he even encourages this practice as a way to mitigate lax sexual habits. For Ḥusayn, the minimum requirement for marriage is puberty of both genders as he argued that sexual intercourse before puberty is physically harmful, and therefore impermissible.

Difficulty of Divorce Leading to Extra Marital Affairs

Very similar to his views on gender mixing, Ḥusayn criticized the difficulty French law placed in obtaining a divorce. French law, most likely following church laws and doctrine on this issue, reserved divorce for certain instances such as adultery and undue hardship and abuse.[77] Ḥusayn also criticized the Roman legal concept of "physical separation" which he argued was more destructive to marriage than divorce.[78] Ḥusayn's point of contention with the French legal notion of divorce was based on two factors. The first was legal and stems from the basic principle that in Islamic law marriage and divorce are based on contract law, not a holy sacrament regulated by the church. Marriage, therefore, is a contract between the husband and the wife, through her legal guardian, and

---

[75] Ibid., 1:159.

[76] See his discussion as well as helpful footnotes from the editors on this topic: Ibid., 1:165–166.

[77] Ibid., 1:249.

[78] Ḥusayn, *al-Muqāranāt*, 1:246.

divorce is nothing more than the breaking of this contract.[79] The second was moral and related to what Ḥusayn referred to as the common occurrence of married couples engaging in extra marital affairs in Europe due to the cumbersome process of divorce. For him the difficulty in a couple receiving a divorce, even for the simple reason that they no longer want to be wedded to one another, helped give rise to these dalliances. This is made easier with the halfway solution of physical separation where there is, essentially, the semblance of divorce minus the legality.

As a counter system, Ḥusayn highlighted the ease of divorce as envisioned by Islamic law, the abuse of which has occupied much of this entire study, as well as, and as may be expected, a defense of polygamy.[80]

The question remains what do these differences mean exactly in relation to Ḥusayn's opinion towards codification of Islamic law, especially in light of his claim that 90% of French law was compatible with Mālikī substantive law? In other words, why did he oppose Sanhūrī's project and what, exactly, was his stance on the codification of Islamic law? Ḥusayn stated clearly that a legitimate political entity, i.e. the recognized legislative branch of a recognized and politically constituted nation-state, has the right to form a code of law and make it have full effect throughout the realm controlled by that particular nation state.[81] He also said that such laws needed to be based on the Sharīʿa, not a foreign legal system.[82] While he does make a distinction between Divine laws (tashrīʿ samāwī) and man-made laws (tashrīʿ waḍʿī), we are left to assume that he would argue for the need of this legal system to be based on the principles of the Sharīʿa. I believe that another way of saying this is that Egypt's code of law, both personal status and civil, cannot be based on a legal system that accidently overlaps with Islamic law, but these laws must be deduced *deliberately* from and adhere to Islamic

[79] This is not to say that there is no moral side to the Sharīʿa conception of marriage and divorce. Rather, my comments are specific to the legal understanding of marriage and divorce as laid out in Islamic law.

[80] Ḥusayn, *al-Muqāranāt*, 1:175.

[81] Ibid., 1:81.

[82] Ibid., 1:79–80.

legal principles, even if the result is nearly the same. While such a notion may seem futile if the final result is the same, it should be kept in mind that the difference is that according to Ḥusayn's understanding of codification, the 'ulamā' would be involved in his form of codification and a precedent would be set for future juristic discussions in which the result may indeed be quite different from European law.

MUḤAMMAD BAKHĪT AL-MUṬĪ'Ī

Muḥammad Bakhīt al-Muṭī'ī (d. 1936) was born in the city of Qaṭī'a in Upper Egypt.[83] Although his family was predominately Mālikī, he himself studied the Ḥanafī school of law, perhaps since this is where upward mobility was vis-à-vis careers in Islamic law at the time. He was a well published and respected 'ālim during his lifetime and although he served in various official capacities, it was noted by his biographers that he never ceased teaching.[84] He served as a judge in the Qalyūb district, al-Minya district, Port Sa'īd, Suez, Fayyūm, Asyūṭ, and Alexandria. He subsequently became an inspector in the Ministry of Justice, then the head of the Sharī'a court bench, and finally the Grand Mufti of Egypt in 1914 until his forced retirement in 1920.[85] In his retirement, he spent more time in the political arena, which caused much controversy and uproar of negative sentiments towards his stances and activities.[86] His po-

[83] Aḥmad ibn Siddīq al-Ghumārī states that there is some discrepancy in the date of his birth and some of his contemporaries argued that he was born in 1254 AH. In addition, al-Muṭī'ī himself changed the spelling of his city from Qaṭī'a to Muṭī'a and therefore popularized this rendition of the family name. See: al-Ghumārī, *al-Baḥr al-'Amīq*, 1:195.

[84] Usāma al-Sayyid Maḥmūd al-Azharī, *Asānīd al-Miṣriyīn* (Abu Ẓabi, Dār al-Faqīh, 2011), 358.

[85] Ibid. Regarding al-Muṭī'ī's forced retirement, al-Ghumari says he was typically stern in the face of the government and might have insulted a certain Pasha (he does not specify who) which caused that Pasha to have the laws of forced retirement, previously not governing the position of the Grand Mufti, apply to Muṭī'ī. See al-Ghumari, *Baḥr al-'Amīq*, 1:199–200.

[86] Al-Ghumari, *Baḥr al-'Amīq*, 200. Al-Ghumārī says, "The reason for this was his engagement in politics and his involvement in some of the

litical interests led him to serve on the constitutional committee of 1923 where he helped draft Egypt's first constitution. In that role he was largely responsible for introducing the language that Islam is "the official religion of the Egyptian nation", a phraseology that lasts until today in defining Egypt's religious character.[87]

It is clear from the few who have written about him that he was extremely popular and served as a direct teacher to many key figures of the early 20th century: Muḥammad Muṣtafa al-Marāghī, Muḥmūd Shaltūt, Aḥmad bin Siddīq al-Ghumārī (d. 1961), Yāsīn al-Fādānī (d. 1990), and many more.[88] Of significant note for this study is that Zāhid al-Kawthārī was a close associate of Muṭī'ī throughout the former's exile in Egypt.[89] Towards the end of his life, the number of non-Egyptian and non-Arab students increased in his circles and he was known to give them extra attention.[90]

Al-Muṭī'ī was an accomplished jurist and teacher throughout the majority of his life. Despite the many positions he held, al-Muṭī'ī's fame grew largely from his public classes. Unlike many of his contemporaries whose lessons were more-or-less monologues, Muṭī'ī promoted class discussion and debate. He was also known to be a highly proficient humorist and used his wit to make difficult subject matters more accessible for a wider audience.[91] However, al-Muṭī'ī was also a student of al-Afghānī and was proficient in log-

---

political groups of the time. People, therefore, became disinterested in him, and rumors about him spread to the point that people labeled him a traitor and biased towards the English. One student said of him one day, 'I believe Shaykh Bakhīt is the most knowledgeable man in the world, and he is a disbeliever (kāfir).'"

[87] Al-Azharī, *Asānīd al-Miṣriyīn*, 361.

[88] Al-Muṭī'ī, Muḥammad Bakhīt, *Fatāwa* (Lebanon: Dār al-Siddīq, 2012), 8. Also see: Syed Junaid Ahmed Quadri, "Transformations of tradition: modernity in the thought of Muhammad Bakhit al-Muti'i" (PhD diss.,, McGill University, 2013); and Jakob Skovgaard-Petersen, *Defining Islam for the Egyptian State* (Leiden: Brill, 1997), 133–140.

[89] Al-Kawtharī, *Maqālāt*, 113.

[90] Al-Ghumari, *Baḥr al-'Amīq*, 1:199.

[91] Ibid., 1:196–200.

ic, western philosophy, and even astronomy.[92] Yet, this should not be mistaken for a reform attitude towards Islam for al-Muṭī'ī was most certainly a conservative and defender of the classical approach and might have even seen the efforts of Muḥammad 'Abduh as a threat to the "purity" of al-Azhar.[93]

GENERAL POSITION AND UNDERSTANDING OF CODIFICATION

Similar to Ḥusayn, al-Muṭī'ī was not opposed to the concept of codifying Islamic law as such but did have a lot to say about how such a process is to properly take place. His basic premise of the need for a code of law in the first place was to ensure that any two litigants would be able to "trust" the law, hence the need for a written code, and know full well that such a law is based on solid jurisprudence, not the whims of man.[94] He saw this not as a rationalization for the codification process already occurring in Egypt during his lifetime (primarily the codification of personal status laws), but rather a function inherent in the power held by those in political authority, a subject I will discuss in detail in the following section.[95] Al-Muṭī'ī's major concern, however, was not with the issue of codification of Islamic law, or more specifically personal status law-he argued that this is a given, but rather what the limits of such a project are vis-à-vis the Sharī'a. His two main writings on the topic serve as a critique of the proposed laws on personal status for their

[92] Ibid., 1:208–209.

[93] Ibid., 1:209.

[94] This is a very interesting notion as it is verbatim what Bentham said about codification (pp. 5–6 above). Muḥammad Bakhīt al-Muṭī'ī, *Raf' al-'Aghlāq 'an Mashrū' al-Zawāj wa'l Ṭalāq* (Cairo: n.p. 1927), 216. A more accessible edition, but one I only discovered after writing this chapter is: Muḥammad Bakhīt al-Muṭī'ī, *Raf' al-'Aghlāq 'an Mashrū' al-Zawāj wa'l Ṭalāq* (Cairo: Dār al-Furūq, 2006).

[95] I find it significant that he does not make this argument as a retroactive support of codification, i.e. since it was already a wave and a reform the *'ulamā'* had to deal with, but rather he states that this was always the case with the Sharī'a even in the time of the Prophet of Islam. Ibid., 36.

misunderstanding of how to form a code of Islamic law, and are not meant to be a critique of codification as such.[96]

Since many of the proposed laws on personal status in Egypt began by claiming to address social problems, al-Muṭīʿī was quick to point out that laws alone cannot produce morality.[97] In other words, he did not find it an acceptable argument as far as the ratio legis of certain laws go that the reason they have been chosen and worded the way they have is to correct people's behaviors. Rather, as al-Kawtharī argued and as I discuss in the previous chapter, moral problems need moral solutions, not legislation.[98]

In a style very similar to both al-Minyāwī and Ḥusayn, al-Muṭīʿī provided commentary on the proposed codes of personal status law. I will pay closer attention to the laws codifying a thrice-pronounced divorce counting as one, revocable divorce, and focus on their opposition to normative sunnī jurisprudence according to al-Muṭīʿī. His goal in doing this, as he stated, was not to argue against the law (qānūn) itself, and hence implied his support for codification,[99] but to point out some of the mistakes the drafters of the code made regarding their interpretation of Islamic law.[100] He equally acknowledged when a particular article was in line with normative sunnī jurisprudence.[101] However, before moving to al-Muṭīʿī's discussion of personal status laws, it is first necessary to discuss his understanding of classical Islamic Law, its boundaries, and the nature of law itself.

---

[96] Muḥammad Bakhīt al-Muṭīʿī, *al-Qawl al-Jāmiʿ fīʾl Ṭalāq al-bidʿī waʾl Mutatābiʿ* (Cairo: n.p., 1320 AH); al-Muṭīʿī, *Rafʿ al-ʾAghlāq*.

[97] Muṭīʿī, *al-Qawl al-Jāmiʿ*, 3; Muṭīʿī, *Rafʿ al-ʾAghlāq*, 33–34.

[98] See my discussion of Kawtharī's point on pp. 145–146 above.

[99] It should be recalled that Riḍā refused to even comment, as he argued that any form of critique and/or commentary would be a tacit form of approval and legitimization for the codification process in the first place. See note 52 in chapter 3.

[100] Al-Muṭīʿī, *Rafʿ al-ʾAghlāq*, 3.

[101] Al-Muṭiʿī, *Rafʿ al-ʾAghlāq*, 184 is one such example.

Classical Islam and its Boundaries

In very similar fashion to Kawtharī, not surprising as they were close friends in Cairo, al-Muṭīʿī believed that classical, normative sunnī Islam was, for the most part, summarized within the confines of the four sunnī schools of law.[102] These four schools represented not necessarily the best legal opinions or jurisprudence, but rather schools of legal thought that have been "effectively preserved" throughout history.[103] Effective preservation for al-Muṭīʿī was a specific historic and scholastic occurrence. It meant that a particular mujtahid imām's legal opinions were copied by his students, catalogued in books that survived the ages, and that these books have been transmitted from one generation of jurists to the next generation in an unbroken chain adding legal discussion and ratio legis at each step. The act of transmission is also itself a specific act, likened to the transmission of ḥadīth texts in the early generations of Islam.[104] For al-Muṭīʿī, this reflected an important point in his legal thinking. Namely that law, as a body of knowledge and way of life, must be learnt from a living teacher and cannot be learnt from books alone. Without a chain of transmission, implying that one has not learned law from a living teacher who himself is part of this chain of transmission, legal opinions could be invalid and heretical.[105] The many other opinions of mujtahid imāms, as well as the schools that formed around them, did not, according to al-Muṭīʿī, received the same level of transmission and therefore represent chains that are cut off.[106] Up until this point, this might reflect a similar opinion of al-Kawtharī. However, al-Muṭīʿī went a bit further to add two important points that make the possibility of tol-

---

[102] Ibid., 7–9.

[103] Ibid.

[104] Al-Muṭīʿī, *al-Qawl al-Jāmiʿ*, 16. Ibn Salāḥ says that the use of the chain of transmission of ḥadīth texts to determine a text's strength is reserved for the early generations of Muslim scholars (until about the 6th Islamic century), an opinion he held in contrast to al-Nawawī and others. See: Nūr al-Dīn ʿItr ed, *'Ulūm al-Ḥadīth li Ibn Ṣalāḥ* (Damascus: Dār al-Fikr, 1998), 17.

[105] Al-Muṭīʿī, *al-Qawl al-Jāmiʿ*, 17.

[106] Al-Muṭīʿī, *al-Qawl al-Jāmiʿ*, 17–18; Muṭīʿī, *Rafʿ al-'Aghlāq*, 9.

lowing non-canonical schools not merely theory, but practical. If one does in fact find a non-canonical opinion that has a sound chain, this opinion can be followed, and such an opinion is only valid for an individual expert to follow and is not meant for mass application via fatwas, *etc.*[107] As we will see in the pages that follow, al-Muṭīʿī never actually criticized codification on the grounds that non-sunnī/non-canonical opinions cannot be followed, but rather critiqued the weak opinions used which, in his opinion, did not add up to actual legal positions that are found in the Sharīʿa.

As has been argued by others found throughout this study, the opinions that form the basis of Islamic law are the opinions of mujtahids, not simply jurists. Part of what determines that a jurist has reached the level of ijtihād is that person is undisputed in his rank and claims. Like al-Kawtharī, al-Muṭīʿī believed that figures such as Ibn Taymiyya, Ibn al-Qayyim, and al-Shawkānī were not universally accepted as mujtahids in all areas and therefore their unique opinions, important here as they form the essence of the three as one divorce issue, do not count as legitimate, non-canonical opinions.[108]

The main regulatory tool that defines and informs al-Muṭīʿī's understanding of classical Islam is the concept of legal consensus (ijmāʿ). Legal consensus determines for al-Muṭīʿī who is a mujtahid, and what schools have been narrated by tawātur. For al-Muṭīʿī this defined ultimately where the boundaries of classical Islam lay.[109] Perhaps more so than any other figure discussed in this study, al-Muṭīʿī's critique of aspects of codified law, not to be confused with his attitudes towards codification in general, stemmed from the violation of legal consensus in some form, be it at a macro principle level, or at a micro ratio legis level, as I will attempt to show below. For he ultimately held the view that the following of weak opinions, even if technically at the very boundaries of orthodoxy, ultimately lead to immoral behavior, which also leads us to our next discussion of what his view of law is in the first place.[110]

---

[107] Al-Muṭīʿī, *al-Qawl al-Jāmiʿ*, 21; al-Muṭīʿī, *Rafʿ al-ʿAghlāq*, 9.

[108] Al-Muṭīʿī, *Rafʿ al-ʿAghlāq*, 137.

[109] Al-Muṭīʿī, *al-Qawl al-Jāmiʿ*, 19–20.

[110] Al-Muṭīʿī, *al-Qawl al-Jāmiʿ*, 32.

The Nature of Law

Al-Muṭīʿī’s theory of the nature of law is deduced ultimately from his theory and understanding of al-siyāsa al-sharʿiyya, a subject I discuss in the next section. While it would make sense to provide a comprehensive overview of his theory of political governance, I think it is important to isolate this section in order to understand how he regarded codification of Islamic law.

For al-Muṭīʿī, the Qur’an offers two clear forms of law: the first are laws related to actions of the universe (*ḥawādith kawniyya*), and the second laws pertaining to social good and bad (maṣāliḥ and *mafāsid* respectively).[111] Laws and actions of the universe are only governed by clear texts of the primary sources (Qur’an and ḥadīth). As for laws pertaining to the benefit of society, these are governed by al-siyāsa al-sharʿiyya. The first type of law can only be known through revelation and, as mentioned in the preceding section, sound narration via tawātur. The interpretation of these primary texts must employ the tools of itjihād (if properly acquired) when a particular issue is not settled via tawātur, taqlīd (when one is not a mujtahid), and ijmāʿ (similar to the discussion in the previous section)[112]. The second type of law, however, is meant to establish justice for all people and, accordingly, deals with temporal issues that are confined by their limits of time, place, and circumstance, all of which a just ruler must act on appropriately.[113] While the first type of law is more the purview of the ‘ulamā’ and therefore ultimately requires a specific level of scholastic training and qualification, the second type relates completely to the realm of al-siyāsa al-sharʿiyya and is therefore up to the discretion of the ruler.[114] In this regard, al-Muṭīʿī upheld the traditional understanding of *ulu’l ‘amr* in the Qur’anic verse 4:59. Namely, those with religious authority (the ‘ulamā’) and those with worldly authority have the right and in fact obligation to regulate laws related to the social good. The ‘ulamā’ advise and articulate the law, while political leadership legislate and

---

[111] Al-Muṭīʿī, *Rafʿ al-‘Aghlāq*, 5.

[112] Ibid., 6–8.

[113] Ibid., 9–10. It should be noted that al-Muṭīʿī here quotes from Ibn al-Qayyim’s *al-Ṭuruq al-Ḥukmiyya fi’l-Siyāsa al-Sharʿiyya.*

[114] Al-Muṭīʿī, *Rafʿ al-‘Aghlāq*, 36, 38–39.

enforce. However, even while al-Muṭīʿī acknowledged this as part of the role of political authority,[115] this type of legislation and governance must take place within the paradigm of the Sharīʿa, not man-made laws. It is on this basis that he critiqued some of the codes of personal status laws offered by the personal status committee.[116]

What, then, is Bakhīt al-Muṭīʿī's opinion of codification of personal status laws? There is no doubt that he supported the concept of codification of personal status law specifically and Islamic law generally. It is within the purview of both political leadership and the judiciary, by the power and authority granted to them via al-siyāsa al-sharʿiyya, to enact, order, and codify laws *compatible* with Islamic legal norms for the betterment of society. This point is demonstrated in al-Muṭīʿī's legal responsa where he often quoted the code of personal status law to illustrate his Sharīʿa opinion.[117] However, this is not a blanket endorsement of the specific Egyptian codification of personal status law project. He was equally quick to point out where certain codes were not compatible with Islamic legal norms, such as the thrice-pronounced divorce counting as one, revocable divorce, and in so doing cast a damning condemnation of the committee of personal status laws insinuating that they were trying to replace God in religious authority![118]

---

[115] Ibid.

[116] The main focus of his work *Rafʿ al-ʿAghlāq* is to offer a critique of the personal status laws and the main focus of his work *al-Qawl al-Jāmiʿ* is to tackle the minutiae of the fiqh arguments of the thrice is one divorce opinion.

[117] Al-Muṭīʿī, *Fatāwa*, 104–105. In this fatwa he provides two clear examples.

[118] Al-Muṭīʿī, *Rafʿ al-ʿAghlāq*, 23. Al-Muṭīʿī says, "[y]ou see from this that the principle [the codifiers] established…demonstrates clearly that what they have written in the third article is a sin and that the codifiers have transgressed [against God] and have sought to have all of Egypt follow them and to be taken as lords instead of God." It is easy from this statement to confuse his critique as a condemnation of the entire codification project.

MUṬĪ'Ī'S OPINION OF THE TRIPARTITE DEFINITION OF CODIFICATION

Al-Siyasa Al-Shar'iyya

The discussion of al-Muṭī'ī's attitudes towards Islamic politics: the role of a legitimate ruler in the legislation process, and the interaction between this ruler and the 'ulamā' (some, not all, of the salient features of al-siyāsa al-shar'iyya that concern this current study) is essentially an extension of his theory of the nature of law. Al-Muṭī'ī argued that there were two types of laws deduced from the Islamic primary sources: a universal moral code that is understood only through Qur'anic texts and sound narrations of ḥadīth. The second type is more temporal and within the realm of the socio-political, and it is the second type of law that concerns the discussion of al-siyāsa al-shar'iyya.

The draft codes of personal status laws that al-Muṭī'ī was commenting on included rationale by both Ibn al-Qayyim (via his *al-Ṭuruq al-Ḥukmiyya f'l-Siyāsa al-Shar'iyya*) and Ibn Farḥūn (d. 799/1397) (via his *Tabṣirat al-Ḥukkām*) allowing political rulers to establish laws and regulations for the benefit of society. To address this point and to demonstrate where the codifiers had overstepped their authority,[119] al-Muṭī'ī elaborated on both these thinkers' conception of al-siyāsa al-shar'iyya using Ibn Farḥūn's outline as a starting point.

Muṭī'ī differentiated between two types of law found within the primary Islamic texts, hawādith kawniyya and maṣāliḥ/mafāsid. Al-Muṭī'ī argued that both Ibn al-Qayyim and Ibn Farḥūn agreed, as well as all major 'ulamā' who have written on the subject, that Islamic law legislates in order to regulate five key aspects:[120]

1. Purification of the self.
2. Protecting lineage
3. Protection against wrongful actions and transactions

[119] Again, my argument is that this is not a denunciation of codification of Islamic law as such, but rather a rejection of some of the codes that the committee of personal status laws drafted.

[120] Al-Muṭī'ī, *Raf' al-'Aghlāq*, 35–37.

4. Promoting moral conduct
5. Laws pertaining to proper politics and protection (siyāsa).

These four areas are what Muṭīʿī referred to as ḥawādith kawniyya and, except in rare occasions, laws regulating these areas are found in the primary texts as well as the legal consensus formed by the mujtahid jurists over the ages. The last area, however, contains six sub categories forming the bulk of legislative areas of al-siyāsa al-sharʿiyya, the second type of law in Muṭīʿī's breakdown:

5. *Al-siyāsa al-sharʿiyya*
   - 5.1. Laws addressing capital crimes
   - 5.2. Laws protecting lineage
   - 5.3. Laws protecting chastity
   - 5.4. Laws protecting property
   - 5.5. Laws protecting intellect and rational faculties
   - 5.6. Laws pertaining to other torts not already mentioned

It is these areas that fall within the purview of political executive leadership (the office of the ḥākim sharʿī) to order, legislate, enact, and, for our purposes, codify laws for the benefit of Muslim society.[121] Again, my reading of al-Muṭīʿī's discussion of siyāsa gives a clear indication that he supported the notion and even defended the right of a legitimate political leader to order and enact laws, particularly when there was no clear text offering legislative precedence. Al-Muṭīʿī' contention with the code of personal status law was that issues of marriage and divorce are not issues of siyāsa in which temporality necessitates human agency and reasoning to deduce laws that are appropriate, but rather issues of *nikāḥ* and accordingly, while they certainly can be codified, they must adhere to sound opinions of known schools of law.[122] Again the critique is not of codification, but the actual code under discussion.

Al-Muṭīʿī's position on al-siyāsa al-sharʿiyya is one of affirmation with limits. In discussion after discussion in his work *Rafʿ al-*

[121] Ibid., 36, 38–39.

[122] Ibid., 38.

'Aghlāq 'an Mashrū' al-Zawāj wa'l Ṭalāq he affirmed that it is indeed within the purview of political authority to codify, order, and structure the law, as well as within the purview of political authority to delegate such powers (to the committee of personal status laws for example), but this is not a carte blanche to enact laws that "are for the benefit of society" and are at the same time against clear rulings found throughout the Sharī'a.[123] Therefore, even though laws of siyāsa allow and require efforts of rational legislation, this must be carried out within the confines of the principles set up by the first four branches of law.

Ijtihād

As alluded to above, al-Muṭī'ī also affirmed the validity and great import of independent legal reasoning, not only as a recognized legal tool of the past, but as one that continues to guide and inform Islamic jurisprudence. It would be easy for one to conclude from al-Muṭī'ī's remarks about the limits of classical Islam that he was antagonistic towards ijtihād. However, similar to his comments on siyāsa, he affirmed ijtihād, and at the same time highlighted the limits of this important legal tool.

Ijtihād for al-Muṭī'ī is linked to the transmission of knowledge in a sound manner. Similar to a scholar of ḥadīth needing to receive texts and traditions according to rigorously authentic transmissions (ṣaḥīḥ), a jurist must receive legal opinions in the same fashion.[124] The reasons for this, according to al-Muṭī'ī are twofold: the first is that the information being transmitted to the jurist allowing him to make an informed legal opinion ultimately reverts to a tradition attributed to the Prophet of Islam or a Qur'anic text. The second reason is that al-Muṭī'ī put a large emphasis on transmission of knowledge as a corner stone of his overall thought of the Islamic sciences. Therefore, and as mentioned in previous sections, the gambit of legal thought is encapsulated in the four sunnī schools of

---

[123] This is essentially his argument against the codifiers saying that a thrice-pronounced divorce should count as one, revocable divorce since this is better for society. Ibid., 51.

[124] Al-Muṭī'ī, *al-Qawl al-Jāmi'*, 17.

law,[125] and the possibility of ijtihād theoretically exists, but must be measured against: legal consensus (ijmā'), sound transmission of knowledge, and the mujtahid himself must fulfill the difficult qualities that only twenty of the Companions were able to fulfill.

Of course, this discussion of ijtihād is restricted only to a certain type of religious knowledge; knowledge that is not already agreed upon through transmissions that are tawātur. In other words, aspects of religion that are "already settled", what one may call the list of ijmā',[126] are areas and subjects that must be accepted as the principles of orthodoxy.[127] And, when one indeed finds an area of law that is not settled, a new occurrence for example, one can exert independent legal reasoning, provided that one is in fact qualified to be a mujtahid, but only use this independently arrived at opinion for oneself.[128]

Talfīq

Despite al-Muṭī'ī's legal conservatism and his commitment to the Ḥanafī school of law, he did acknowledge and even argue for a much more liberal approach to legal eclecticism. He acknowledged that there are two sides to the talfīq debate: those like Kamāl ibn Humām (d. 861/1456) who allowed talfīq absolutely, and those more conservative Ḥanafīs who argued against it.[129] In either case, al-Muṭī'ī made it clear that the possibility of talfīq only exists for mujtahids, and not commoners, as the commoners' source of legal authority comes from the opinion of their mufti, not their own independent legal efforts.[130]

However, in his fatwa dealing with the issue of ijtihād and talfīq mentioned in the previous paragraph, he stated his own in-

---

[125] Ibid., 18.

[126] Two examples of books that list points of *ijmā'* are: Ibn Mundhir Al-Naysabūrī, *al-Ijmā'* (Cairo: Dār al-Ithār, 2004); Ibn Ḥazm al-Ẓāhirī, *Marātib al-Ijmā'* (Beirut: Dār Ibn Hazm, 1998).

[127] Al-Muṭī'ī, *al-Qawl al-Jāmi'*, 9–10.

[128] Ibid.

[129] Al-Muṭī'ī, *Fatāwa*, 432–33.

[130] This is summarized in the common statement, "*madhhab al-'āmmī muftīh*". See: Ibid., 434.

terpretation as arguing that the only form of talfīq that the jurists universally reject is when all mujtahids equally criticize the legality of an action under investigation. In other words, when one engages in a form of talfīq in committing a particular action, if all the mujtahids from whom this act is taken say that the act under question is not valid (meaning that each mujtahid has found an error in the act according to their legal principles), then such an act, being universally denounced, is not valid.[131] The implicit argument, one is left to deduce, is that were one to engage in an act that is *not* universally invalidated, such an action would be accepted. I infer this conclusion from al-Muṭī'ī's repeated statement throughout this particular fatwa that the definition of talfīq is to create a third opinion when only two exist.[132] While his discussion of talfīq is brief, it is a rule that, when applied, explains many of his harsh critiques of specific conclusions of the code of personal status, and also explains why, at least theoretically, he supported the notion of codification and the concept of creating a "third" opinion.

AL-MUṬĪ'Ī'S CRITIQUE OF THE THREE AS ONE POSITION

Al-Muṭī'ī's inclusion in this chapter would not be complete without concluding with a section demonstrating how he, at times, found fault with actual codes of personal status law, while at the same time upholding the concept of codification of Islamic law. His work Raf' al-Ighlāq 'an Mashrū' al-Zawāj wa'l Ṭalāq is essentially a commentary on the personal status laws issued in 1929,[133] and while he agreed with some articles and disagreed with others, it is perhaps most logical to discuss his treatment of article 6 which codified a thrice-pronounced divorce counting as one, revocable divorce. Before continuing, however, it is important to make one introductory remark. Muṭī'ī's response to this position, both in Raf' al-Ighlāq 'an Mashrū' al-Zawāj wa'l Ṭalāq as well as *al-Qawl al-Jāmi' fi'l-Ṭalāq al-Bid'ī wa'l Mutatābi'* offers many of the same arguments used by al-Kawtharī whom I discuss in the previous chapter. There

---

[131] Ibid. For examples of this, see my discussion pp. 140–144 above.

[132] Ibid., 437.

[133] Which I discuss in chapter 1 above.

are, however, some unique additions that al-Muṭīʿī adduced which are significant vis-à-vis the overall legal discussion. In what follows, I will limit the discussion to those areas that al-Muṭīʿī adds to the discussion, rather than repeat the arguments made by al-Kawtharī.[134]

One of al-Muṭīʿī's main critiques as is it relates to personal status law was that marriage and divorce are not matters of *siyāsa*, but contract law. Indicating that it would be difficult to find areas were the opinions of non-canonical schools would apply. In addition, and similar to al-Kawtharī, al-Muṭīʿī argued that the problems of marriage and divorce, problems that we see discussed by ʿulamāʾ in previous chapters, are not solvable by laws alone and are themselves symptoms of larger social issues.[135] He went as far as to say that men who constantly marry and divorce are in fact committing a form of adultery.[136] Therefore, he was pointing out the severe limitations of the arguments allowing a thrice-pronounced divorce to count as one, revocable divorce.

As far as a three as one divorce being an argument held by others in the past is concerned, al-Muṭīʿī fully acknowledged that there are indeed those amongst the ʿulamāʾ who have upheld this position, specifically the Ẓāhirīs, Ibn Taymiyya, Ibn al-Qayyim, and al-Shawkānī.[137] This position, al-Muṭīʿī was quick to point out, is entirely based on the story of Rukāna, which I discussed earlier in some detail.[138] However, al-Muṭīʿī narrows this story to two main ḥadīth texts:

1. The ḥadīth narrated by Muḥamad ibn Isḥāq that Rukāna divorced his wife by way of a thrice pronouncement in one instance, was saddened by this, and the Prophet of Islam,

---

[134] It should be noted that in actuality it is al-Muṭīʿī who preceded al-Kawtharī in these arguments. Both works by Muṭīʿī were written in 1927 and 1902 respectively. While al-Kawtharī's book on the subject was written in 1956.

[135] Al-Muṭīʿī, *al-Qawl al-Jāmiʿ*, 3.

[136] Ibid., 75.

[137] Ibid., 36.

[138] See pp. 150–153 above.

after enquiring about this, instructed him that this is in fact one, revocable divorce.

2. The ḥadīth narrated by 'Abd al-Razzāq that the thrice-pronounced divorce counted as one, revocable divorce until the time of 'Umar who subsequently made it count as three and therefore rendered such a divorce irrevocable (*al-bātta*).[139]

To settle this issue, al-Muṭī'ī argued that the first narration was not reliable enough to serve as a proof text because Muḥamad ibn Isḥāq and his teacher are considered questionable narrators.[140] As for the second text, this narration is sound and is found in the collection of Muslim, but does not indicate that there is a scholarly debate on the issue amongst the Companions (khilāf). Rather, it demonstrates that there was an abrogation (*naskh*) of the ruling that took time to communicate amongst the Companions and this is why, for example, none of the Companions critiqued 'Umar's decision later during his Caliphate.[141] For al-Muṭī'ī this latter ḥadith text and its subsequent treatment by *mujtahid* Imāms in similar fashion, i.e. that it represents abrogation, is also an implicit argument that there is consensus (ijmā') as to the abrogator (nāsikh) as well. To this effect, al-Muṭī'ī added to his argument other ḥadith texts that demonstrate this point.[142] In addition, he also demonstrated that there are other ḥadith that indicate that a thrice-pronounced divorce has full effect, including the ḥadith narrated by Ibn 'Abbās that he and three other Companions asked about a virgin who is divorced in a thrice pronouncement, and they were told this is an irrevocable divorce.[143] He concluded that the soundest of narrations regarding the story of Rukāna, according to Bukhārī, is with

---

[139] Al-Muṭī'ī, *al-Qawl al-Jāmi'*, 49–50.

[140] Ibid.

[141] Ibid.

[142] Ibid., 55–56. Al-Muṭī'ī here brings in several other situations where similar wording indicates that the Companions had agreed that an abrogation of a ruling took place.

[143] Ibid., 61.

the wording al-bātta, not thrice, therefore indicating that the divorce pronouncement was irrevocable, not revocable.[144]

Another discussion area for al-Muṭīʿī regarding the problematic nature of the three-as-one opinion is the action of Ibn ʿAbbās himself as a Companion. He established in numerous places that Ibn ʿAbbās's own opinion was that a thrice-divorce pronouncement had full effect.[145] Therefore, and as a legal principle, al-Muṭīʿī argued that a Companion could not hold one opinion, yet narrate the opposite since only one of two conclusions could be made if such an occurrence were to take place: the Companion is not morally upright (*fāsiq*), which cannot be the case since the sunnī principle is that *all* Companions are morally upright in their ability to narrate matters of religion, or the narration in question is itself weak, which is what al-Muṭīʿī leant towards regarding Ibn ʿAbbās. This also furthers al-Muṭīʿī's argument that the decision of ʿUmar reflected a clear sign of consensus (ijmāʿ) regarding abrogation.

Of course, al-Muṭīʿī's arguments regarding the two main discussion areas noted above are long and highly detailed. He spared no examples, cross examination, and rhetoric to establish what for him was the simple fact that this is a seriously flawed opinion that represented a serious lapse in legal scholarship by those who have held it in the past. This is, I believe, the most significant part of his overall argument and where, for example, he distinguished his opinion from that of al-Kawtharī. Al-Muṭīʿī did not hesitate to heavily critique not only the position of a thrice-pronounced divorce counting as one, revocable divorce, but also the legal argumentation of Ibn Taymiyya, Ibn al-Qayyim, and al-Shawkānī. In fact, one is almost left feeling after reading al-Muṭīʿī's discussion that these three were not in fact qualified jurists. He is emphatic that this position is indefensible from the point of view of the classical legal structure and full of errors of interpretation of the primary texts. Yet, he also defended them individually, particularly Ibn Taymiyya and Ibn al-Qayyim, as luminaries and restricts his criti-

[144] Ibid., 116.

[145] The proof being that all the narrations of the Rukāna story except one narrated by Ibn Ṭawūṣ demonstrate that a change took place during ʿUmar's reign. Al-Muṭīʿī, *al-Qawl al-Jāmiʿ*, 61.

cism to "those known areas in which they made mistakes," rather than castigating them completely and utterly. In a fatwa responding to his opinion of Ibn Taymiyya and Ibn al-Qayyim, al-Muṭīʿī wrote:

> [They] were from amongst the very senior scholars of sunnī Islam. They were also shaykhs of the Ḥanbalī school of law. There is no dispute that Ibn Taymiyya was Shaykh al-Islam during his lifetime. However, there are some issues in legal methodology, theology, and law in which Ibn Taymiyya, and he was followed in this by his student Ibn al-Qayyim, made mistakes and went against the pious ancestors (al-salaf al-ṣāliḥ) and his contemporaries criticized him for this…therefore we are to avoid these issues and not fall into them, and at the same time we offer them praise for their efforts and other opinions.[146]

He does not, therefore, argue that they are not mujtahids, but says they are not an absolute mujtahid (mujtahid *muṭlaq*),[147] and is quick to point out that he is in no way against following other than the four canonical sunnī schools of law, but that the conditions he lays forth (sound narration of opinions, undisputed mujtahids, and preserved schools) need to be met for this to take place.[148]

---

[146] Al-Muṭīʿī, *Fatāwa*, 400.
[147] Al-Muṭīʿī, *Rafʿ al-ʾAghlāq*, 140.
[148] Ibid., 142.

CONCLUSION

I began this study with an understanding of codification as the reduction of the whole of the law, whether statue law or common law, into a systematic form. I also established the importance of selecting authoritative works of law as well as the role jurists must play in this selection process in order to the draft a code of law. As I discussed the example of the French civil code in the introduction, I also observed that the concise nature of a legal code almost always necessitates what legal experts' term juristic discussion in order to provide needed commentary as the law evolves. While there were efforts in the past to organize, catalogue, and codify Islamic law, it was not until the modern period that the codification of Islamic law became a subject of wide discussion amongst the 'ulamā'. This was particularly influenced by the fact that by the middle of the 19th century Islamic law's influence had been restricted to issues of personal status.

In discussing the opinions of the 'ulamā' towards the codification of personal status law, I have attempted to demonstrate that the 'ulamā' can be thought of as belonging to one of the following four categories:

1. Those who wrote codes of law.
2. Those who supported the theory of codification but did not write codes.
3. Those who were against codification.
4. Those who accepted the theory of codification but criticized aspects of the code of personal status.

I selected at least two 'ulamā' from each category to establish their arguments from a theoretical point of view, as well as their attitudes towards the specific issue of a thrice-pronounced divorce counting as one, revocable divorce in order to provide a practical example to follow throughout the study.

In discussing the opinions of the ʻulamāʼ towards codification of personal status laws, I identified three variables that, for the ʻulamāʼ, constituted the framework of codification: ijtihād, talfīq, and al-siyāsa al-sharʻiyya. These three issues had to be reconciled and deemed valid for a particular ʻālim to approve of codification. When one or more of these caused problems, however, the outcome was a rejection of codification. Since codification of law often requires jurists to rethink legal norms against realities, it is not surprising that the codification of personal status law in Egypt called for a greater use for ijtihād as well as the need for an eclectic approach to Islamic law (talfīq). Although not all the ʻulamāʼ I discussed had an equal understanding of ijtihād and talfīq, none of them denied their import or their use in the Islamic law tradition. The debate was, however, concerning the limits of these legal tools. Law 25 of 1929 brought this into focus by taking the concept of ijtihād and talfīq to a new level that caused some ʻulamāʼ, like al-Kawtharī and al-Muṭīʻī, to reject their new use. However, the codification of personal status law, a process that took place roughly from the 1860s to the 1920s, happened against the backdrop of Egypt's colonial experience with the British. It is in the realm of al-siyāsa al-sharʻiyya that many of the ʻulamāʼ found the greatest level of debate regarding the permissibility, or lack thereof, of codification. This is not to say that the other two variables were not debated. Rather, my point is that the political context, the right afforded by the Sharīʻa to the government, and the role of the ʻulamāʼ as the interpreters and protectors of Islamic law caused the greatest concern. While there was no disagreement regarding the right of the sovereign to enact laws in theory, what was not equally understood was how to interpret Egypt's political situation and how to deal with issues legislation. This is, in my view, where the greatest discrepancy in their opinions lay.

While I used a precise definition of codification throughout this study, the ʻulamāʼ examined did not share a uniform definition to taqnīn. For some (al-Minyāwī and ʻAbduh for example) it was akin to references in books of siyāsa to laws that a sovereign is allowed to enact. For others (Riḍā and Shākir for example), it was a clear usurpation of the Sharīʻa and secularization of Egypt's legal system. But in all cases, the ʻulamāʼ analyzed above took their own understanding and projected this on the three variables of codification to arrive at their conclusion. None of them, unfortunately, provided a definition of codification as it relates to Bentham's project and its use in other legal jurisdictions. Accordingly, I would argue that there is a significant gap between what codification means for law as envisioned by European jurists, and the 'ulamā's understanding of taqnīn.

In my discussions of the 'ulamā', I often referred to what they observed was an accidental overlap between the codified personal status law and their corresponding rulings in Islamic law. This particularly concerned the 'ulamā' who did not accept the process and result of codification, but it was noticed by all of them. The accidental overlap highlights that while the laws of personal status resembled Sharī'a rulings, they may have been codified despite the 'ulamā' and despite Islamic law. That the 'ulamā' were not involved in codification entirely and that there was no clear, transparent methodology provided by the government for codification of personal status laws was of great concern to the 'ulamā'. As we saw in the introduction, half of the codification process involves the decision of what authoritative legal sources are to be used to make law. However, the other half of codification involves the jurists themselves who are needed to undergo the codification process. It is clear that the process of codification of personal status laws in Egypt did not involve, at least directly, many of the 'ulamā'. While different 'ulamā' interpreted the result of codification differently, they universally observed that they were not a part of the process. While this indeed questioned the veracity of the codification process, especially for certain 'ulamā', it underscored that there was no clear process of codification to begin with, nor a clear understanding of what the point of a code of law was. We know from analyzing the explanatory note to Law 25 of 1929 in chapter 1 that there was certainly an attempt to explain how certain laws were established, but I found no clear articulation of the process of codification, which caused an array of responses from the 'ulamā'. Furthermore, I found that the 'ulamā' were more concerned with their lack of inclusion than they were with the code of law produced. Codification was much more than cataloguing Islamic rulings for them. Codification was part of their greater societal role as protectors and interpreters of the Sharī'a.

The absence of the 'ulamā' from the official committees of personal status law did not mean, however, that they were not actively discussing codification. As I demonstrated in the introduction, the juristic discussion surrounding law is part and parcel of the codification process. Also, as discussed in the introduction, scholars who commented on the codification of personal status laws during and past the laws' enactment all form part of the juristic discussion, or, as I have chosen to call it, the intellectual footprint of the 'ulamā'. These writings, some of which I examined above, form an essential part of the codification story, and ultimately define how the authority of legal texts is established. This is where I believe some scholars have missed the mark in describing codification as the end of the Sharī'a in the modern world. Perhaps this is due to the fact that many of these writings were reactionary and not necessarily measured legal discussions. However, as I have attempted to show, specifically regarding the issue of a thrice-pronounced divorce, these works are essential to understanding the process and mechanics of codification and signal the vibrancy of Islamic legal discourse amongst the 'ulamā'.

Another part of the intellectual footprint of the 'ulamā' I discussed in chapter 2 was the impact the feminist movement had on issues of codifying personal status law. We should appreciate that scholars who have written and debated these issues may not consider these discussions a serious engagement by the 'ulamā' on issues of gender, marriage, and divorce. My inclusion of these discussions should not be thought of as an endorsement of their engagement or an argument that these discussions by the 'ulamā' satisfied and enhanced the feminist movement of Egypt throughout the 20th century. Rather, the inclusion of these discussions demonstrates that the calls for gender equality and reform in marriage and divorce practices by leading feminists in Egypt in the late 1800s and first quarter of the 1900s impacted the juristic discussion of the 'ulamā' regarding codification of personal status laws. Again, I would argue that these discussions are part and parcel of the intellectual footprint of the 'ulamā' and must be considered part of the codification story.

From these proceeding remarks one may think that I am attempting to paint a story of antagonism between the 'ulamā' and codification. There was certainly a great deal of tension involved in the codification process. However, I am of the opinion that this tension was a result of not including the 'ulamā' directly in the process of codification, much more than it was the effects of codification on Islamic law. This is why the subtitle of chapter 4 asks a question if the 'ulamā' who supported the concept of codification but rejected aspects of the code of personal status law could be thought of as the silent majority, which I believe they can. While some 'ulamā' like Riḍā were concerned with the substance and name of the code, there is no indication that this was a widely held notion amongst the 'ulamā'. Accordingly, I believe that codification, despite its challenges in the space of Islamic law, only sought to catalogue the object of Islamic law, what I argued in the introduction as the rulings (aḥkām) of the Sharī'a. Islamic law's subject, the methodology of interpreting the primary Islamic sources, remained intact and, if one considers the juristic discussion of the 'ulamā', saw a resurgence, not a death, due to codification. While there is no poll that I can point to in order to say definitely that there is a silent majority, I can point to the fact that the code of personal status law continues to be accepted in Egypt by the 'ulamā', is used in court cases, and given as proof texts in fatwas issued by the National Fatwa Office. In addition, the writings criticizing codification and the code itself have diminished over time. Today, the code of personal status law and the issue of codification of Islamic law in Egypt is an accepted fact.

In conclusion, I have attempted to demonstrate throughout this study the importance of approaching the topic of codification of Islamic law with a holistic definition of codification and the impact this definition had on the Sharī'a. With great political changes throughout the Middle East, particularly Egypt, the interaction of the 'ulamā' with the state and the role of Islamic law in modern legislation will most likely continue to be a topic of much discussion.

BIBLIOGRAPHY

'Abd al-'Āṭi, Muḥammad Ḥilmī, *al-Mabādi' al-'Āmma fī Tashrī'āt al-Aḥwāl al-Shakhṣiyya* (Cairo: Maktabat al-Qāhira, 1962).

Abdel Kader, Soha, *Egyptian Women in a Changing Society, 1899–1987* (London: Boulder & London, 1987).

'Abduh, Muḥammad, *al-Islām Dīn al-'Ilm wa'l Madaniyya* (Cairo: Dār al-Hilāl, n.d.).

'Abdullah, 'Abdullah Rabī'a, Muḥammad, *Madā Taghyīr al-Aḥkām bi Taghyīr al-Jihāt al-'Arba'a* (Cairo: Ministry of Endowments, n.d.).

Adams, Charles C., *Islam and Modernism in Egypt* (London: Oxford University Press, 1933).

Ahmad, Ahmad Atif, *Structural Interrelations of Theory and Practice in Islamic Law: a study of six works of medieval Islamic jurisprudence* (Leiden: Brill, 2006).

Ahmed, Leila, *Women and Gender in Islam: Historical Roots of a Modern Debate* (New Haven: Yale University Press, 1992).

Anderson, J.N.D., *Islamic Law in the Modern World* (New York: New York University Press, 1959).

Āṣāf, Yūsuf, *Mir'a al-Majalla*, 2 vols., (Cairo: al-Maṭba'a al-Amiriyya, 1894).

al-'Asqalānī, Aḥmad Ibn Ḥajar, *'Fatḥ al-Bārī bi Sharḥ Ṣaḥīḥ al-Bukhārī*, 14 vols., (Cairo: al-Maktaba al-Salafiyya, 1380 AH).

al-Azharī, Usāma al-Sayyid Maḥmūd, *Asānīd al-Miṣriyīn* (Abu Dhabi, Dār al-Faqīh, 2011).

'Amāra, Muḥammad ed., *al-'Amāl al-Kāmila li'l Imām Muḥammad 'Abduh*, 5 vols., (Cairo: Dār al-Shurūq, 1993).

———, *al-'Amāl al-Kāmila li Qāsim Amīn* (Cairo: Dār al-Shurūq, 1989).

———, *Islāmayāt al-Sanhūrī Bāshā*, 2 vols., (Cairo: Dār al-Wafā', 2006).

———, *Rifā'a al-Ṭahṭāwī Rā'd al-Tanwīr fī'l-'Asr al-Ḥadīth* (Cairo: Dār al-Sharq, 2007).

Amīn, Qāsim, *Les Ègyptiens* (Cairo: Jules Barbier, 1894).

———, "al-Mar'a al-Jadīda" in *al-'Amāl al-Kāmila li Qāsim Amīn*, ed. Muḥammad 'Amāra, 419–517 (Cairo: Dār al-Shurūq, 1989).

———, *Taḥrīr al-Mar'a* (Cairo: Maktaba al-Jāmi'a, 1928).

Asad, Talal, "The Idea of an Anthropology of Islam," *Occasional Papers Series, Center for Contemporary Arab Studies*, (Washington D.C, Georgetown University Press, 1986).

Azūzī, Idrīs, *al-Shaykh Aḥmad Zarrūq wa Arāuhū al-'Iṣlāḥiyya* (Morocco: Maṭba'at Fāḍila, 1998).

Badran, Margot, *Feminism in Islam* (Oxford: Oneworld Publications, 2009).

Badran, Margot and Cooke, Miriam eds., *Opening the Gates* (London: Virago Press, 1990).

Bannā, Ḥasān, *Majmū'at Rasā'il al-Imām al-Shahīd Ḥasan al-Bannā* (Beirut: Dār al-Andalus, 1965).

Baring, Evelyn (Earl of Cromer), *Modern Egypt*, 2 vols., (London: Elibron Classics, 2005).

Baron, Beth, *The Women's Awakening in Egypt: Culture, Society, and the Press* (New Haven: Yale University Press, 1994).

———, *Egypt as a Woman* (Berkeley: University of California Press, 2005).

al-Bayjūrī, Ibrāhīm, *Ḥāshiyat al-Bayjūrī 'ala Sharḥ al-'Allāma Ibn Qāsim*, 2 vols., (Beirut: Dar al-Fikr, n.d.).

———, *Tuḥfat al-Murīd 'ala Jawharat al-Tawḥīd* (Cairo: Dār al-Salām, 2006).

Bazian, Hatem. "Religious authority, state power and revolutions: Recent events in the Arab and Muslim world are redefining the role of religious scholars." *Aljazeera*, September 15, 2013, http://www.aljazeera.com/indepth/opinion/2013/09/201391 06443895282.html.

Bechor, Guy, *The Sanhuri Code, and the Emergence of Modern Arab Civil Law (1932–1949)* (Leiden: Brill, 2007).

Bentham, Jeremy, *The Collected Works of Jeremy Bentham*, 11 vols., (Edinburgh: William Tait, 1838–1843).

———, *Theory of Legislation* (Boston: Weeks, Jordan & Company, 1840).

Berkes, Niyazi, *The Development of Secularism in Turkey* (New York: Routledge, 1998).

Berkey, Jonathan P., *The Formation of Islam* (Cambridge: Cambridge University Press, 2003).

———, *The Transmission of Knowledge in Medieval Cairo* (Princeton: Princeton University Press, 1992).

Black, Henry, Campbell, *Black's Law Dictionary*, 6th ed. (St. Paul, West Publishing, 1990).

Bousquet, G.-H. and Schacht, Joseph eds., *Selected Works of C. Snouck Hurgronje* (Leiden: E.J. Brill, 1957).

Brinton, Jasper Yeates, *The Mixed Courts of Egypt* (New Haven, CT: Yale University Press, 1968).

Brunner, Rainer, *Islamic ecumenism in the 20th century: the Azhar and Shiism between rapprochement and restraint*, trans. Joseph Greenman (Leiden: Brill, 2004).

Cannon, Byron, *Politics of Law and the Courts in Nineteenth Century Egypt* (Salt Lake City: University of Utah Press, 1988).

Cevdet, Ahmed, *Teẓākir.* 3 vols., (Ankara, Türk Taīīh Kurumu Basimevī: 1953).

Chambers, Richard L., The Education of a Nineteenth-Century Ottoman Alim, Ahmed Cevdet Pasa", in *International Journal of Middle East Studies* 4(1973): 440–464.

Coulson, N.J, *A History of Islamic Law* (Edinburgh: Edinburgh University Press, 1964).

Dahlawī, Shāh Wali Allah, *Ḥujjat al-Allah al-Bāligha*, 2 vols., (Cairo: Dār al-Jīl, 2005).

Debs, Richard D., *Islamic Law and Civil Code* (New York: Columbia University Press, 2010).

Donahue, Charles, "Historical Introduction: Comparative Law Before the Code Napoléon", in *Oxford Handbook of Comparative Law* eds., Mathias Reiman & Reinhard Zimmermann (Oxford: Oxford University Press, 2006): 3–32.

———, "Law without the State and During its Formation", in *The American Journal of Comparative Law* 56 (2008): 541–565.

Drewes, G.WJ., "Qasim Amin, Egyptisch Feminist: (1865–1908)" *Bijdragen tot de Taal-,Land-en Volkenkunde,* Deel 114, 1ste/2de Afl (1958): 55–71.

Egypt, *al-Kitāb al-Zahabī lil Maḥākim al-Ahliyya*, 2 vols., (Cairo: Maṭba'at Bulāq, 1937).

Elgawhary, Tarek, "Codification of Law" in *The Oxford Encyclopedia of Islam and Law*. Oxford Studies Online http://www.oxfordislamicstudies.com/article/opr/t349/e0033 (accessed September 26, 2013).

Elgawhary, Tarek and Friedlander, Nuri trans., *Responding from the Tradition* (Louisville: Fons Vitae: 2011).

Encyclopedia of Islam 2nd edition (Leiden: Brill, 1960–2002).

Fadel, Mohammad, "The Social Logic of *Taqlīd* and Rise of the *Mukhtaṣar*" *Islamic Law and Society* 3,2 (1996): 193–233.

France, *Code Napoleon or The French Civil Code*, (Baton Rouge: Claitor's Book Store, 1960 reprint of the original 1804 unnamed translation).

Friedrich, C.J., "The Ideological and Philosophical Background," in *The Code Napoleon and the Common Law World*, ed. Bernard Schwartz (Westport: Greenwood Press, 1956): 1–18.

Geuthner, Paul and Massignon, M.L. eds., *Revue Des Études Islamiques* (Paris: Librairie Orientaliste, 1929).

Al-Ghiṭā', Muḥammad al-Ḥussayn Āl Kāshif, *Taḥrīr al-Majalla*, 2 vols., (Najaf: Iraq, 1359 AH).

Al-Ghumārī, Aḥmad ibn Siddiq, *al-Baḥr al-'Amīq fī Marwiyāt Ibn al-Siddīq*, 2 vols., (Cairo: Dār al-Kutbā, 2007).

Goiten, S.D., *Studies in Islamic History and Institutions* (Leiden: Brill, 2012).

Goldziher, Ignaz, *Die Richtungen Der Islamischen Koranauslegung* (Leiden: E.J. Brill, 1952).

Gunasti, Susan, "Approaches to Islam in the Thought of Elmalili Hamdi Yazir (1878–1942)" (PhD diss., Princeton University, 2011).

Haddad, Mahmoud, "Arab Religious Nationalism in the Colonial Era: Rereading Rashīd Riḍā's ideas on the Caliphate," *Journal of the American Oriental Society* 117, no.2 (1997): 253–277.

Hallaq, Wael, *Sharī'a: Theory, Practice, Transformations* (Cambridge: Cambridge University Press: 2009).

———, *The Impossible State: Islam, politics, and modernity's moral predicament* (New York: Columbia University Press, 2013).

———, *The Origins and Evolution of Islamic Law* (Cambridge: Cambridge University Press, 2005).

———, "Was the Gate of *Ijtihād* Closed?" *International Journal of Middle East Studies 16* (1984): 3–41.

Ḥaydar, 'Alī, *Durar al-Ḥukām Sharḥ Majallat al-Aḥkām*, 4 vols., (Beirut: Maktabat al-Nahda, 1970).

Haykel, Bernard, *Revival and Reform in Islam: the Legacy of Muhammad al-Shawkani* (Cambridge: Cambridge University Press, 2003).

Heyworth-Dunne, J., *An introduction to the History of Education in Modern Egypt* (London: Luzac & Co., 1938).

Hill, Enid, "Al-Sanhūrī and Islamic Law: The Place and Significance of Islamic Law in the Life and Work of 'Abd al-Razzāq al-Sanhūrī, Egyptian Jurist and Scholar, 1895–1971," part I & II *Arab Law Quarterly* 3(1988): 33–64 and 182–218.

Horten, M., "Muhammed Abduh: Sein Leben und seine theologisch-philosophische Gedankenwelt-Eine Studie zu den Reformbestrebungen im modernen Ägypten (parts I and II)," in *Beiträge zur Kenntnis des Orients* (Halle: Gebauer-Schwetschke Druckerei und Verlag, 1916): 83–114 and 74–128.

Ḥijāzī, Maḥmūd Fahmī ed., *Uṣūl al-Fikr al-'Arabī al-Ḥadīth 'ind al-Ṭahṭāwī ma'a'l-Naṣṣ al-Kāmil li-Kitāb "Takhlīṣ al-Ibrīz* (Cairo: al-Hay'a al-Miṣriyya al-'Āmma lil Kitāb, 1974).

Holmes, Oliver Wendell, "The Path of the Law", in *Harvard Law Review*, 110(1997): 991–1009.

Hourani, Albert, *Arabic Thought in the Liberal Age* (Cambridge: Cambridge University Press, 2008).

Hoyle, Mark S.W., *Mixed Courts of Egypt* (London: Graham & Trotman, 1991).

Hunter, F. Robert, *Egypt Under the Khedives 1805–1879* (Cairo: American University in Cairo Press, 1999).

Ḥussayn, Sayyid Abdallah, *al-Ajwiba al-Fiqhiyya fi'l Madhhab al-Sāda al-Shāfi'iyya* (Cairo: al-Maktaba al-Maḥmūdiyya al-Tujāriyya, n.d.).

———, *al-Ajwiba al-Khafīfa fi'l Madhhab al-Imām Abī Ḥanifa* (Cairo: al-Maktaba al-Maḥmūdiyya al-Tujāriyya, 1958).

———, *al-Ajwiba al-Tīdiyya fi'l Madhhab al-Sāda al-Mālikiyya* (Cairo: al-Maktaba al-Maḥmūdiyya al-Tujāriyya, 1965).

———, al-*Muqāranāt al-Tashrī'iyya*, 4 vols., (Cairo: Dār al-Salām, 2006).

Ibn 'Ābidīn, Muḥammad Amin, *Radd al-Muḥtār 'ala al-Durr al-Mukhtār (Ḥāshiyāt Ibn 'Ābidīn)*, 12 vols., (Beirut: Dār al-Ma'rifa, 2000).

Ibn Athīr, 'Ali 'Izz al-Dīn *Usd al-Ghāba fī M'arifat al-Ṣaḥāba*, 7 vols., (Cairo: Majala Kitāb al-Sha'b, 1970).

Ilbert, Courtenay, *The Mechanics of Law Making* (New York: Columbia University Press, 1914).

'Itr, Nūr al-Dīn ed. *'Ulūm al-Ḥadīth li Ibn Ṣalāḥ* (Damascus: Dār al-Fikr, 1998).

Jansen, Nils, *The Making of Legal Authority* (Oxford: Oxford University Press, 2010).

Jokisch, Benjamin, *Islamic Imperial Law* (Berlin: Walter de Gruyter, 2007).

Jumu'a, 'Alī, *al-Ḥukm al-Shar'ī 'ind al-Uṣūliyīn* (Cairo: Dār al-Salām, 2002).

———, *al-Madkhal ilā Dirāsat al-Madhhāhib al-Fiqhiyya* (Cairo: Dār al-Salām, 2004).

——— ed., *Fatāwā al-Imām Muḥammad 'Abduh* (Cairo: al-Jam'iyya al-Khayriyya al-Islāmiyya, 2005).

———, *al-Kalim al-Ṭayyib: Fatāwa 'Aṣriyya*, 2 vols., (Cairo: Dār al-Salām, 2005).

———, *Fatāwā al-Bayt al-Muslim* (Cairo: Dār al-Imām al-Shāṭibī, 2009).

Al-Juwaynī, Imām al-Ḥaramayn, *al-Giyāthī: Ghiyāth al-'Umma fi'l Tiyāth al-Ẓulam*, ed., 'Abd al-'Azīm Maḥmūd al-Dīb (Beirut: Dār al-Minhāj, 2001).

Kafāfī, Ḥusayn, *al-Khadīwī Ismā'īl wa Ma'ashūqatuhu Maṣr* (Cairo: al-Hay'a al-Miṣriyya al-'Āmma lil Kitāb, 1997).

Karīm, Muḥammad 'Izzat, *Tārīkh al-Ta'alīm fī 'asr Muḥammad 'Alī* (Cairo: Maktabat al-Nahda al-Miṣriyya, 1938).

Al-Kawtharānī, Wajīh ed., *al-Dawla wa'l Khilāfa fi'l Khitāb al-'Arabī Ibbān al-Thawra al-Kamāliyya fī Turkiyya* (Beirut: Dār al-Ṭal'iyya li'l Ṭibā'a wa'l Nashr, 1996).

Al-Kawtharī, Zāhid, *al-Ishfāq fī Aḥkām al-Ṭalāq* (Cairo: Maṭba'a Majalat al-Islām, n.d.).

———, *al-Ishfāq 'ala Aḥkām al-Ṭalāq* (Cairo: al-Maktaba al-Azhar lil Turāth, 1355 AH).

———, *Muqadimāt al-Imām al-Kawtharī* (Damascus: Dār al-Thurayya, 1997).

———, *Maqālāt al-Kawtharī* (Cairo: Dār al-Salām, 1998).

Al-Kaylānī, Shams al-Dīn, *al-Imām Muḥammad 'Abduh* (Cairo: al-Ahlī li'l Ṭibā'a wa'l Tawzī', 2001).

Kedourie, Elie, *Afghani and 'Abdud: An Essay on Religious Unbelief and Political Activism in Modern Islam* (London: Frank Cass, 1997).

Keller, Nuh, *Reliance of the Traveler* (Beltsville: Amana Publications, 1994).

Kerr, Malcolm, *Islamic Reform: The Political and Legal Theories of Muḥammad 'Abduh and Rashīd Riḍa* (Berkeley: University of California Press, 1966).

Khadduri, Majid, "Marriage in Islamic Law: The Modernist Viewpoints," *The American Journal of Comparative Law* 26 (1978): 213–218.

Khayrī, Aḥmad, *al-Imām al-Kawtharī* (Cairo: Maktabat al-Azhariyya lil Turāth, 1999).

Koc, Yunus, "Early Ottoman Customary Law: The Genesis and Development of Ottoman Codification" in *Shattering Tradition: Custom, Law and the Individual in the Muslim Mediterranean* eds., Walter Dostal and Wolfgang Kraus (London: I.B. Tauris, 2005): 75–121.

Knysh, Alexander, *Ibn 'Arabi in the Later Islamic Tradition* (New York: State University of New York Press, 1999).

Kuwait, Ministry of Religious Endowments and Islamic Affairs, *al-Mawsū'āt al-Fiqhiyya*, 45 vols., (Kuwait: Maṭābi' Dār al-Ṣafwa, 1993).

Layish, Aharon, "The Contribution of the Modernists to the Secularization of Islamic Law", *Middle Eastern Studies* 14(1978): 263–277.

MacIntyre, Alasdair, *After Virtue* (Indiana: University of Notre Dame Press, 2007).

———, *Three Rival Versions of Moral Enquiry* (Indiana: University of Notre Dame Press, 1990).

al-Mahdī, Jawda Muḥammad Abū al-Yazīdī ed., *Manāqib al-Qutb al-Rabānī Sayidī 'Abd al-Wahhāb al-Sha'arānī* (Cairo: al-Dār al-Jūdiyya, 2005).

Mahdī, al-'Abbāsī, *al-Fatāwa al-Mahdiyya fi'l Waqā'i al-Miṣriyya*, 6 vols., (Cairo: al-Maṭba'a al-Azhariyya, 1301 AH).

Al-Manār (Cairo), "Bāb Uṣūl al-Fiqh: Risālat al-Ṭūfī fi'l Maṣlaḥa." 9(1906): 745–770.

———, "Madaniyat al-Qawānīn." 23 (1922): 539–548.

———, "Muḥāwarāt al-Musliḥ wa'l Muqallid." 10 (1901): 361–371; and 22(1902): 852–866.

———, "Musāwāt al-Mar'a lil Rijāl fī Ḥuqūq al-Wājibāt." 30(1930): 777–783.

———, "al-Mutafarnijūn wa'l al-Iṣlāḥ al-Islāmī." 10(1918): 404–408.

———, "al-Ta'līm al-Qaḍā'ī." 2(1899): 117–121.

Mardin, Sherif, "Some Explanatory Notes on the Origins of the 'Mecelle'" in *The Muslim World* 51(4) 1961: 275.

———, "The Mind of the Turkish Reformer 1700–1900" in *Western Humanities Review*, 14(1960): 420–23.

Al-Māwardī, Muhammad, *al-Aḥkām al-Sulṭāniyya* (Cairo: Maṭba'a al-Ḥalabī, 1973).

McGregor, Richard J.A., *Sanctity and Mysticism in Medieval Egypt* (New York: State University of New York Press, 2004).

Meron, Ya'akov, "The Development of Legal Thought in Hanafi Texts", in *Studia Islamica* 30 (1969): 73–118.

Messick, Brinkley, *The Calligraphic State* (Los Angeles, University of California Press, 1993).

Michel, B. and Abdel Razik, Moustapha trans., *Rissalat al-Tawid du Cheikh Mohammed Abdou* (Paris: Librairie Orientaliste Paul Geuthner, 1925).

Al-Minyāwī, Makhlūf, *Ḥāshiyat al-Minyāwī 'ala Sharḥ Ḥulyat al-Lub al-Maṣūn* (Cairo: al-Bābī al-Ḥalabī, 1357 AH).

———, *Commentary on the Basmallah*, King Sa'ūd University collection, Manuscript 3617, 20 fols.

———, *Muqāranāt al-Tashrī'iyya*, 2 vols., (Cairo: Dār al-Salām, 1999).

Mitchell, Richard P., *The Society of the Muslim Brothers* (London: Oxford University Press, 1969).

Muḥammad, 'Abdallah Rabī'a 'Abdallah, *Madā Taghyīr al-Aḥkām bi Taghyīr al-Jihāt al-'Arba'* (Cairo: Ministry of Endowments, n.d.).

Muṣṭafa, 'Umar, *Uṣūl Tārīkh al-Qānūn* (Cairo: Mu'assasa al-Maṭbū'āt al-Ḥadītha, 1960).

Al-Muqaffa', 'Abd Allah, *Āthār Ibn al-Muqaffa'* (Beirut: Dār al-Kutub al-'Ilmiyya, 1989).

Al-Muṭī'ī, Muḥammad Bakhīt, *Fatāwa* (Lebanon: Dār al-Siddīq, 2012).

———, *al-Qawl al-Jāmi' fī'l Ṭalāq al bid'i wa'l Mutatābi'* (Cairo: n.p., 1320 AH).

———, *Raf' al-'Aghlāq 'an Mashrū' al-Zawāj wa'l Ṭalāq* (Cairo: n.p. 1927).

———, *Raf' al-'Aghlāq 'an Mashrū' al-Zawāj wa'l Ṭalāq* (Cairo: Dār al-Furūq, 2006).

Nadolski, Dora Glidwell, "Ottoman and Secular Law" in *International Journal of Middle East Studies* 8(4) 1977: 517–543.

Al-Nawwawī, Muḥyi al-Dīn, *Sharḥ Ṣaḥīḥ Muslim*, 18 vols., (Beirut: Dār al-Ma'rifa, 2006).

Al-Naysabūrī, Ibn Mundhir, *al-Ijmā'* (Cairo: Dār al-Ithār, 2004).

New York Times, "New Sultan Breaks Moslem Traditions," May 11, 1909.

Newman, Daniel L., trans., *An Imam in Paris* (London: Saqi Press, 2004).

Niẓām, Shaykh, *al-Fatāwā al-'Ālamkīriyya al-ma'rūf bi-al-Fatāwā al-Hindiyya fī madhhab al-Imām al-A'ẓam Abī Ḥanīfa al-Nu'mān*, 6 vols., (Cairo: Bulāq Press, 1892).

Peters, Rudolph, "What Does It Mean to Be an Official Madhhab? Hanafism and the Ottoman Empire," in *The Islamic School of Law*, eds. Peri Berman, Rudolph Peters, and Frank Vogel (Cambridge: Harvard University Press, 2005): 147–158.

Peterson, Samiha Sidhom trans., *The Liberation of Women and the New Women* (Cairo: The American University of Cairo Press, 1992).

Qadrī, Muḥammad, *Murshid al-Ḥayrān ila Ma'rifat Aḥwāl al-Insān* (Cairo: al-Maṭba'a al-Kubra al-Amīriyya bi Bulāq, 1891).

———, *Qānūn al-'Adl wa'l Inṣāf li'l Qaḍā' 'ala Mushkilāt al-Awqāf* (Cairo: al-Maṭba'a al-Amīriyya, 1909).

———, *al-Aḥkām al-Shar'iyya fi'l-Aḥwāl al-Shakhṣiyya*, 4 vols., eds., Muḥammad Aḥmad Sirāj and Ali Jumu'a (Cairo: Dar al-Salām, 2006).

Quadri, Syed Junaid Ahmed, "Transformations of tradition: modernity in the thought of Muhammad Bakhit al-Muti'i" (PhD diss., McGill University, 2013).

Al-Qurtubī, 'Abd al-Barr, *al-Isti'āb fī M'arifat al-Aṣḥāb*, 4 vols., (Beirut: Dār al-Kutub al-'Ilmiyya, 1995).

Radding, Charles, *The Corpus Iuris Civilis in the Middle Ages: Manuscripts and Transmission from the Sixth Century to the Juristic Revival* (Leiden: Brill, 2007).

Al-Rāfi'ī, 'Abd al-Raḥmān, *'Asr Ismā'īl*, 2 vols., (Cairo: Dār al-Ma'ārif, 1987).

Riḍā, Rashīd, *al-Wahhābiyūn wa'l Ḥijāz* (Cairo: Maṭba'a al-Manār, 1344 A.H.).

———, *Tafsīr al-Qur'an al-Ḥakīm al-Mushtahir bi Tafsīr al-Manār*, 12 vols. (Cairo: Dār al-Manār, 1947–54).

———, *Tarīkh al-Ustādh al-Imām al-Shaykh Muḥammad 'Abduh*, 3 vols., (Cairo: Dār al-Fadīla, 2006).

Rutherford, Bruce, *Egypt After Mubarak: Liberalism, Islam, and Democracy in the Arab World* (Princeton: Princeton University Press, 2008).

Ṣabrī, Muṣṭafā, *Qawlī fi'l Mar'a* (Beirut: Dār al-Qādirī, 1993).

Safran, Nadav, *Egypt in Search of Political Community* (Cambridge: Harvard University Press, 1961).

Al-Sanhūrī, 'Abd al-Razzāq. *Le califat, son évolution vers une société des nations orientale* (Paris : P. Geuthner, 1926).

———, *al-Waṣīt fi sharḥ al-Qānūn al-Madanī*, 10 vols., (Cairo: Dar al-Nahda al-'Arabiyya, 1964).

———, *Fiqh al-Khilāfa wa Taṭawuriha li Taṣbaḥ 'Uṣba Umam Sharqiyya* (Cairo: Al-Hay'a al-Miṣriyya al-'Āmma lil Kitāb, 2013).

Al-Sanhūrī, Muḥammad Aḥmad Faraj, *al-Qawānīn al-Miṣriyya al-Mukhtāra min al-Fiqh al-Islāmi*, 2 vols., (Cairo: Maṭba'a Misr, 1949).

Al-Sanhūrī, Nādiya ed., *al-Sanhūrī min khilāl Awrāqihī al-Shakhsiyya* (Cairo: Dār al-Shurūq, 2005).

Sanūsī, Abū 'Abduh Muḥammad bin Yūsuf al-Sanūsī, *al-Manhaj al-Sadīd fī Sharḥ Kifāyat al-Murīd, taḥqīq Muṣtafā Marzūq* (Algeria: n.d.).

Sarkīs, Joseph Ilān, *Mu'jam al-Maṭbū'āt al-'Arabiyya wa al-Mu'āraba*, 2 vols., (Cairo: Sarkīs Press, 1928).

Sartain, E.M., *Jalāl al-Dīn al-Suyūṭī Biography and Background*, 2 vols., (Cambridge: Cambridge University Press: 1975).

Al-Sayyid, Riḍwān, *Jawānib min al-Dirāsāt al-Islāmiyya al-Haḍītha* (Dār al-Fanak: Casablanca, 2000).

———, "al-Imām Muḥammad 'Abduh wa'l Iṣlāḥ fi'l Awqāf wa'l Maḥākim al-Shar'iyya" in *al-Imām Muḥammad 'Abduh Mi'at 'Ām 'ala Raḥīlihi*, eds., Ibrāhīm al-Bayyūmī Ghānim and Ṣalāh al-Dīn Elgawhary (Cairo: Dār al-Kitāb al-Miṣrī, 2005).

Schacht, Joseph, *An Introduction to Islamic Law* (Oxford: Clarendon Press, 1982).

Schofield, Philip and Harris, Jonathan, eds., *The Collected works of Jeremy Bentham: Legislator of the World: Writings on Codification, Law and Education* (Oxford: Clarendon Press, 1988).

Sedwick, Mark, *Muhammad Abduh* (Oxford: Oneworld, 2010).

Shafīq, Aḥmad, *'Amālī b'ad Mudhakkirātī* (Cairo: Maṭba'at Miṣr, 1941).

Shafīq, Duriyya, *Taṭawwur al-Nahḍah al-Nisā'īyah fī Miṣr min 'ahd Muḥammad 'Alī ilā 'ahd al-Fārūq* (Cairo: Maktabat al-Ādāb, 1945).

Shaham, Ron, *Family and the Courts in Modern Egypt: A Study Based on Decisions by the Sharī'a Courts, 1900–1955* (Leiden: Brill, 1997).

Shākir, Ahmad, *Abḥāth fī Aḥkām* (Cairo: al-M'ārif, n.d.).

——— ed., *Alfiyyat al-Suyūṭī fī 'Ilm al-Ḥadīth* (Cairo: Maktabat al-'Ilmiyya, n.d.).

——— ed., *al-Bā'ith al-Ḥathīth Sharḥ Ikhtiṣār 'Ilm al-Ḥadīth* (Cairo: Dār al-Turāth, 2003).

———, *Ḥukm al-Jāhiliyya* (Cairo: Dār al-Istiqāma, 1992).

———, *Kalimat al-Haqq* (Cairo: Dār al-Kutub al-Salafiyya, 1408 AH).

———, *al-Kitāb wa'l Sunna Yajibā an Yakūnā Maṣdar al-Qawānīn fī Miṣr* (Cairo: Dār al-Kutub al-Salafiyya, 1986).

——— ed., *Musnad al-Imām Aḥmad ibṇ Ḥanbal*, 16 vols., (Cairo: Dār al-Ḥadīth, 1995).

———, *Niẓām al-Ṭalāq fī'l Islām* (Cairo: al-Nahḍa, 1354 AH).

——— ed., *al-Risāla li Imām al-Shāfi'ī* (Beirut: Dār al-Kutub al-'Ilmiyya, n.d.).

———, *Taqrīr 'an Shu'ūn al-T'alīm wa'l Qaḍā'* (Cairo: Maktabat Imām al-Bukhārī, 2009).

Sha'rāwī, Hudā, "Dawr al-Mar'a fī Ḥarakat al-Taṭawwur al-'Ālī" (A speech given at the American University in Cairo November 12, 1929).

———, *Muḥādarāt Dawr al-Mar'a fī'l Nahḍa al-Sharqiyya* (Cairo: al-Maṭba'a al-'Aṣriya, 1935).

———, *Harem Years* (New York: The Feminist Press, 1986).

Al-Shināwī, 'Abd al-'Azīz, *al-Azhar Jāmi'an wa Jamā'atan*, 2 vols., (Cairo: Anglo-Egyptian Bookshop, 1983).

Skovgaard-Petersen, Jakob, *Defining Islam for the Egyptian State* (Leiden: Brill, 1997).

Snyder, David V. "Private Law Making", in *Ohio State Law Journal* 64 (2003): 371–449.

Susa, Nasim, *The Capitulatory Regime of Turkey: Its History, Origin, and Nature* (Baltimore: The Johns Hopkins Press, 1933).

Suyūṭī, Jalāl al-Dīn, *Ḥusn al-Muḥādara fī Akhbār Miṣr wa'l Qāhira*, 2 vols., (Cairo: al-Maṭba'a al-Mawsū'āt, n.d.).

———, *Ḥusn al-Muḥādara fī Akhbār Miṣr wa'l Qāhira*, 2 vols., (Beirut: Dār al-Kutub al-'Ilmiyya, 1997).

———, *al-Radd 'ala man Akhlada ilā al-'Ard wa Jahila anna al-Ijtihād fī Kul 'Aṣr Farḍ* (Beirut: Dār al-Kutub al-'Ilmiyya, 1983).

———, *Taqrīr al-Istinād fī Tafsīr al-Ijtihād* (Alexandria: Dār al-D'awa, 1983).

Talal, HRH Ghazi Muhammad Ibn, *True Islam and the Islamic Consensus on the Amman Message* (Amman: n.p., 2006).

Tedeschi, G., "'Personal Status' and 'Statut Personnel'", in *McGill Law Journal* 459(1969): 453–4.

Al-Tirmidhī, Abī 'Issa Muḥammad bin 'Issa bin Sawra, *Sunan al-Tirmidhī*, 2 vols., (Germany: TraDigiital Stuttgart GmbH, 2000).

Tucker, Judith E., *Women in Nineteenth Century Egypt* (Cambridge: Cambridge University Press, 1985).

———, "Revisiting Reform: Women and the Ottoman Law of Family Rights, 1917", in *Arab Studies Journal* 4(1996): 4–17.

Tunic, Andre, "The Grand Outlines of the Code," in *The Code Napoleon and the Common Law World*, ed. Bernard Schwartz (Connecticut: Greenwood Press 1956): 19–45.

Turkey, *al-Majalla : wa-hiya taḥtawī 'alā al-qawānīn al-shar'īyya wa-al-aḥkām al-'adilīyya al-muṭābiqah lil-kutub al-fiqhīyya* (Beirut: al-Matba'a al-Adābiyya, 1884).

'Umar, Ṭūsūn HRH, *al-Bi'thāt al-'Ilmiyya fī 'Ahd Muḥammad 'Alī thumma fī 'Ahdi 'Abbās al-'Awwal wa Sa'īd* (Alexandria: Maṭba'at Ṣalāḥ al-Dīn, 1934).

van den Boogert, Maurtis H., *The Capitulations and the Ottoman Legal System* (Leiden: Brill, 2005).

Vogel, Frank E., *Islamic Law and Legal System* (Brill: Leiden, 2000).

Weiss, Bernard, *The Spirit of Islamic Law* (Athens: University of Georgia Press, 2006).

Winroth, A., *The Making of Gratian's Decretum* (Cambridge: Cambridge University Press, 2000).

Al-Ẓāhirī, Ibn Ḥazm, *Marātib al-Ijmā‘* (Beirut: Dār Ibn Hazm, 1998).

Zaman, Muhammad Qasim, *Religion and politics under the early ‘Abbāsids: the emergence of the proto-Sunnī elite* (Leiden: Brill, 1997).

———, *The Ulama in Contemporary Islam: Custodians of Change* (Princeton, Princeton University Press, 2002).

———, *Modern Islamic Thought in a Radical Age* (Cambridge: Cambridge University Press, 2012).

Zebri, Kate, *Maḥmūd Shaltūt and Islamic Modernism* (Oxford: Clarendon Press, 1993).

Ziadeh, Farhat, *Lawyers, the Rule of Law, and Liberalism in Modern Egypt* (Stanford: Hoover Institution on War, Revolution and Peace, 1968).

INDEX

ARABIC AND TURKISH TERMS

PEOPLE & PLACES

www.ingramcontent.com/pod-product-compliance
Lightning Source LLC
LaVergne TN
LVHW011522200926
848484LV00001B/111
9781463239084